CALLING OUT THE SHADOWS:

A FATHER'S STAND AGAINST THE CURRENT

NEAL WINSOMER
PUBLISHING LLC

Calling Out the Shadows:
A Father's Stand Against the Current

Clarity over comfort.

Transparency over secrecy.

Structure over spin.

Love over anger.

A chronicle of overcoming disappointment and adversity; defining legacy not by what broke me, but by how I chose to respond.

NEAL WINSOMER

First edition, 2026
6x9 Trim
$19.99 USD

Published by:
Neal Winsomer Publishing LLC
State Business ID: 0008090264
1333 College Pkwy #1037
Gulf Breeze, Florida 32563 United States
Ph: (904) 736-5175
Em: hello@NealWinsomerPublishing.com
Website URL: NealWinsomerPublishing.com
Website 2 URL: NealWinsomer.com

ISBN 979-8-9953351-1-5 (paperback)
ISBN 979-8-9953351-6-0 (hardcover)
ISBN 979-8-9953351-7-7 (eBook)
ISBN 979-8-9953351-3-9 (skimmer's edition ebook)
ISBN 979-8-9953351-2-2 (audiobook)
ISBN 979-8-9953351-0-8 (library audio edition)
ISBN 979-8-9953351-4-6 (large print edition)

Library of Congress Control Number: 2026907360

BISAC Subject Codes:
1. BIO026000 Biography & Autobiography / Personal Memoirs
2. FAM015000 Family & Relationships / Divorce and Separation
3. FAM013000 Family & Relationships / Conflict Resolution

Thema Codes:
DNB - Biography & True Stories / Autobiography: general
VFVG - Family & Relationships / Coping with / advice about divorce, separation, bereavement
VFX - Family & Relationships / Parenting: advice and issues

Table of Contents

*To those who preferred this story stay
in the shadows, your efforts are
appreciated and documented.*

NOTE ON AI AND WRITING TOOLS

This book was written by the author through human drafting and revision between July 15, 2025, and March 12, 2026, over approximately 837 hours of focused writing time. From February 16 to March 12, 2026, the manuscript was edited in collaboration with one additional reader and a series of grammar, formatting, and AI editing programs, for roughly 162 hours of concentrated editorial work. Those programs were used only for grammatical editing, proofreading, and consistency checks, not to generate creative scenes, characters, or chapters. All narrative content, interpretations, and decisions about wording remain the author's own.

The audiobook was recorded by the author over eleven days, from Saturday, March 21, 2026, through Tuesday, March 31, 2026, at the Stewarding Springs Casita. Recording time totaled 51 hours and 33 minutes across many takes to reach the flow, tone, and emphasis he thought the book should carry. The finished, unabridged audiobook itself runs 14 hours and 9 minutes.

Post-production was handled by an audio and mastering engineer. EQ, compression, a noise gate, and a limiter were added during that process. Final mixing and mastering followed, bringing the recording to the technical standards required for audiobook distribution. Some AI tools were used by the engineer to reduce pops, lessen extended spaces, cut louder breaths, and remove any additional background noises.

No words were generated, replaced, or scripted by artificial intelligence. What you hear is the author's voice, reading his own words.

ACKNOWLEDGMENTS

Ashley, Aubrey, Brent, Brian, Bryant, Chris, Chuck, Clara, Crystal, Daniel, Derek, Diana, Don, Doug, Ed, Erica, Erin, Faye, Gary, Haze, Jackie, James, Jane, Janelle, Janis, Jennifer, Jeremy, John M, Jon, Karen (a real one, not the slang term), Katherine, Keith, Kimberly, Laura, Lyndsay, Mark A, Mark S, Megan, Michael, Nicole, Patrisha, Phil, Renata, Robin, Ruth, Scott, Shannon, Stephanie, Steve, Taylor, Ted, Terry, Thom, Tiffany, Tim, Will and Yeshua.

Airbnb, Albertsons, American Airlines, Barnes and Noble Café, Bowker Publishing Services, Breathe Right Nasal Strips, Canva, Carmex Classic Lip Balm, Chili's, Corporate Tools, Dollar Tree, Dropbox, editGPT, GarageBand, Grammarly, IngramSpark, iPostal1, MacBook Air 15 Inch M2 2023, Marriott Hotels, Microsoft 365, Miller's Ale House, Namecheap, Notarize Inc, Northwest Registered Agent, Panera Bread, PPBL Author Portal, Reedsy, Shure MV88 USB-C Stereo Microphone, Stewarding Springs Casita, Square, Starbucks, Tim Horton's, Tor Browser, Turo, United States Copyright Office, Wordpress, VapoRub, 180 Medical

PREFACE.
Authoring a Blueprint to Protect Truth and Story

Opening Thought

My writing began without a clear direction, guided by the responsibility to express what was true and personal. I prioritized substance over surface, aiming for clarity, structure, and authenticity to honor my daughter and convey this message. What followed became an account shaped by transparency, compliance, calm, and care, designed to withstand interpretation and preserve integrity.

Vulnerability demands exposure. These pages contain my experiences, feelings, pain, humility, and the humiliation I endured. The narrative reflects my voice, intentions, and recollections over many years. My book consists of interconnected stories and experiences, arranged to reveal patterns and lessons instead of following chronological order. This comes from a real, living, breathing author, not from someone adding scattered thoughts to a prompt or relying on an app that can produce a book in minutes. I dislike how those "books" are created and uploaded to popular selling websites in hours, then made available to the public later that same day.

I tracked every hour across writing, editing, research, and finalization. The work required 999 hours and 9 minutes. I stopped there on purpose. Nine carries a weight of finality in scripture, and I felt it fitting to close this effort at that mark. Somewhere past the 950-hour mark, I told myself I would not cross into a thousand. I could have kept writing, revising, and refining for months longer. Setting that boundary though, marked the close, made the finish line visible, and pressed me to stand behind what I had built instead of endlessly reworking it.

I subdued my voice to honor my daughter and maintain necessary subjectivity. My goal is to share my story while adhering to safety principles to avoid potential legal issues. I present a format that carefully focuses on how a sensitive story can be shared, using subjective, humble tones rather than asserting verified facts. I explain these personal experiences while pulling back on some emotions and assertive edges. I believe this approach offers a level of protection, allowing authenticity to emerge with greater security for a broader audience.

I avoided sarcasm entirely, as any hint of it could be taken out of context from the intention of the words and allow for misinterpretation.

With continued focus on stability and integrity, I removed crutch words, fillers, banned words, exaggerations, and language that could raise legal issues. These restricted words are not included in the manuscript, though I share the categories, definitions, and a complete list in Appendix G and Appendix H.

Unlike my previous books, where longer chapters could span over 30 pages, most of these chapters are only a few pages long. I'm exploring a new understanding of what a chapter means to me, approaching it as a collection of pieces of me, with interconnecting thoughts and stories derived from diverse experiences over many years.

> *"Details document patterns rather than people, supporting records can counter spin, and calm responses can meet*

> *escalation, so that my daughter's peace, not a parent's pride, sets the standard."*

This book has a format substantially different from what I initially expected. As I started organizing it, I chose a method for introducing and concluding each story, including an opening thought, a closing thought, and the strongest pull quote I felt was in that chapter. My reasoning was for the skimmer and for an approach I used in a previous book.

Readers could skim each chapter by reading the title, opening thought, pull quote, and closing thought, then decide whether to explore that chapter further or move on. This is why I chose this format. I am not asking anyone to read the whole book from front to back. If they choose to, that is welcomed and appreciated. Still, I used this form to consider the skimmer, the scanner, and the person not invested, and to honor them as well. My blueprint reflects this intention to document patterns from this experience in full.

About the Title

"Calling Out the Shadows: A Father's Stand Against the Current" reflects a personal reckoning to shine a light on information that was obscured or presented misleadingly. It spotlights truth, transparency, and the experiences that have been disregarded, dismissed, or distorted by a person in my life. In this context, shadows represent the denials, and gaps that can leave individuals feeling lost and vulnerable, while harm quietly builds in the background.

In these pages, shadows refer to areas where darker influence thrives behind selective replies, erased context, withheld details, and strategic silence. "Calling out" signifies a deliberate act of documenting, dating, and preserving facts without rage or spectacle.

Shadows are not only the absence of light to me; they are spaces where ambiguity quietly resides, distorting reality through vague answers, false claims, unhealthy communication, and the silence between the lines. Still, there is a paradox in shadows. While they can blur reality, they also help shape it.

Shadows can define edges, prompting us to focus and consider the boundaries that invite deeper questions about what is present and what may be concealed. I have learned that strategically documenting, dating, and preserving facts without anger or impatience can, in time, reveal the shape of the shadow itself. In that act, the blurred lines become clearer, and the silence that once felt like a refuge for misunderstanding loses its grip.

The Subtitle

I chose the subtitle "Stand Against the Current" because it works in both literal and figurative ways for me. From a literal standpoint, it represents an upstream stance resisting pressure to conform to narratives. From a figurative standpoint, it indicates a deliberate nonconformity when widespread sentiment favors comfort, equivocation, and short-term memory over accountability, perseverance, and verifiable evidence.

That stance forms the backbone of this story, a father's pursuit to document challenges, resist instigation, prioritize faith, stand in accountability, protect his daughter's peace, and secure truth through evidence and lawful structure by choosing clarity, transparency, and love over comfort, secrecy, spin, and anger.

The Tagline

To me, "Clarity over comfort. Transparency over secrecy. Structure over spin. Love over anger." distills the method and motive into four disciplined choices that recur throughout this narrative and my experiences of the last several years.

Clarity over comfort rejects vague stories, blurred intelligence, and confused understanding.

Transparency over secrecy replaces silence, back channels, and selective disclosures with verifiable timelines, accountability, and truth.

Structure over spin focuses on how I structured my reactions, as well as the careful, strategic collection and organization of experiences, emails, texts, and evidence to show the patterns. The emphasis is on actions and documented records rather than emotional appeals or slanted interpretations.

Love over anger maintains a calm tone, prioritizing my daughter's well-being, and is anchored in love, patience, wisdom, and faith. From here, I worked to stay grounded, focused, and calm with each instigating attack, empty claim, or awful ordeal that I have gone through or that my daughter has experienced for herself and shared with me.

Each element of the tagline traces back to my goal of making what was obscured in the shadows visible, legible, and provable, without becoming what the conflict seeks to press, pressure, and push forward.

Against the Current, By Design

"Against the current" is both a posture and a practice. To me, it involves rejecting the momentum, resisting peer pressure to accept a preferred view as truth, and pushing upstream with a tenacity that endures when false sentiments shift. It can signify nonconformity to the easy path taken by many.

I also intended to avoid theatrics or negative tactics by shining a clear light on a steady archive that allows my daughter and other readers to weigh what happened against what was claimed in the dark.

This is why I wrote the book this way. I intended for it to exist at the intersection of narrative and proof. I believe that details document patterns rather than people, supporting records can counter spin, and calm responses can meet escalation, so that my daughter's peace, not a parent's pride, sets the standard.

Intended Result

The title conveys the chronicle's goal of calling out what was hidden in the shadows. The subtitle frames the stance of standing against the current and the crowd.

And the tagline commits to the method. Clarity, transparency, structure, and love are the consistent threads that run through each page.

Together, my goal was to have this title and tagline reflect my story's arc: a father who rejects secrecy, resists instigation, maintains faith, and keeps records, ensuring that this account holds when memory fades and pressure mounts.

My daughter will not receive the full book for many years to come. I plan to share this with her when she is old enough and ready to see another side of the story and read it with a foundation and clear understanding of the intention behind it.

What began as a journal has turned into a detailed account, one I wish to share with those who may relate to it and perhaps with those who could benefit from it. My hope is that it could also inspire those who have been cautious or apprehensive about sharing their stories to know that it can be done with humility, protection, strategy, and care when addressing and amplifying challenging circumstances and events.

This is the foundation of my book. I built it this way to protect it in truth, authenticity, and humility. I hope this becomes a piece of my legacy for my daughter, and that it resonates with other readers as well.

Closing Thought

Steadfast faith, unwavering truth, transparency, and strategic protection became the principles guiding the organization of this book. I removed language that could be misunderstood or viewed negatively, including overused terms, fillers, expressions conveying heightened emotion, aggression, or weakness, and phrasing that could create problems down the line. I focused on presenting my story and feelings with a strategic calm and a faithful humility. My record is built on honesty, balance, and protection rather than insults, retaliation, or instigation.

AUTHOR'S NOTE.
Practicing Restraint and Responsible Editing

Opening Thought

Growth rarely comes easily or on a preferred schedule. This book was written with deliberate care. I shaped the narrative thoughtfully and strategically, making careful decisions about which details to share, which words to use, and which to avoid. The goal has been to balance honesty with protection to create a clear, meaningful, and enduring story of record. I hope these pages reflect a commitment to conscious restraint, strategic sharing, and a process designed to offer transparency, clarity, and accuracy from start to finish.

Restraint shaped every word choice in these pages. Each decision about language and structure was made to protect the narrative and those involved, carefully determining which words and phrases to include and which to omit. This restraint strengthened clarity and intention, while pushing me to express myself with humility, security, and integrity.

Every challenge faced and every truth uncovered has been part of an undertaking of endurance to create a lasting light for my daughter and to exchange shadows for clarity, transparency, accountability, and love.

Legacy for my daughter matters more than competition, one-upping, or trying to make someone look bad. These pages exist for the long-term endurance of this narrative, so she can see another perspective and a bigger picture, whether I am here or gone. In specific instances, rather than defending a particular position, I chose to edit, adapt, and remove language to maintain authenticity, while ensuring responsible accuracy. I see it as shaping words with care and conviction instead of adding hype and noise.

Today's writing world offers so much trendy and automated language that can distance stories from authentic human experience. In my writing and editing, I prioritized meaning, removed commercial jargon, eliminated vague or emotional expressions, and filtered terms with any legal or interpretive risk. The focus is on a narrative grounded in honest reflection, purpose, and respect for all readers.

24 Deflective and Evasive Communication Patterns

Later in the book, after the narrative chapters, I highlight certain communication styles that can emerge when conversations become difficult or when someone feels cornered or pressured. These patterns are less common among individuals with healthier communication habits, but more common among those with poor communication habits, relational issues, and a resistance to resolution.

In Appendix A, I compiled a list of 24 deflective and evasive communication patterns. I encountered many of these styles in discussions with my former wife and observed similar patterns in her other relationships. Throughout the book, I reference specific patterns by name, not as judgments, but as identifiers that signal when dialogue has shifted away from the possibility of resolution and moved toward deflection or avoidance. Appendix A provides brief definitions and examples for each pattern. If you find yourself feeling confused in conversations or questioning your perceptions, this resource may help you put a name to what you are experiencing and hopefully find more informed ways to respond to that person's communication style.

My Restricted Language List

2,150 Words and Phrases for Narrative Clarity and Compliance

To maintain integrity, accuracy, and protection in this book, a broad set of words and phrases has been omitted, replaced, or excluded from the outset.

This complete framework appears in Appendices G and H at the end of the book. Appendix G explains the 12 categories into which these words and phrases were placed and my definitions of these categories. Appendix H provides the complete alphabetical list of all 2,150 terms.

Clarifying the Scope of Restraint

To be transparent and precise, not a single restricted word or phrase from this 2,150-term list appears in this book until the appendices.

All front matter pieces are free of these terms, including the Preface, this Author's Note, and the Introduction. The numbered narrative chapters also contain no restricted language. The Conclusion, Epilogue, Letter from Daddy, and Coda maintain this same restraint.

These restricted terms appear only within eight of the ten appendices. In those eight sections, I used a limited number of those words and phrases from the restricted language list. This is by design for technical definitions, observable trait descriptions, and direct examples that required blunt clarity.

Their tone prioritizes directness and utility for the reader. My goal is for the appendices to serve as educational resources and reference tools, differentiating them from the personal narrative. This distinction preserves the protective restraint and subdued voice throughout every narrative, reflective, and personal section, while allowing the appendices to function with the clarity and frankness their reference purpose requires. This means the full 2,150-term list serves as a boundary and a reference tool, not as language sprinkled through the narrative to intensify it.

The exception to my rule is in Appendix I, which contains the personal titles of the items in the digital gift basket of content pieces I sent to my daughter. In that appendix, there are more objective, positive-style words in the titles that were written for and directed at her.

Purpose and Practice

This language boundary list serves as a practical tool for strengthening truth and clarity in narratives where compliance, interpretation, and responsible storytelling are at stake.

The challenge seemed simple at first. Could I tell a story with purpose and authenticity while avoiding overused, reactive, or ambiguous language? I hope each chapter shows how thoughtful language choices can add substance and expression, while strategic, subjective word selection can support and secure a narrative.

Each chapter or section in this book is built around five anchors: the title, the opening thought, the first sentence that follows, the pull quote, and the closing thought. Across the full work, 349 distinct first words open those anchors. Each was chosen with attention to what stands before and what comes after, so that if these pieces were read alone, they would still point to the heart of that section.

"Legacy for my daughter matters more than competition, one-upping, or trying to make someone look bad. These pages exist for the long-term endurance of this narrative, so she can see another perspective and a bigger picture, whether I am here or gone."

I also created a shortened version of each chapter or section's title, opening thought, pull quote, and closing thought to test whether the opening, middle, and closing moments still held together as a clear, compact idea. My hope is that someone who only skims those elements can still understand what each section holds, while those who read every page feel the deeper connections that run through the structure. I have also created this for initial connection purposes, allowing people to read these short segments and then decide if they want to dig deeper.

This process involved finding the right words and framing this narrative without resorting to oversaturated language that can reveal weakness. These words and phrases include banned terms that cannot be used on specific social media sites without penalties. They also include language that can hold a person accountable or create potential problems for what they wrote, regardless of whether it is true.

Many of the words and phrases removed have added a layer of protection and compliance to the book's delivery. My intention is to make it clear that this is written by a human, in humility and transparency, with all my imperfections and limited formal writing training. You will find mistakes. In that, though, I hope you will find my voice too.

This word-conscious, subtraction-based approach may also support stories from writers focusing on accountability, honor, and the humble consideration of how language can be perceived beyond the writer's intention.

As I've shared before, "Clarity over comfort. Transparency over secrecy. Structure over spin. Love over anger." By removing many of these words and phrases, each page became an opportunity to practice patience and grace, document with clarity, and create space for love and transparency. I believe real strength grows not from getting every detail right, but from steady correction and sincere integrity throughout the process.

Closing Thought

Humility, truth, and accountability continue to teach me. Progress is not about flawless execution but about continuous awareness, honesty, and deliberate correction. Each day presents another chance to practice patience and grace, lead with love, and remain transparent through both effort and tender vulnerabilities. Through this experience, I've come to understand that real strength and growth take root here.

INTRODUCTION.
Grounded in Truth and Love Through Fatherhood

Opening Thought

Truth emerges as the narrative shifts from confusion and chaos to clarity and accountability, painting a fuller picture and offering a broader view for my daughter and others sharing their stories. I strive to convey my experiences with assertive, humble honesty, making clear the choices rooted in honor, respect, and transparency at every stage of this journey.

Perspective shapes what follows, filtered through a father's memory, lessons learned, and evidence gathered over years where stories diverged, and truths sometimes became obscured. Above all, I hope to provide my daughter with both perspective and protection.

The intention is not to attack, divide, or blame. Instead, this writing aims to document how repeated stories, evolving perspectives, and unexamined patterns can shape our perceptions of truth. Every detail and decision in these pages is meant to safeguard the clarity, transparency, and integrity of this story. I hope it serves as a lasting record that supports healing, growth, and understanding for my daughter and possibly others.

As my daughter grows, I know she will encounter moments that echo those in this narrative. I hope that by reading this, she and others can identify patterns, become more empathetic listeners, and develop the resilience to engage with compassion and forgiveness. This book is not meant to sway her to my side but to gently broaden her perspective and equip her to recognize influences that may otherwise obscure her experience.

For years, chaos and lack of accountability dominated our broken family. I endured repeated misunderstandings, shifting accounts, constant communication breakdowns, and an ongoing clash of memories that rarely matched. Through questioning, presenting evidence, and striving for open communication, I learned how silence, avoidance, or deflection makes genuine connections difficult. My former wife often forgot what had transpired, reacted unpredictably, and sometimes seemed unaware of how her actions affected others. Amid this turmoil, finding common ground or mutual understanding often felt elusive.

Moments documented include not only personal experiences but also efforts made toward truth, accountability, and peace. These steps were taken so my daughter is not left holding only half the story. Much of what is shared here comes from the perspective of someone whose health and future were uncertain when I began writing. These reflections offer guidance and comfort for my daughter and for anyone trying to rebuild from similar confusion, silence, or imbalance. I believe that a stable, loving future can be built on lessons from the past if we are willing to bring them to light, offer support, and make space for change.

> *"Moments documented include not only personal experiences but also efforts made toward truth, accountability, and peace. These steps were taken so my daughter is not left holding only half the story."*

This work aims to reveal what was hidden for those who may one day seek to understand more than what was initially shown to them. With my former wife, I chose, over time and through learning, to respond more patiently rather than react impulsively.

I gradually shifted toward writing and responding with quieter, substantiated opinions instead of loud emotional declarations, and this book is grounded in those steady reflections, painful lessons, and prayers for renewed hope. I seek to provide my daughter with a new foundation of understanding and wisdom, as well as for others who may relate to similar circumstances.

Comfort can obscure clarity, secrecy can hide truth, spin can distort structure, and anger can displace love. These pages detail my efforts to resist those tendencies and, as much as possible, move toward clarity, transparency, structure, and love.

Closing Thought

Renewal emerges when challenges are met with deliberate, respectful steps that build understanding, welcome other viewpoints, and cultivate stability. As I pray for cooperation, endurance, and strength in the days ahead, may these words inspire others to embrace transparency, courage, and determination to follow a path of love, honor, and light.

CHAPTER 1.
Clarity Earned Through Chaos and Patient Response

Opening Thought

Difficult truths can emerge slowly through chaos, documentation, and steady reflection, bringing into focus patterns that were once easy to miss. This story does not claim to be rare or special, but it exists so my daughter and others can see another side of events, grounded in records, restraint, and a father's decision to respond with clarity instead of reaction.

Wisdom from this story is not fully clear, including whether observers will see only drama or a chance to recognize patterns in their own lives. The story makes no claim to originality, but it felt necessary to share. Whether it helps anyone or opens eyes to what has emerged remains unknown.

For this book, my daughter will be referred to as Zoey, and my former wife as Anya.

Throughout it all, particularly because of Zoey, I find it hard to hold onto regret. I still reflect on the past and work toward forgiveness, for the situation, for Anya, and for the chaos that unfolded despite the many warning signs. I was either unaware of them or shielded from recognizing them. The latter seems far more likely.

All this learning and experience seemed necessary for me to understand my relationship with Zoey and her mother. From my experience, I perceived her as mentally and emotionally unhealthy in several ways, marked by anger and what felt like irrational vengeance toward me. Over time, it grew clearer that traits of revenge and cold-heartedness were becoming more pronounced. I grappled with the intensity of her anger and emotional turmoil.

It all seemed aimed at me. I don't wish to depict her solely as mean-spirited, but I remain focused on telling what happened with clarity and transparency. Many of the signs I later recognized should have been visible from the start. Despite considering myself a good judge of character, able to read most people's emotions and identify patterns in business relationships easily and quickly, I couldn't see any of it in her then, though the signs were evident throughout. If any of these elements had changed or been different during that period, I don't believe I would be the person I am today. Zoey would not have been born, because I would not have stuck around.

> *"Despite considering myself a good judge of character, able to read most people's emotions and identify patterns in business relationships easily and quickly, I couldn't see any of it in her then, though the signs were evident throughout."*

When Anya launched her attacks, criticisms, and rants, I sent emails saying, "I'm praying for you, for your healing, and for your happiness." The immediate responses felt like a brush-off. She wrote back, "I'm fine, I'm doing great, I don't want your prayers." Despite her protests, she could use all the prayers she could get. One prayer I am consistent with asks for her heart to be softened, her mind to be strengthened, and her negativity to be released.

I hope this book may one day help Zoey understand my perspective, especially given the health challenges and personal trials I'm navigating, as well as the distance I'm facing from her. From my viewpoint, the narrative shared with Zoey doesn't reflect my experiences or my side of the story; another perspective has overshadowed and reshaped it. This book exists so Zoey can one day see another side of the story for herself. It is also about a woman who chose to conceal aspects of herself, distorting reality to present a version of herself that was the opposite of who she was. Perhaps that's where it all starts.

Closing Thought

Embracing each task, including the difficult ones, allowed for greater growth, support, and direction in my journey. If these reflections resonate with those who seek them, I hope they offer guidance, encouragement, and a sense of shared experience rooted in honest documentation and calm response.

CHAPTER 2.
Red Flags Hidden in False Starts and Blind Pursuits

Opening Thought

Whispered doubts can arrive quietly, bringing warning signs many choose not to see. Working in scripted reality entertainment taught me how false narratives take hold, but I missed those same patterns emerging in my own life. This path brought my daughter into my life despite the shadows I failed to acknowledge when they first appeared.

Uncertainty marked that period on the West Coast. I had finished a book festival where I was speaking and doing a book signing when I met Anya. I had launched my book a few months earlier and was preparing for a book tour. I was also figuring out where to settle and what to pursue next. After writing the previous book, I felt drawn away from my current career and eager to explore new opportunities.

As I prepared for the upcoming tour, a question bounced around about returning to the West Coast afterward. I landed firmly on no. I viewed the tour as an opportunity to travel across the country and determine the right place to settle, which was not the West Coast. It wasn't that I didn't enjoy the West Coast or felt too old for it, but I was ready to leave.

I remembered one of my last sessions on the West Coast in a studio that felt hollow. I had enjoyed my work in entertainment, but I was tired of seeing the same patterns and personality types. It was discouraging to see different individuals taking identical shortcuts with misguided optimism. I would hear comments like, "This is going to be big," or "This will be a chart-topper." It wasn't a criticism of them personally; it reflected my understanding of the industry's complexities. Based on their work and their beliefs about how the industry was supposed to operate, I felt that so many didn't have what it takes to stand out and succeed.

The "overnight success" stories that sold so many people on the industry rarely held up. Most had financial backing, marketing, and behind-the-scenes staging that went unseen. An ungrounded attachment to false narratives, a pattern I saw often in the industry, became a theme I noticed in Anya from the beginning.

At a small dinner party, I encountered her for the first time. Hearing the host, who was preparing the dinner, speaking negatively about her seemed off to me. I thought to myself, "If you feel this way, why invite her?" I was accustomed to this style of talk, but it still felt different. When she and the others arrived, the conversation quickly shifted from criticism to hugs and expressions of joy at seeing each other. That duplicity bothered me, though it was common in that city.

We met at this dinner party, and it wasn't a particularly special connection at first. It was refreshing to meet someone outside of entertainment who didn't seem to know much about it and wasn't impressed when I was introduced with my career credentials and recent book. I appreciated not being seen for certain accolades or accomplishments.

We spoke a fair amount that evening and shared what I thought was attraction, though it may have been comfortable conversation and not much else. Still, in that moment, I enjoyed the interaction. We discussed connecting further, and there was a hug at the end of the night. She had consumed a fair amount of alcohol, which I recognized but didn't dwell on then. It would later prove to be a significant issue.

The next day, I tried to look her up online. I couldn't find much about her. This stood out, but I also found it intriguingly mysterious. When she called that day, we connected and talked. Later that evening, there was a first kiss.

I was drawn to her, though she wasn't the type I had gone for in the past. I was seeing a different woman during that period, not exclusively, but someone much more my type. This woman was successful, intelligent, beautiful, gregarious, and outgoing while also showing a seemingly shy side. She was accountable for her actions and transparent. I liked her, still, without a clear reason, I continued pursuing the connection with Anya.

She mentioned having to leave town but was vague about why. Another warning sign I chose to ignore. I now realize I had no practical reason to continue the relationship. In any other case, I believe I would have recognized the red flags right then and walked away. I now see, in faith, that it was all about Zoey coming into my life. I was blinded for a reason.

As a man of faith now, I see that blindness as part of that journey. I still felt frustrated by how I had overlooked clear signs and struggled to identify patterns of poor communication, discord, and negative behaviors she displayed toward others and family, despite having learned to spot these issues in other people.

> *"Deflection became her signature move, redirecting inquiries about herself back to me or focusing solely on the present moment, as if the past didn't exist."*

There was a period of anger and self-loathing for feeling foolish for not seeing what was there, thinking of the many signs I had ignored and missed. Still, I came to understand that this was necessary for me to have Zoey. I had to go through this experience to have her, and that realization changed my anger into acceptance.

We continued texting while she was away, and our conversations grew more romantic. Distance and the initial ease of messaging drew me in further. Still, each time I asked about her past or her interests, she would turn most of those questions back toward me. Deflection became her signature move, redirecting inquiries about herself back to me or focusing solely on the present moment, as if the past didn't exist.

She had erased her past, or she could no longer recall it with accuracy. The conversations felt more enjoyable as she adapted to my communication style and began mirroring it. I mistook that reflection for real contribution and connection.

It appears it was mostly a reflection of who I was. Because I didn't look deeper, I missed the mirroring signs and traits. I didn't get the chance to learn who she was, and only later understood that throughout our entire relationship, I hadn't known her at all.

She was constructing a narrative of what she thought I would prefer to see. Many months later, as I watched her shift her conversational style away from mirroring toward her own way of communicating and relating, I found there was little about this woman that felt authentic.

When she returned from her travels, and I was preparing for my tour, I suggested she join me. After spending more time together and trying to work out what this relationship would or would not be, I asked her, "Why not get in the car and figure this out together, experiencing each other and seeing where this relationship goes?" She was immediately enthusiastic about coming along for the tour.

There were levels of comfort-based connection rather than electricity or passion. There were no arguments, disputes, or differences at first, which made me curious about where the friction would be or might arise. I wasn't looking to start arguments, but I was confused by how few differences there seemed to be. I have consistently valued understanding how people operate. I watch their communication during disagreements, their conflict resolution strategies, and how they handle difficult days. I have found that learning someone's true communication skills during difficult times can show more about who they are, rather than a facade that many present in more favorable circumstances or easier moments.

During our initial connection, which included pleasant, non-conflict conversations, enjoyable interactions, intimacy, meals, and discussions about news and politics, I did not experience any real friction. That changed partway through the book tour when another huge warning sign appeared for me.

Closing Thought

Authenticity requires peeling back illusions and embracing uncomfortable honesty about what we may have overlooked, missed, or didn't want to see. In that clarity, humility, and resolve, missteps can become corrected steps toward growth.

CHAPTER 3.
Conflicts Echoing Through Cycles I Sought to Understand

Opening Thought

First disagreements can reveal not only who we share space with but also who we become in those moments. Sometimes it is not the raised voices or heavy silences that stay with us, but the underlying cycles that signal deeper relational challenges ahead.

Friction emerged shortly after we arrived in the Midwest for a book tour stop, marking our first real conflict together. I don't remember exactly what ignited the argument; my focus was on the conflict itself and the early signs of learning who this woman genuinely was.

I felt a pull toward resolution, comfort, understanding, and a middle ground. I was already working to address communication issues with someone I'd known for only three months, and it felt as if we'd been together for years, dealing with long-standing and unresolved problems.

Her defensiveness began to rise, and the argument shifted toward retaliation. As we were on our way to the hotel for the night, I recall pulling over, meeting her gaze, and trying to bring calm. I expressed what became a recurring theme, evident in our emails and interactions today.

"I am not attacking you. That is not my intention. I am not trying to hurt you or prove superiority. I hope to understand the feelings at play and the reasons behind them, and to have my own perspective heard and understood. With that, we might find agreement and move toward a healthier resolution. We could work to avoid repeating this sequence of conflict in the future."

Growing up in an unpredictable and, at times, corrosive communication environment, I was determined that cycle wouldn't repeat itself in my relationships. Communication, connection, and understanding matter deeply to me. It was remarkable to me how these three elements seemed to take a back seat with Anya.

Sitting in the front seat, I worked to cultivate some level of understanding as I shared. I repeated what I had already shared, that this was not an attack, and asked what she was feeling. I've consistently emphasized the difference between facts and opinions, especially with Zoey now.

I watch so many people make false claims these days, presenting them as truth when they are not. How much healthier could we be if we expressed feelings like "I feel this is happening" or "It appears this is what you are doing"? Can we talk about that? Maybe your intention is different; perhaps my perception is wrong. But can we build from your understanding of how it feels to me while I learn what you genuinely feel or mean?"

I believe that is how real resolution is built.

But that didn't happen.

It also revealed these physical reactions in her arguing. She shut down, her shoulders tensed as they rose upward, and her face appeared to shift and turn into the ugliest expression I had ever seen. Her face would clench the instant she heard words she didn't like. From that point forward, it appeared both physically and mentally, she was preparing her response rather than listening.

Early signs of consistent self-absorption began to show up. Instead of recognizing these traits in herself, she would talk about her mother's issues. She routinely commented on her mother's self-absorbed behavior, her sister's similar tendencies, and how her seemingly non-confrontational brother had relocated to a distant state to avoid their mother. It appeared this unhealthy family communication structure had been in place for a long time.

"Swinging from attack and deflection to complete self-blame eradicates any chance for resolution or understanding."

Anya expressed this apprehension many times, as if it were a mantra. "I don't want to turn into my mother." Fast forward to the end of that year, past that first argument in the Midwest. We stayed together in a place in the Southeast. She was on the floor crying. She rarely cried, saying, "I don't want to become my mother."

I got to know Anya's mother over time and observed some unsettling, self-centered tendencies. It raised another red flag. Still, I hoped that Anya was working through her issues. I hoped she was recognizing some of the same detrimental elements I had experienced in my own family's communication habits growing up, and that she wouldn't repeat them, as I was determined not to.

I mentioned to her that I couldn't see her reaching anywhere near her mother's level of self-absorption issues. I hoped to reassure her with those words then. Now, more than a decade later, she seems to have developed tendencies that have surpassed her mother's in a troubling way. Those same signs would later become part of what I set out to understand in greater depth.

Back to the first argument, we finally reached our hotel. She appeared to go through a process of denial and defensiveness, followed by some hurtful comments. Eventually, she listened for a moment, calming somewhat, but another round of deflection and confusion followed. It felt as though the blame shifted from being entirely my fault to being entirely Anya's fault.

As I worked to correct those misconceptions and stimulate better communication, I was turned off by her negativity. "No, I'm not saying this is all your fault. I see an issue here, and I don't want to argue about it. We can talk calmly about it. Let's address it together and improve our communication. I'm open to your perspective. I also hope to be heard. I hope we can resolve this so that we can manage our disagreements in the future without having to revisit this same topic."

It was one of the few times she cried, saying, "This is me, this is all me. I'm the one at fault." It bothered me because I recognized the pattern in her. I believe swinging from attack and deflection to complete self-blame eradicates any chance for resolution or understanding. From that point, she followed a common cycle for her, moving into the critical statements: "I'm sorry, it's me, I'm a terrible person." This style was disconcerting.

I shared with her, "It's okay; you feel what you feel, and we can work through this together. We can communicate and learn. You're not a terrible person, and it's not all your fault. I am aware of and take responsibility for contributing to some of the friction here as well. We can both take responsibility and accountability for where we are."

I tried to build her up to reach some point of calm, then reiterated: "So, am I clear that this is what you feel or think? I'm not trying to take the conversation backward. I'm trying to clarify so we can conclude, define the issue, and close this out. Creating a result where we both cooperate, coordinate, and compromise on a healthy solution allows us to gain clarity so we don't have to revisit this topic. It may also help us identify and understand what keeps recurring, so we can recognize and address it as it arises and reach a faster resolution."

We stepped into the hotel, and a sense of ease began to settle in. Her shoulders loosened, her face softened. We shared a kiss. After handling a few room details and then moving toward the lobby for a drink, the atmosphere between us gently shifted. In that instant, the earlier conflict faded into the background, and its heaviness gave way to a cautious calm.

It appeared to be a resolution, but it still seemed as though it wasn't. Was what happened addressed and fully resolved now, or was it being pushed down and ignored by her, setting the stage for it to happen again?   Is this a major communication breakdown that could become a recurring and long-standing issue? In time, the answer to that question was yes.

Closing Thought

Overlooking early issues seldom prevents their return. Unaddressed, those cycles gain strength and repeat. I've learned that genuine bonds form when we acknowledge patterns, accept unease, and tackle difficult moments before they become routine.

CHAPTER 4.
Recognizing the Patterns Within Repeating Sequences

Opening Thought

Naming a pattern does not fix it. Still, for some, it can make it real enough to face, especially when both people are willing to see what keeps repeating and why. I requested quiet recognition over loud claims, trusting that patient attention might open healthier paths toward resolution. Those requests were denied.

Cycles like this played out over many years. She disliked the word "pattern" when I brought it up during arguments. I did not use it in a mean way; I used it to address what was being repeated. I would say, "Let's look at what keeps recurring here and where it's gone. How do we change this together?"

That would anger her. The word "pattern" would cause her face to tighten with anger and resentment, and a counterattack would commonly follow. Puzzled, I thought, "I'm seeing these themes and traits keep cycling back. We're having this same argument again and again. By naming it and getting to the root of it, couldn't that help us change it?"

It apparently couldn't, and it became a deflected situation where she took it as me attacking her, putting her down, and implying she was a bad person. This was all her interpretation. With her, balance rarely felt possible. We were going to look at it her way. In most instances, if an approach doesn't work with her perspective, it won't work for her. This became the defining shape of our communication. It continued until she filed for divorce and began routing all communication through her lawyer. Then she was able to attack freely and shield herself with legal protection.

Fast forward to the present day. She hasn't spoken a word to me in over two years. When she chooses to respond, it's generally via email, and she tends to avoid topics she does not want to address. Communication now flows primarily through her attorney, creating another layer of distance between us.

Her argumentative approach had been evident for years, sometimes far more intense depending on the topic. At times, while pleading for her to listen, I asked, "Could we record this argument so you can hear it later?" She took that as an insult. I didn't know what else to do.

She would sometimes go into rants and display cycles of self-absorption that were becoming more frequent, launching harsh criticisms, only to insist later that it was entirely her fault. I thought of asking but didn't, "If this is your fault most of the time, as you seem to claim, then why do you continue to allow this behavior? Why do you deny what keeps happening?" I understood that it wasn't solely her fault in our arguments. Still, it was part of the same repeating cycle.

The pattern I experienced was...

Dispute.

Locking up and shutting down any potential information or alternative viewpoints.

Counterattacking.

Slowing down to a point when she felt she wasn't being attacked.

Reaching a point where it seemed we might head in a healthier direction.

Then the bottom would drop out, and she appeared to take all the blame.

It's revealing to see how her acceptance and responses have shifted over the past decade. She moved from rarely expressing her feelings through tears to moments when she was overwhelmed, sitting on the floor and crying. At first, she would say, "I don't want to turn into my mother." Later, she confided, "I don't know how my mind is going to be in a few years. I don't know what I'll remember. I forget important details."

An issue beyond the emotional

I learned about an accident she had been in when she was younger. It was apparently bad and resulted in an injury that included an intense blow to the head. I spent some time researching the injury and its effects, both in the short and long term.

Details about this accident and its potential long-term effects were also being revealed. In a moment of problem-solving that was later forgotten, she asked whether some of these recurring arguments could possibly be related to or influenced by unresolved issues and her injury from the accident years ago. Unfortunately, following the same path Anya had committed to, the follow-through did not happen.

I researched potential outcomes. These elements could emerge later in life, contribute to memory issues, and lead to future problems. She was open to this discussion, but right around the time she filed for divorce, all of this became denial. She reverted to saying, "This doesn't affect me at all. I'm fine."

I observed drastic changes in communication over time with her. I say this not to be unkind, but because it appears to me that her mental and cognitive state may have been affected by physical challenges she's faced. In this apparent denial, I am concerned about what may be difficult for her to acknowledge or understand.

One of the aspects that raises questions for me about her behavior is her drinking. I noticed this early on, before we left the West

Coast, during our conversations before the book tour. I remember her becoming inebriated, and it was unsettling to see how she seemed to struggle with alcohol.

> *"Balance rarely felt possible. We were going to look at it her way. In most instances, if an approach doesn't work with her perspective, it won't work for her."*

It is not about the right to drink or indulge; that is entirely her choice. What troubles me is that she seems unable to recognize when she's had too much. This started when we first began living together and has not shifted since. When I am not around, particularly when she is alone with Zoey without someone else providing a ride, that weight grows for me. I have seen her get into a car after drinking. She may believe she was not impaired, but I question whether she fully understands, or is willing to accept, how affected she was.

There were frequent moments of tension when she returned from drinking with the neighbors when we were living together. I witnessed her speech coming off garbled and her balance unsteady. She insisted she "didn't have that much to drink" and "wasn't impaired." When I tried to point out what I observed, I asked, "Do you hear yourself mumbling? Should I record this so you can hear it? You're holding yourself up on the counter right now. Do you see any of this?" She would commonly dismiss my concerns. We fell into a recurring cycle. Eventually, she might say, "Oh, I am impaired," but it seemed as though it would then fade away a moment later, as if it hadn't happened.

She went out with a friend after the book tour while we were first living together. She returned, appearing unwell and unsteady that evening. She insisted, "Nope, I am fine. What do you mean?"

"Fine" shifted to "not so fine" as she threw up multiple times that night and was hungover and under the weather for the entirety of the next day.

This continued to concern me throughout our relationship. Jumping from one emotionally intense side to another added to the cognitive and mental issues, and now her health, how she got sick, and the frequency of her illnesses were all part of that same cycle.

Closing Thought

Rejection of patterns meant those cycles continued. I couldn't change her perception, but I could change my responses. It is sobering to see how easily denial becomes comfort, and how much time is lost when we look away from what might lead to resolution.

CHAPTER 5.
Shadows That Shaped a Father by Choosing Care Over Anger

Opening Thought

Pursuing a meaningful connection with my father shaped my values and approach to parenting. The patterns and behaviors I witnessed taught me to forgive, not for his benefit, but for mine and my daughter's. Holding onto anger would have robbed me of the grace I now carry.

Fathers shape some of us in complex ways. I was fine with the notion of having a Daddy issue or two, though my experiences differed from Anya's. She faced her own challenges when it came to bringing up her dad, and often in a negative light. I felt that the way I worked through, accepted, and let go of any negativity regarding my issues with my dad positively contributed to my growth as a father.

When it comes to Anya, there wasn't much shared about her father, aside from a passing mention of a terrible incident. On the occasions that I sought to understand more, the conversation would dwell on that one negative aspect. I also noted that Anya's mother viewed most men from Anya's past, every previous relationship, and male figures in general in an unfavorable light.

I had done my best to address my relationship with my father, but despite genuine effort and perseverance over time, the distance remained. I can't claim to be more mended than Anya when it comes to fathers, but stepping away from direct communication offered a sense of release. I made the attempt, then moved forward. The question of closure with her father remained unaddressed in our conversations.

Reflecting on my father and the men in my life, my earliest memories are of my grandfather on my mother's side. He faced challenges with drinking in the past and often had a stern demeanor toward my mother. As I got to know him more, I encountered a more troubling side of him. Visiting him sometimes felt obligatory, and I didn't have a meaningful conversation with him at any point that I recall. I carried a sense of frustration over how he treated my mother during her upbringing.

After my maternal grandfather's passing, I felt strongly about not attending his funeral. I know I could have been more supportive of my mother by going. Still, I was resolute in my decision not to honor someone who had caused my mother so much pain.

By comparison, my grandfather on my father's side was an honorable, kind, loving, and disciplined man. His influence in my early years overshadowed my father's. I felt a genuine connection with my grandfather, and his love was tough but warm.

I thought about how my father might have turned out differently if he were more like his dad, given the solid upbringing he had. I did not see my grandfather's influence on my father at all. They were close while also being distant. My father's unreliability puzzled me, especially considering how my parents went through a tumultuous cycle of separating and reuniting. I remember hoping they would stay together at first, but I came to realize it would be best for them to stay apart for good. The constant back-and-forth was exhausting.

I also had reasons to believe my father may have been unfaithful, which made me want to defend my mother, but as I reflect, there was likely much more to the situation than I could fathom. Still, my relationship with him was limited; we did some activities together, he did not feel especially connected to me.

Being around me looked more like a required task than a preferred choice. I tried to connect with him and engage him by playing football to gain his approval when I was younger, but it didn't pan out as I had hoped. When I got into music, I sought his validation too. I remember sharing my performances, inviting him often, but his responses shifted from "This place is too small" to "This place is too big." These appeared to be the justifications for not coming to see me perform. I don't believe he owns any of my books or albums. My attempts to connect didn't bear fruit.

There was a brief time when he was eager to connect again, but he married someone who I felt controlled him. He showed many signs of being submissive to her, and she didn't like me for reasons I couldn't comprehend, though she appeared not to have issues with my younger brother. I suspect some of her feelings were tied to my efforts to bond with my father. He would occasionally express a desire to spend time together, but those words rarely turned into action. Promises were made without any follow-through, and I gradually distanced myself from those words.

I initially felt angry about it, but I let that feeling go. Early on, I thought, "If I ever have kids, I don't want to be like that." He offered little besides financial support when I was younger. As I reflect on love and connection, I have few, if any, fond memories of my father. I hoped his words would stand the test of truth, and I yearned for that father-son connection.

Still, it was unrealistic and did not materialize. As I distanced myself, I found healing, not in a way that meant I was cutting him out forever, but I refused to be sidelined by empty promises and exhausted hopes. So, we drifted apart, and he seemed fine with it, making no effort to communicate apart from a few happy birthday emails over the years that stopped altogether long ago.

After Zoey was born, I felt a desire to try to mend our relationship. I imagined my father having and wanting a connection with his grandchild, especially since my brother wasn't planning to have kids. This was an opportunity for him outside the family he married into, which already had children. I reached out through my aunt, his sister, and my mother, inviting him to meet his granddaughter, hold her, and get to know her. I made it clear I wouldn't be there; my mother, Anya, and Zoey were present.

I had hoped this would be meaningful and allow for a new connection with Zoey, potentially paving the way for us to connect, but it didn't turn out that way. I heard from Anya that he held her briefly, asked a few questions, and then got distracted by his phone, which seemed to give him a reason to leave. I found that disappointing, but I let it go.

When my brother got married, it presented another chance for my father and me. By then, I was starting to embrace faith and forgiveness, feeling less anger toward my father and his actions or inactions from the past. I was more focused on what I had learned, not in an insensitive way, but in the sense that I had come to understand the father I had to be and the father I would be. I recognized what I would not repeat and held myself to a higher standard as a father. I would not have gained those perspectives if my father had been different, and I felt a sense of gratitude for both his actions and his failures, which helped shape me into a better father.

> *"Learning that I could forgive my father, while realizing I did not have to let the aspects that I found unhealthy, disrespectful, and wrong continue, brought peace. It was liberating when I could forgive the man, but could also distance myself from elements that I had no reason to experience or engage with anymore."*

At the wedding, I attempted to hug him, but his wife, still holding onto some unclear and unfounded resentment she seemed to have toward me, appeared to scoff as I embraced him and would not look me in the eye when I acknowledged her and said hello. His embrace was brief and distant. Throughout the event, Zoey seemed to want to connect with her grandfather. Her only other experience was with my mother's current husband, who I felt deserved the special title I gave him for grandfather, which was the same one I called my father's dad when I was little. He spent some time with her, and Zoey was having a great time; still, it was tough because the next day, Zoey asked, "What am I doing wrong that your dad doesn't want to know me or see me?"

Hearing that question, my heart sank. I reassured her that it was not her fault at all and mentioned that this might present an opportunity for her connection with him in the future. Still, I remained cautious about raising her hopes too high, sensing he would slip away once more, and that is precisely what unfolded.

It was painful, but by that point, I had already forgiven my father for his past behavior. I celebrated him for the growth I attained through those experiences, which helped me become a better father for Zoey. I also resolved not to let his disrespect extend to her. So, I left a door open, but he chose to stay distant. I haven't spoken to him in years, and he hasn't reached out to me or Zoey.

She occasionally asks why her grandfather does not want to know her, and that still stings. I no longer care about my relationship with him, but he is losing out on connecting with an outstanding girl who is loving, sensitive, and kind.

Watching Another Form of Giving Up

For the grandfather Zoey knows and spends time with, I value what he adds to her life, and I also notice a long-standing sadness in my mother and her husband. From what I've seen, my stepfather seemed to stop trying years ago, and with his health issues now, it feels as if he has let go entirely.

This pattern causes me to pause about Zoey witnessing that type of behavior in her grandfather. He's good at hiding it, but it's notable how Zoey has asked, "Why does he go to bed early so often?" Yes, he has some health issues, still, he appears to be a man who gave up long ago and is waiting to pass on rather than trying to heal and live life.

As for my daddy issues, I don't view them as an excuse. I am grateful for those experiences and wouldn't wish to change a single one of them. Through those challenges, I gained clarity about the type of father I would be, what I hoped to avoid, and what I should be cautious of. Despite the past turmoil with my father, I have found it in my heart to forgive him. I can still say I love him. While we don't communicate, I honor him as my father and respect the lessons he's taught me to be a better parent to Zoey, shaped by my experiences with him.

In that forgiveness, there was freedom and a great release. Learning that I could forgive my father while realizing I did not have to let the aspects that I found unhealthy, disrespectful, and wrong continue, brought peace. It was liberating when I could forgive the man, but could also distance myself from elements that I had no reason to experience or engage with anymore.

Closing Thought

Forgiveness released judgment and gave me direction. Watching promises fade and actions fall short taught me to choose presence over absence, accountability over anger, and to become the father I had to be by not repeating what I saw.

CHAPTER 6.
How Repeated Sicknesses Signaled What Denial Tried to Hide

Opening Thought

Wellness doesn't begin when we feel better; it starts when we face the habits and cycles that made us worse. Recognizing how we get sick, how often it happens, and what surrounds it can teach us to protect our bodies through sickness, health, weakness, and recovery.

Frequent illness defined much of what I witnessed, leaving her down for long stretches. While these issues no longer affect me, I remain concerned about her ability to care for Zoey. When she fell ill, which was often, it seemed to take a significant toll.

She routinely found herself unwell, and I noticed some recurring themes and signs in her illness. There were times when she struggled to recognize when she had too much to drink. This sometimes led her to match the pace of others who could handle far more and knew their own limits, while she seemed unaware of hers. Recovery from social gatherings often took a long time, commonly affecting her the next day. On several occasions, it affected her for many days afterward, which she denied had any connection to the drinking.

"Acknowledgment remained absent long-term. She would push to the point of sickness through drinking and activities that made recovery more difficult. She would refuse to rest, often requiring extended recovery, would acknowledge the issue briefly, then forget and repeat it."

Given the alcohol issue and her lack of self-care while drinking (possibly stemming from not recognizing how intoxicated she was), one might think she would want to take better care of herself, especially as a mother. Having to remind a grown woman was absurd. I would say, "We've seen this happen several times, where your next few days have been ruined. Maybe you should have some water or food." She responded dismissively, "I don't require that," a phrase she often used to deflect.

Then the consequences became evident. Whether from dehydration or other factors, she would be wrecked. Later, when visiting neighbors (who were unaware of the extent of Anya's issues), they would see her drinking but not see the full picture or the problem. Only part of the story was shared, and different approaches to alcohol consumption raised questions about her well-being. I'm not labeling the neighbors in any specific way. They had a better grasp of moderation and the effects of intoxication. Still, they drank with a woman who had no idea how to do the same. This was not helping the situation or her accountability.

When COVID-19 emerged, or many illnesses for that matter, she was left bedridden for extended periods. Illness was a recurring challenge during our time together, with times where self-care was not prioritized and physical health was often disregarded.

I understood she wasn't feeling well, and I did all I could to take care of her. I changed the sheets, brought her food, medicine, and water, along with other items, drinks, or food she requested. Despite consistent encouragement, witnessing her require reminders left me unsettled. Without reminders, concepts related to staying hydrated, eating, and taking simple steps to support her health were ignored. She became resigned to feeling unwell, allowing discomfort to persist rather than seeking to improve her condition.

Perhaps there was some uncertainty and concern about missing out. Still, acknowledgment remained absent long-term. She would push to the point of sickness through drinking and activities that made recovery more difficult. She would refuse to rest, often requiring extended recovery, would acknowledge the issue briefly, then forget and repeat it. Anya often looked miserable, to the point that Zoey would comment, "Mommy looks upset" or "Mommy doesn't look happy." Zoey made these observations often.

When I brought this up, I said, "I'm noticing this pattern and wanted to share my reasons. Would you consider holding off tonight, maybe drinking less, having a glass of water between drinks, or eating a snack of some kind?" The response felt defensive. My intentions centered on well-being; still, my concern was met as though I was crossing a line. In place of a collaborative approach to improving health, the conversation slipped into, "You're attacking me," and any effort to discuss this faded away.

Specific issues remained difficult to address during our relationship and appear to have left her with unhealthy habits and traits from my viewpoint. These same habits continue today, reflected in what Zoey shares with me.

When Zoey talks about neighborhood gatherings or parties that turn into late nights, the next day she will often say, "Mommy is resting, Mommy's taking a nap, Mommy has to be left alone right now," or "Mommy doesn't feel well." Zoey also mentions that she spends much of her time alone in her room, often on her iPad for long stretches on many weekends after party nights. More recently, she has shared that she doesn't like when Mommy drinks too much or how she acts with her. She has also said she is not supposed to talk about that with Mommy and that topics like this are not meant to be discussed between kids and adults.

While I don't wish for her to be sick, I notice that after what I would guess are her heavier nights, Zoey reaches out more often and wants to talk for longer on those days, and from what she shares, Anya is often still resting or Zoey is left by herself. Although I am not pleased with the situation, I appreciate the increased contact I get to have with her on those days. I love that in those moments Anya is not managing the iPad, turning off the internet, or preventing FaceTime as much, and that I have more opportunities to connect with Zoey.

It is unfortunate and questionable that she keeps getting sick the way she does and shows little accountability for the illnesses she could have prevented or for caring for herself. Considering all she has been through, including the car accident and several mental and cognitive factors, I pray for her growth and hope she will recognize what her health requires, for her sake and Zoey's.

Closing Thought

Healing begins when we stop making excuses and start taking responsibility. Accountability matters at every phase. A commitment to health requires facing what wore us down, not waiting until we feel good enough to care for our bodies.

CHAPTER 7.
Façades Built to Shield What Avoidance Still Protects

Opening Thought

Refusal to face the truth can wear down both those who turn from it and those who love them. People who refuse reality can cling to fantasies and false narratives for so long that they can lose any firm grip on what is true.

Avoiding exposure of vulnerable parts of herself became a dominant pattern shaping her choices and behavior. Among the many aspects she hid from others, including from herself, this stood out as central. This issue challenged our relationship and, I believe, continues to shape her interactions with the world.

I think about this aspect of Anya when it comes to Zoey, because she shows signs of remarkable brilliance. When she asks questions that are dismissed or ignored, I sense she will either quickly become disillusioned or, more likely, start digging deeper to find the truth. In time, I pray she will see the whole picture so she can make her own decisions. I am already astounded at how intuitive she has become and what she has been able to identify at such a young age.

I look forward to those aspects growing further within her, allowing her to distinguish what is true from what is false.

Early on, I sensed a mysterious side to Anya that was both alluring and attractive. That mystery slowly morphed into a more negative, falser front as she would have to make phone calls away from me or go into a bank and say, "Don't come in with me."

Shreds of Secrecy

There was one evening that became a turning point in trust, or rather, in the lack of it. I had come home early from writing. My routine for my third book involved writing in the mornings on the beach, then going to a café for coffee and more writing. I would make a few phone calls, and if I was writing in the evening, I would go to a bar now and then.

Returning home earlier than expected that evening, I found Anya with a shredder set up in the kitchen. She had boxes of documents and was methodically shredding them, without any prior mention that she planned to do this. As I approached her, she became protective and defensive, asking me to leave the room. That was a turn-off. In that moment, as I tried to trust and understand, I gave her that space, but the secrecy gave me pause.

Now, I'm curious what else she was hiding from me. Based on what she shared about specific experiences, I question what was going on because I don't know. That moment, less than a year into our relationship, created trust issues that I later addressed by saying, "I don't feel good about this. This seems problematic. Can we talk about this?" Despite that, those concerns were not discussed, and worse, they were dismissed.

New Friends. Old Walls

When we first started having problems, it was still early in the relationship. I asked her, "Would you talk to somebody? Would you talk to a friend?" She didn't have many friends; she spoke to one person occasionally and had few connections. While she did contact a few people, there was a great deal of solitude surrounding her. I tried to encourage her to connect with others, saying, "Okay, let's get out more and meet people," especially after Zoey was born. I hoped we could connect with others, but she remained withdrawn and more isolated.

Later, after we moved farther north, she gathered with a group of neighbors and quickly became friends with them. Then, as she developed these friendships, I began spending more time away from the group. It wasn't about or against them. I thought giving her space to build new relationships in my absence could help her. There was so much friction between us and so little joy that I thought her time with others, without me, could benefit her, but also Zoey and me as well.

Hiding in Plain Sight

I liked these neighbors, but if there was going to be a "who do you get" aspect in a breakup, I consciously spent more time away to allow her to forge those connections. Part of my intention was that learning to be social might improve our connection, not as far as the marriage was concerned, that was long over, but it could enhance our communication.

During my time with them, I remember one neighbor saying, "We see her pretty often, but I have no idea about her." There were jokes about how "she is a complete mystery." I could relate to that, as it mirrored my own experience. She was a complete mystery, but it was no longer alluring or intriguing; it was hiding.

She may still be hiding a great deal from those around her. She can present any version of herself she chooses in the moment, obscuring the aspects she does not want seen or known. Without me nearby, she may feel it's easier to create and believe a narrative based on her perception, regardless of whether it reflects the truth. Allowing these neighbors and friends to see only what she wants them to see is not helping her growth, healing, transparency, or commitment to truth.

I've sent emails in the past saying, "I pray for you, and I pray for your healing, and I love you." I send them because I know I'm supposed to love her, not as a partner from the past, but as someone of faith. Her responses have come in wild emails: "I don't want your prayers. I'm happier than I've ever been. I have great friends who see me for who I am. No one else sees the problems you saw."

My first response in that moment would have been defensive, so I chose not to send it.

"They don't see it because you've continued to hide it."

She presented different versions of herself in various social contexts. What if the person she is currently with eventually sees through this façade? Will she be able to continue hiding this side of herself and keep up appearances? Hiding became a way of life for her. I don't know if she knows who she is, but I do know she knows how to hide.

This persisted as we were separating. Zoey was not two years old when I brought it up with my mother to keep her in the loop; we had a better connection then. My mother, though, much like Anya, could not hear the truth of the situation.

When it came to Anya's mother, Anya did not mention the separation or the difficulties in our relationship for several years. She continued to keep this hidden. When we visited her mother, it was requested that I refrain from speaking about our struggles. She wasn't ready to discuss it. She still has not shown willingness to face or address many of the true aspects of our shared history.

In her hiding, in her inaccuracies, and in what she's concealed about me, recasting me as an awful person in her narrative, it doesn't bother me because I know who I am. I understand the objective truth of the situation, including the actions and substantiated elements that occurred. As I've already shared, I can accept that reality, while I don't believe she can.

I find that unnerving because she has constructed a universe that works for her and presents it to others as she wishes. I don't feel compelled to call her neighbors and friends to say, "No, here's what's going on." I've received some side-eyes from them, but that doesn't trouble me. I won't defend myself to those who have chosen to see only one side without considering another. What good would that serve?

It's hard to watch someone in deep pain ignore the facts, evidence, and truth that confront them daily, denying reality at any cost to maintain the illusion of comfort and control. Anya may have withdrawn into a world of inaccuracies, perhaps misguiding herself and holding onto a fantasy that she believes in.

So, when she responds, "I'm happier than I've ever been. I didn't have these kinds of problems with anyone else. It was all you," she seems to erase the woman who once sat on the floor crying, saying, "I have to improve my communication. I see the traits. I see the signs. I see the issues; please help me."

> ### *"Hiding became a way of life for her. I don't know if she knows who she is, but I do know she knows how to hide."*

As the arguments persisted, she occasionally realized that she wasn't being attacked. She understood that I wasn't trying to one-up her but rather to improve the situation. When she expressed a desire for better communication, there was a brief moment, a ray of light, a sense of hope. It was as if she were coming out from the shadows into the light. Still, it was not long before she retreated to a comfort zone that allowed her to do what she wanted and see the world as she wanted to see it.

One of the main issues, and this is why I am careful with naming traits, characteristics, and elements I experienced, as well as how I present this book, is this:

I believe Anya might do all she could to stop this book from getting out there.

She would want to avoid being seen from a view that contradicts hers.

I've sometimes thought about sharing the emails she wrote me with her mother, my mother, or her friends, not to expose them, but to offer a different perspective. I might say, "Look at the person you think you have a full picture of, and here is how they respond privately and some of the hurtful words that have been directed at me." Still, I recognize that doing so would serve no constructive purpose.

Seeing and Blindness

Some readers may be earlier in this story than I was. If any of this connects to where you are now, it may be worth sitting with and pausing for a moment to make a plan, before the strings become harder to untangle. To reach the place where you can say, "I don't think this will get better, and I don't see a way for it to improve," and act on that, takes honesty that gets harder the longer you wait. I wouldn't change a single event, experience, or day that led to Zoey's birth, and I would go through it all again. Still, if someone else can identify the signs sooner and make a different choice, maybe it is time.

One cornerstone of this record is for Zoey to hear my side, my views, and my perspective beyond the facade, the presentation, and the problems routinely disregarded, dismissed, and forgotten.

For someone else, this may help you recognize when you are being blinded. It may equip you to step away from the wrong situation, find the right person, and build a foundation grounded in healthy communication, transparency, and a positive connection. And if the window for that has already passed, perhaps this record becomes more than that, a way to show a son or daughter that one parent saw the full picture, documented with care, and chose to stand in the light regardless of the cost.

It saddens me that Zoey must navigate this divorce and its many challenges. I wish her experience could be different. While I can't change her mother's actions, and, despite her previously stated desire for improved communication and greater openness, Anya's long-standing misgivings have contributed significantly to what unfolded.

I pray that transparency and honesty become possible for her healing and Zoey's benefit, and that she faces accountability for her actions and choices. To date, these are challenges she has chosen not to face and seems unwilling to confront.

Closing Thought

Helping another break free from a self-made prison becomes far more challenging when they believe they are already free and content within the confines of their own misconceptions and the make-believe reality they have created.

CHAPTER 8.
Choosing Clarity Over Comfort to Protect Her Future

Opening Thought

Prioritizing truth over temporary peace sometimes requires sharing what may be difficult to hear. Here, it means leaving a record that clarifies rather than conceals, trusting that understanding today becomes healing over time.

Writing this message for Zoey means documenting what she deserves to know when she's ready to understand it. What follows moves between addressing her directly and documenting what others in similar situations may recognize or relate to. Zoey, I am concerned that you might see it as an attack on your mother, and that is not my intention.

I hope that your love, trust, and knowledge of me will help you understand my perspective and see the clarity, honesty, transparency, and humility in how I am sharing this with you and others.

Some of what I share may be difficult to hear. This message is written for you and for anyone experiencing communication issues with someone else. It could help them, allow them to relate, or lead them to find peace amid their struggles. If they have a child as extraordinary as you, they can better understand the situation and decide on the next steps without regret. If they don't have that, and it's a situation they can leave, then it may be time for them to do so.

This may be the piece that sparks someone to say, "Oh, okay, I recognize this. I have to change this." They may notice recurring signs and relate to them, and see that it is time to shift.

The other piece is for you, Zoey. It's about my experiences. There are many moments and details I couldn't share with you directly. We've had an outstanding level of connection and transparency in our communication, and I've mentioned that there are matters I cannot discuss due to the parenting plan. When shared from a subjective perspective, this information could still be turned against me. Anya has, at times, twisted my words and made inaccurate claims, but that is not where the focus belongs right now.

What matters to me is for you to understand where I'm coming from. I don't think your mother is a bad person. I've told you, Zoey, that regardless of your mother's feelings toward me or what she has said to you, I will continue to love your mother. She gave birth to you, and she is important to you, which is important to me. This is part of my faith and what is required of it. I don't want to be with her, and I'm not going to try anymore, but I will strive to love her because of you and my faith.

That has been challenging to commit to, but I continue to do it. Her actions have been difficult for me, but I don't want you to stop loving her, and I don't want this to pull you away from her. My purpose is to enlighten you and help you recognize specific behaviors. If any of these traits or communication styles arise between you two, I hope you will be more forgiving, acknowledging that this could be a mental health issue and that it's not about you.

I hope that by observing these traits, you won't distance yourself from your mother, but instead, perhaps grow closer by recognizing some of her unaddressed challenges. Please understand what I'm sharing here and the root of my intention. This is about my experiences, my feelings, and what I went through. It is about why I kept pushing through and why I tried to build a stronger foundation of understanding within our family, all of it tied to, and focused on, you. My efforts were for you, my love, working to support communication, not only for her and me but for you and her, for all of us.

> *"Regardless of your mother's feelings toward me or what she has said to you, I will continue to love your mother. She gave birth to you, and she is important to you, which is important to me."*

Unfortunately, that open communication and willingness to change didn't happen. By the time you read this, you might no longer call her "Mommy"; you will more than likely refer to her as "Mom." As you get older, you might see certain unhealthy behaviors in her that, while they seem focused on you, likely have roots elsewhere. I hope that you'll reach a place where you can say, "Maybe this isn't her mistreating me. Perhaps it's a struggle she's trying to manage internally, and it isn't about me."

Unable to Face or Feel the Discomfort

There was a time when Anya expressed concern about her behavior. She acknowledged her self-absorption and stated that she wanted to avoid ending up like her mother. She also experienced unease regarding the lingering effects of a car accident. Over time, her expressed concerns about self-improvement seemed to fade, replaced by statements that no issues or problems existed with her at all.

To me, this denial seemed both sad and alarming. I gently suggested to Anya that being aware of these issues and actively working to improve them could make a significant difference. Still, what I hoped would shift remained consistent despite our discussions.

I offered her some problem-solving ideas and encouraged her to create a list of ways to address the issues she sometimes recognized. Still, most of our discussions remained as words, rather than leading to actions that could bring about improvement or healing.

Zoey, you once told me, and I loved this so much, that you wanted to be a problemsolver during a talent show at summer camp, and you are. I love that because it reflects what I was doing throughout my time in entertainment, finding the right parts, pieces, or changes, and communicating across all sides of an issue to bring about the best work.

A key part of the work I did centered on problem-solving, specifically on how to help people communicate effectively with one another, across those who knew each other and those who did not, those who got along and those who did not, and across a range of different personalities, ideas, and expectations.

I see myself as an excellent problem solver and wanted to support Anya in that role. In one moment, she would say she had to change and solve the problems she claimed she saw and had, and in the next, she would insist there were no problems at all, and that I was in the wrong.

When I shared ideas, it was not about being right or claiming that she was wrong. It was about creating a mutual understanding together with her. As you may recognize some of the lessons described here, I hope you will be mindful of these nuances and watch for them in any relationship, whether professional or personal.

When you start to see these signs, you may realize that this is a person to avoid, a business to steer clear of, or a friend to step back from. If resolution seems too far out of reach, if communication is not clear, or if any sense of love, honor, transparency, or accountability is missing, it may be time to communicate with the goal of creating change or creating distance.

By learning those lessons and recognizing those signs and traits early on, you might find yourself more prepared for what comes next.

So, to my love, Zoey, my rock and the true reason for my life, this all comes down to you. Please understand that my intention is to share my perspective, help you recognize these traits, and encourage you to be forgiving toward your mother when her actions or traits suggest that the issue may not be about you, but rather behaviors and traits she exhibits.

She hasn't been held accountable, and she's gotten away with it, so she continues in the same way. It's not against you; it's how she operates. Understanding this may make it easier to love her in times of friction and confusion about who she is, and to forgive her for words or actions that feel hurtful or out of character. I hope that makes sense to you. I love you. And that's the intention of this. I hope you carry that intention with you as you read through this and experience a touch of what I went through.

Closing Thought

Revelation motivated by protection matters more than silence preserved for comfort. This record shows patterns and offers perspective, trusting that what is documented today can guide my daughter's awareness and discernment tomorrow.

CHAPTER 9.
Surrounded by Voices That Refuse to Question the Story

Opening Thought

Problematic and unhealthy influences are not only those who encourage poor choices, but also those who surround someone with approval while refusing to challenge a single version of what they have been told. When comfort replaces curiosity, inaccuracy can become accepted as truth.

Observed over time, the support around Anya showed that some people genuinely tried to help, while others, unaware of their role, deepened her detrimental behavior. Reflecting on Anya's situation, I considered her choice of lawyer, who seemed to resonate with her beliefs and communicate in a similar style. I felt that this approach, while perhaps comforting to Anya, was also misguided and inadvertently helped to compound her selfish behavior.

With some knowledge of the law, I've come to appreciate the complexities involved in communicating with her lawyer.

When I was served with the divorce papers, some questions came to mind.

Why this approach?

Why now?

It was frustrating to see this conflict stem from baseless claims that I intended to take Zoey away, which wasn't true.

That only reinforced Anya's distorted perception of reality.

The lawyer's approach allowed Anya to view the situation solely from her own perspective, which seemed to uphold Anya's lack of accountability and responsibility. It appeared that the lawyer, perhaps unintentionally, reinforced her misconceptions, making it seem acceptable for Anya to express untruths and act on inaccuracies. While Anya may have been aware that these actions were misguided, she likely felt a newfound sense of support for her choices, her inaccuracies, and her disdain, without any form of accountability to the truth. Unhealthy patterns arise from narratives Anya has created, which have allowed her to present a version of events that appears to line up with her wishes.

My Mother

No one seemed to hold her accountable for her behavior toward my mother or me. While I am not blaming Anya for the distance that grew between my mother and me, I do recognize and observe how she seemed to contribute to it.

My mother chose to prioritize her granddaughter over our relationship, and I can understand that decision, as I suspect she had reservations about losing her bond with Zoey because of her unease about what Anya might have done if my mother had decided to raise questions about what had occurred.

"Unchallenged affirmation from those who
accept an incomplete story harms her.
Hidden truths remain concealed as she
refutes all other claims."

Fast forward a year and some since we had last spoken, I met my mother while on a visit to see Zoey the next day. I listened sincerely to her concerns about Anya, what she had observed, and her perceptions of what happened from her view. I had hoped I could connect, share my experiences, and be heard, but the conversation was unproductive. My mother, much like Anya, was not ready to listen to what I had to say. That day, as we attempted to reconnect, it brought up memories of when I first told her I didn't think this marriage would work out. I saw her cycle through anger, sadness, and guilt-tripping tactics, telling me I couldn't do this to my baby daughter. Then, like Anya, denial set in, and we didn't speak of it again for some time.

My mother may have had concerns about losing her bond or spending time with Zoey if she had spoken up. That may have influenced her decisions or the conversations that followed. I don't hold this against her, and I've found a way to forgive her. It pains me to think about the relationship my mother and I are missing out on and how she seemed to yield to a seemingly well-supported but misguided view of Anya. Still, I understand why my mother felt compelled to act the way she did.

Support without Question

Anya's confidence appeared to grow with this new support system. She was surrounded by a circle of friends in the neighborhood who primarily heard her side of the story, perhaps without fully grasping the complete context. They embraced her narrative, seemingly unaware of the importance of considering different perspectives, which might have influenced her actions.

This environment allowed Anya to express herself more freely and fictionally while avoiding challenges to her views. What she freely constructed seldom squared with what the record showed. Unchallenged affirmation from those who accept an incomplete story harms her. Hidden truths remain concealed as she refutes all other claims.

While she might be aware of some of her inaccuracies, I've begun to question whether there is a part she struggles to understand, accept, or believe exists. There were moments when this distortion crystallized around specific issues, such as her pursuing legal action over a simple image of Zoey and me that was lawfully shared as part of a podcast tribute to our daughter. Once confronted with the actual law and documentation, those legal claims dissolved into silence; still, her perception did not shift. Episodes like this showed how quickly she could move from attack to retreat without ever acknowledging the underlying truth.

I recognized I couldn't address these issues directly; I was trying to resolve matters with someone who lacked the openness and humility to confront realities supported by evidence. Knowing this, I understood that if I presented proof, she would deny it. She would initially reject it, then acknowledge it, only to forget that acknowledgment the next day and revert to her inaccuracies from before.

The attributes Anya settled into have allowed her to remain stagnant, avoiding acknowledgment of her ongoing issues and continuing to conceal aspects of herself or actions she does not want others to see. It appears that she continues to avoid facing the truth, arranging and authoring a reality that allows her perspectives to comfortably line up with her desires, seemingly without regard for narratives or facts that may contradict her own.

Closing Thought

Voices that echo only what they have been told often offer false comfort in place of true clarity. When those close to someone accept one version without ever considering another, empty approval can fill a space where honest reflection might otherwise have grown.

CHAPTER 10.
Living as an Obstacle to Her Preferred Narrative

Opening Thought

Reduced to a problem rather than being seen as a person can expose the fragility of another's account. When your silence maintains their story, you may stop existing as a human to them, becoming an inconvenience, a disposable barrier blocking the path they want.

Absence would make her version easier to maintain without challenge. While she would likely deny it for appearances' sake, I sense her story depends on my silence. Considering how fiercely Anya protects her narrative, the version of reality she wants Zoey to see carries significant weight. Without me present, her version of events would go unquestioned. She could continue presenting what she wants to be seen as accurate, with no accountability to the truth.

My passing would leave her version of events unopposed. This is not an overdramatic claim. She has constructed a narrative that allows her to view the circumstances in a particular way, sharing only the specific details of her choosing and accepting falsehoods that form a story based on her beliefs over the facts. It would be much easier for her if I were not around to maintain and amplify that story with no one to question or contradict it.

This became clear when she hired a lawyer. In her mind, the blame had shifted from being her fault to all my fault. Playing out a denial of the past, she has overshadowed any positive memories, substituting them with her anger and perspective, leaving me feeling like the rival in her narrative.

Anya shares what she wants others to see, regardless of whether it is true or false. I've looked back at emails that show contradictory and harsh tones, such as "I wouldn't do this," when she had done exactly that many times, and "I wouldn't say that," when I have texts and emails proving she wrote those words, alongside jabs like "I don't know if you love Zoey" and the power play of "You have no right to have any control over Zoey."

The Ice Cream No Go

I asked her via email to consider working together to improve our connection for Zoey's benefit numerous times. I suggested that we spend some time together, the three of us, as Zoey had requested, and I proposed going out for ice cream. This could show Zoey that we could share moments together. Though she is the last person I'd choose to spend time with, for Zoey's sake, I was prepared to do this for her. I hoped it might improve the co-parenting connection, but Anya didn't respond to any of those emails.

We could have gone for a walk or to a small ice cream shop nearby. Zoey asked for exactly that. Still, in Anya's seemingly self-centered state, the focus was not on Zoey; it landed on her own desires and perceptions, and in most cases, little else seemed to matter.

In her hesitation, it appears Anya struggled to consider committing to that, let alone respond. Still, it feels significant that Zoey sought and continues to seek that connection and time with the three of us together. In her selfishness, Anya could not and would not offer it. She will not respond when Zoey or I ask her. To me, this reveals a great deal about her character and her lack of consideration for Zoey's wishes. It seems to reflect a narrowed focus that cannot extend past her own viewpoint.

"Playing out a denial of the past, she has overshadowed any positive memories, substituting them with her anger and perspective, leaving me feeling like the rival in her narrative."

If she were to face these realities, put in the effort, and be willing to sit down with the three of us in a social setting, I don't know if she could handle it. It might unravel her. Given that she can't address, respond to, or handle a simple, short outing with the three of us getting ice cream highlights a critical flaw in her ability to move past her selfish requirements and one-sided perspectives. This is not denying me or my requests; this is denying Zoey and what she wants.

Regardless, I Will Keep Trying

I will not stop asking for and pushing toward a positive and healthy relationship with Anya, regardless of how she ignores my requests. I am committed to building a cooperative, transparent, and respectful coparenting relationship that benefits my daughter and allows us to communicate, compromise, and connect in the best way possible, thereby forming the strongest mutual support system.

This includes the ability to communicate honorably for Zoey's benefit, as well as how she speaks with Zoey. Anya's inability to do that, along with her anger and her desire to erase all other narratives in favor of her own, presents problems.

Perhaps that's one reason why I'm writing this book: to share information that allows others to understand, and for Zoey to grasp a fuller truth than the version that makes her mother comfortable.

One of my goals is for Zoey to be able to reflect on aspects of her mother, recognize patterns and attributes, and understand what is happening. This is about wisdom and awareness for Zoey. For her emotional safety, she should be able to name these behaviors and know how to navigate them. This is not about taking her away from her mother; it's about helping her identify these behaviors and understand that they are not her fault.

I wish for Zoey to see these elements and learn how to respond in the healthiest way possible, with the understanding that these issues may mostly come from her mother. I hope this knowledge and awareness can help Zoey maintain a healthier relationship with Anya.

Closing Thought

Realizing you've been erased from someone's record while you still exist in their life creates a chilling reality. They've rewritten what happened to exclude you, choosing the world where you no longer matter or exist.

CHAPTER 11.
Marrying in Haste
for Parenthood Over
Partnership

Opening Thought

Vows can be made to the person standing right in front of us. They can also be made to the hopes we carry within us, to the dreams of a family we long to create, or to the child who awaits birth. Through this experience, I learned that a vow and a covenant are not the same, and it now seems contradictory to me that, when two people wed, a simple spoken vow is all that is asked, rather than the deeper commitment a covenant of action would require.

Distinguishing whether I should have married her, versus whether I should have been with her at all, matters. In my heart, I know that the difficult path I traveled with Anya was the specific, destined road I had to take to receive the divine gift of my daughter. All the tumultuous, unpredictable experiences, the awful moments, and the arguments were necessary for me to have her. But the question remained: did I have to marry Anya?

With a different perspective now, I see events with greater understanding. She found out she was pregnant before a trade show event where I was a speaker. There was a new spark inside me that I couldn't define, intense feelings, and an underlying, undeniable element to it all. I remember tears of joy. I also recall her limited emotions, but I was more focused on the experience of becoming a father.

A New Focus and Shift

In that moment, I turned toward wanting to have a child. What I once thought was not possible suddenly seemed doable. Intense, energetic emotions washed over me as I considered what being a father would mean. Still, I noted that the same fervor was absent when it came to the concept of marriage. I sensed that this was what she wanted.

Throughout my time with her, my primary focus was on making her happy. She was giving me a child, this dream, and in return, I thought I should give her a ring. So, I proposed.

The proposal stayed with me, though not in the way I had hoped. I aimed to make it special by choosing the beach and getting down on one knee. The weather, the beach, the time of day. Those details stayed clear.

The restaurant afterwards, a short walk from our place, drew warm responses from those we told.

This whole experience felt less about us and more about the act of getting married, as if it were tied to her happiness and the child we were expecting. It didn't feel like it was for me.

Now I see it. Committing to the concept of parenthood with a partner for the child, rather than the partnership of two people helping and loving each other. It was about becoming a father, not becoming a husband. I know I should not have gotten married, still having Zoey, yes, but not marrying Anya.

In hindsight, would it have been better for Anya if we hadn't tied the knot? Would that decision have affected Zoey differently? Would the situation altogether have turned out better if we had understood that this wasn't meant to be a marriage but could still have been another type of family?

Yes, we could have been together and raised Zoey, but there might have been a clearer and healthier separation early on. Instead, we lived behind a false front, with the word "married" applied to us and few actions to support it.

Zoey grew up seeing us in separate rooms for the bulk of her life. She witnessed arguments and didn't see a couple who were close as parents. Would it have been better for her if the lines had been drawn more definitively, instead of this effort to appear happy or present ourselves in a way that was not truthful?

I'm impressed by where Zoey is now; she has a great understanding of the situation. Still, I question if it would have been better for her to see the relationship in a different light earlier on.

The Ocean's Answer

After we got the rings, I decided to wear mine, though we weren't married then. I was testing both the ring and the idea of being a husband. A few weeks later, while swimming in the ocean, a significant wave tossed me. It was not huge by East Coast standards, but it was enough to knock me over and pull the ring off my finger.

As soon as I recognized the ring had come off, I knew it was gone. Clenching my fist and realizing the ring was not on my hand filled me with a mix of disappointment, while another part of me asked, "Is this a sign?" I looked around, trying to find the ring, feeling my way through the water, searching for it, but knowing I was not going to find it.

I got another ring ordered, and during that time, I wasn't wearing it; I wasn't missing it. My focus was still on the baby coming, and in those moments, the question of whether getting married was the right step for me, for us, or if this was only about the baby kept circling. This uncertainty lingered.

Amid some arguments and poor communication, shaped by my upbringing in a family of divorce, I began to think about how to build our relationship in the best way possible for our child.

It's a Girl.

I came back from a morning of writing at the beach while Anya was at an appointment. She went through many experiences alone, choosing for herself what to share and what to keep. At this appointment, she learned our baby's gender without me. It was another instance of her keeping what she wanted to herself, with little consideration that this might be an experience for us to share together.

I would have liked the chance to share that experience with her and learn the gender together, but given that she often didn't act as a partner and made decisions like that on her own, I wasn't given that respect or opportunity.

> *"Committing to the concept of parenthood with a partner for the child, rather than the partnership of two people helping and loving each other. It was about becoming a father, not becoming a husband."*

She returned to our place with a shiny silver bag shortly after I got home and handed it to me. Inside, there was some white tissue paper covering an item I could not make out. At the edge of the tissue, I noticed a hint of what appeared to be white lace. My first thought was that this might be some form of lingerie. We had been trying to work on our intimacy, which was far from good, but she did seem at times to want to improve it. As I began to open the package, I thought, Okay, this has got to be lingerie. Nice.

As I pulled it out, I saw it was a onesie. That was when I found out it was going to be a girl.

In that moment, I can still place exactly where I was standing in the living room. Every angle, every smell, the details have stayed with me. I had thought it would be a boy. I figured it would be easier, a buddy I could be rowdy with, and we could be the two guys, early out of the gate. He could be cute but strong, and an array of other ideas that floated around after I found out Anya was pregnant.

But a second after learning it would be a girl, a part of me gave way all at once. It was remarkable how quickly it all shifted, from all my ideas of having a boy to, without a doubt, feeling so glad it was a girl.

I cherished that realization, thinking, yes, I'm going to be a girl dad. The anticipation, the exhilaration, and the intensity of it all, along with the knowledge of being a father to a daughter... I still do not have the words to describe it.

Becoming a dad became profoundly significant to me. It meant more than the world to me.

Then we got married. As we traveled from the southeast to the northeast for the wedding, the entire ride felt different. I experienced a mix of emotions I was reaching for and others I couldn't name. I thought to myself, okay, I'm going to get married. There was a clear difference between what was going on in her mind and mine. Still, this didn't feel like a joyous occasion.

The idea was not to have a big wedding, and we decided that a small, intimate ceremony would be fine. I also saw there were mental aspects to consider, especially regarding her. She didn't have many people available to share it with. A larger wedding would have included a host of people and potential issues, so we settled on the concept of elopement.

I suggested a beautiful bridge not far from where I grew up in the northeast. As a child, I remembered it as a crappy old, abandoned train bridge that had been renovated into a bike path and walking bridge. Halfway out, overlooking the water and the woodwork, it looked great and offered an excellent view of the river and the foliage on both banks.

As a kid, I visited the bridge on late weekend nights when it was in disrepair. We had to sneak under a "do not trespass" sign to get there. It was hazardous, but we did it for the rush. We would navigate the broken boards and climb down to a small island in the middle. It was reckless, especially when we added alcohol into the mix.

That High, for a Moment, is Where I got Married.

That morning stayed with me. I was at my friend's house, the one who was officiating the ceremony. My anticipation was not about my soon-to-be bride or the ceremony. She was pregnant and wore a dress that made her glow and accentuated her bump. The small child making up that bump held my attention more that day.

Standing there, I was drawn more to her stomach than her eyes. Taking our vows, looking into her eyes, my gaze kept drifting down. I was looking at my child, or at least where my child was then, and feeling an intense connection. In a way, those vows of love, protection, and forever felt directed at the child inside Anya, rather than the woman standing in front of me.

From the moment we found out she was pregnant, to that day on the bridge, to Zoey's birth and the years that followed, I did my best to create a family for Anya and Zoey. I tried to work through all the issues for both of them, but our relationship slipped into a strange cruise-control mode that was not a marriage of love, or much of a marriage at all. Anya shared vows and words that gave me hope, but the lack of action kept it from becoming more.

Appearances did not ring true.

There were times when I took off the ring. The first time stayed with me. It wasn't a year into our marriage. During an argument, and although I'm not an aggressive person, I took off the ring and threw it across the room, declaring, "I'm not wearing this. This isn't real. I'll keep up appearances for your mom."

Later, in our separation and trying to address the issues, Anya seemed more concerned about how it all looked. It was astounding to hear, in the middle of an argument aimed at finding a resolution, that she cared more about how it looked to her mother than about working toward common ground and connection between us. She seemed more focused on making sure I was wearing the ring when we visited her mother than on sharing the truth about the issues and problems we were facing. It all felt like a presentation and a performance.

It was years after our separation before she finally stopped wearing her ring. She was agitated when I suggested it was time to sell the rings. "I plan to keep this," she said. But was it only about holding on to memories? There weren't many good times to recall. Our strongest connection centered on our shared love for Zoey, which was why I didn't understand why she wanted to keep the ring.

Many signs. Many Warnings

I've questioned at times if I ever got the best out of her, though the best of her didn't feel like much or show up all that often. If I had to do it all over again, would I? Maybe I would have drawn a line in the sand, saying, "I'm going to take care of you. We'll make this work; we'll live together and raise our child as co-parents rather than a couple."

Were all the signs there that it would be a mistake in the long run, including the issue with the ring, the lack of feelings, and the blank look on her face during the ceremony?

When I brought it up later, she dismissed my concerns, saying, "Oh no, I was feeling so emotional." I responded, "How so? What emotions were you feeling?" The response was the all-too-common one-two punch of unhealthy engagement with her, my questions were disregarded (punch one), and I was dismissed (punch two).

After the ceremony, we had lunch that afternoon. Dinner that evening included cake and the scripted act of smashing it in her face at a friend's house, but it all felt contrived. I tried to create a meaningful experience for her to build on, but it wasn't there.

The real bond was about Zoey and what lay ahead for us.

So, should I have gotten married? I can see now the answer was no.

I did it for Anya.I did it for the baby on the way. And I did it for my mother. I didn't do it for me.

Closing Thought

Mistakes carry different costs. Mine was believing that wanting love to work and giving my all to it meant it would. Love cannot be created by sheer will alone, nor can it be sustained when only one side holds the weight for two.

CHAPTER 12.
Rewriting a Past to Conserve Comfort and Dodge Consequences

Opening Thought

Belief cannot take root where promises are treated as disposable, rewritten, or erased the moment they become uncomfortable. When commitments are abandoned for convenience, genuine connection may disappear. Trust requires memory, accountability, and consistency, none of which survive when convenience becomes the only priority.

Letting go of guilt and remorse too quickly can shortcut the growth that working through them builds. Throughout my relationship with Anya, I recognized a recurring cycle. Authentic regret for the hurtful actions between us was seldom present. Apologies were rare outside of conflict. During heated moments, it seemed that responsibility was routinely shifted or deflected onto me. As tensions began to settle, I observed a distinct change. Suddenly, I would hear repeated apologies, such as "I'm sorry, it's my fault, it's all my fault," expressed reflexively rather than as an acknowledgment of sustained accountability.

But once this cycle completed itself and the dust settled from our latest confrontation, I found that she carried no lasting weight from what had happened. The hurtful actions she took went unacknowledged. I observed no ownership, no real reflection, and no lasting effect on her conscience. It felt as though she had devised a way to dismiss these experiences, as if erasing them from her memory would render it all acceptable again.

This showed itself in her memory issues, her approach to managing difficult situations, and the ways she handled circumstances that perhaps overwhelmed her capacity to cope. She moved forward unburdened, as though those experiences had been overwritten entirely.

When confronted with significant inaccuracies and misleading statements, when she was caught in clear contradictions, I saw no regret. I observed no promise that "I won't do that again" and no commitment to any positive change. It was both sad and fascinating to witness this complete absence of accountability.

One incident before her pregnancy demonstrated this. She had gone out with a friend, and when she returned home, she was heavily intoxicated. She brought herself home without a call or cab, operating a vehicle in no condition to do so, placing herself and others on the road in jeopardy.

I had encouraged her to go out with this friend because I hoped she would socialize more, connect with people, and get out of the house. She had been increasingly isolated, rarely communicating with others, and when she did interact, it commonly happened away from me without explanation.

This friend of Anya's lived close by. She could handle her alcohol well. She drank heavily but came across as a person who did so responsibly. Anya's friend seemed to know her limits and, more so, understand the effects. I watched Anya struggle with both. She often appeared unaware of her own state or limitations.

When she stumbled through the door that night, I felt a mix of anger and concern for her well-being and safety. I attempted to address what had happened, but she seemed so far gone that I understood the conversation would have to wait. I turned my attention to getting her water and food and eventually helped her to bed. The next day, I hoped for acknowledgment of what had transpired, perhaps a recognition of the risk she had placed herself and others in.

> *"Eliminating guilt and remorse, by removing these experiences from her emotional architecture altogether, she granted herself the freedom to return to the comfort zone she desired."*

Instead, there was only silence. I didn't want her to drown in self-reproach; I hoped she could understand the recklessness of her behavior. We had started discussing the possibility of trying for a child down the line around then, and it might be fundamental for her to realize that such incidents shouldn't happen again. Still, she carried none of it forward. It was as if the situation from less than 12 hours earlier had slipped entirely from her mind.

Her response was dismissive. "It wasn't that bad. I'm fine. I won't drink and operate a vehicle." Her actions that evening and her lack of responsibility were brushed aside, as if they hadn't happened. And, true to form, it happened again.

This avoidance of responsibility appeared in countless other situations. For a few moments, she would own up to a false statement, an unfounded accusation, or an irrational conclusion.

But in most cases, I wouldn't call it holding herself accountable in any lasting way. It was more like she was mirroring my concerns back to me as a deflection tactic, offering enough acknowledgment to end the conversation. She would say she felt resolved and thought it was covered, then move on immediately. Though as those traits reappeared, it was clear that it wasn't true.

I've often found that some of the most unsettling people aren't those who refuse to feel remorseful. They're those who don't understand why they should, no matter how much harm they leave in their wake, and who alter their script to end the conversation without regard for truth, responsibility, or authentic resolution.

This pattern of claiming it is good without making it good highlighted concerns about her problem-solving, honesty, and transparency, both in the moment and for the future.

I found it puzzling. Eliminating guilt and remorse, by removing these experiences from her emotional architecture altogether, she granted herself the freedom to return to the comfort zone she desired. I have not encountered anyone who could so easily move past their mistakes without owning any of it or showing any effort to make a real change.

Closing Thought

Yesterday's promises become today's rough drafts when avoidance takes precedence over commitment. I don't believe trust can survive such constant revision. When those feelings are erased rather than experienced, patterns can persist unchecked. Accountability then dies in the editing process, leaving only a revised version tailored to protect the editor, not the record.

CHAPTER 13.
Navigating Blind Spots When Denial is Behind the Wheel

Opening Thought

Denial can create a gap in awareness, making it difficult to recognize the effects of one's choices. When a person fails to acknowledge the signs of their own struggles, the consequences remain concealed beneath the surface. If left unaddressed this pattern can erode trust, undermine protection, and keep meaningful solutions out of reach.

Subtle signals hide in plain sight, whether behind the wheel or woven into daily life, especially when avoidance shadows perception. Sometimes, what appears to be unreasonable caution or hesitant action is more than a habit; it can reflect an internal struggle and a lack of awareness of one's own limitations.

These moments, visible to those paying close attention, invite more profound questions about the choices we make and the truths we may be avoiding. I had already seen how her choices around alcohol and illness affected our home, which I describe in more detail elsewhere in this book.

Have you ever been in a car with someone operating a vehicle under the influence or felt uneasy about their handling of the car altogether? Perhaps you've noticed someone who looks or acts too tired to be steering. A compounding carefulness can signal unhealthy overcompensation and, while not necessarily problematic, may prompt questions about what might be hidden or masked.

Highway behavior showing this tendency might include following other cars at a more than considerable distance. Drivers stay too far behind, act too passively, and become overly cautious to the point that their amplified safeguards could become unsafe. These kinds of behaviors are what some experienced police officers learn to spot. Overcompensation indicators can expose specific elements and behaviors that may be off, prompting further investigation and, on occasion, a traffic stop.

I observed this pattern repeatedly with Anya, and when I think about her behind the wheel with Zoey, it still concerns me today. She was uncomfortable in cities, and there were numerous occasions when we found ourselves in urban areas, and she would immediately ask, "Can we switch places? Can you take the wheel?" Instead of openly sharing that she was not comfortable in higher-traffic, higher-population areas, she would offer excuses like, "I'm feeling tired," or, "You handle this area better; would you mind switching now?"

During the times I was in the car as a passenger, notably one time when she picked me up from the airport after a work trip, I sat in the back with Zoey to reconnect after being away. She displayed clear signs of unease and imbalance. The choices I witnessed her make on the road appeared shaky and unreliable.

There were occasions when I was in another car, observing her from a distance, and the way she handled her vehicle troubled me. This situation led me to broader questions about licensing and safety protocols. In the state where I lived, licenses are renewed without adequate checks on current capabilities. This has been an issue not only regarding Anya but also for many older individuals whose capabilities may warrant reassessment.

The effort it seemed to require for her to maintain focus concerned me, and this included times when she wasn't drinking. When alcohol entered the picture, my concerns about safety for Anya and Zoey increased dramatically. I know that Zoey attends various weekend parties, gatherings where kids hang out together while adults drink. I feel Zoey is much safer when these events occur within a small cluster of three or four houses in her neighborhood. There, I know Zoey will not be in a car while most of the adults are drinking.

> *"Safety matters more to me than causing Anya to feel uncomfortable. What would bother me a great deal is if someone got physically hurt because I was too concerned about hurting feelings to ensure competency, safety, and protection."*

It might be helpful for Anya to undergo cognitive testing, though I am sure she would dismiss the idea. The circumstances surrounding her car accident and the injury she claims is no longer affecting her do not add up. I believe it is affecting her, and that it could be valuable for her to be retested now, including an evaluation of whether she is capable of obtaining a license and of her alertness in traffic. Zoey has also shared on numerous occasions that her mother has made some quick stops or been honked at, creating uneasy moments in the car, which Anya has blamed on other drivers.

Still, there were times when I didn't feel comfortable riding in the car with her operating the vehicle. I'm not arguing for someone's license to be revoked arbitrarily, and I understand these parallel concerns about older people on the road. A common saying is, "I've been on the road for sixty years," which is fine, but decades of experience don't necessarily ensure current ability. If someone poses a risk to themselves or creates a significant risk to others, including Zoey, then they should lose their license.

This apprehension prompted me to speak with a politician from that state during my time there. Their response was immediate, as if it had been shared many times already: "If we tried to push a bill like this, we would lose votes." The implications of that political calculation took me aback. There was hesitation to risk upsetting some voters by requiring license retesting for older people who still hold their licenses, and the financial burden of implementing such a program felt daunting. I began to question the potential cost savings from preventing accidents. What about the lives that might be saved?

That same reluctance applies to requiring retesting after certain injuries. The hesitation is that such requirements might upset people and be perceived as unfair. My response to that is simple and straightforward: be uncomfortable with the idea if you must, take issue with it, but take the test. Prove that you're either capable of being safe, alert, and aware, or that you're not.

Safety matters more to me than causing Anya to feel uncomfortable. What would bother me a great deal is if someone got physically hurt because I was too concerned about hurting feelings to ensure competency, safety, and protection. I didn't see Anya as solid or reliable behind the wheel. I believe she is adequate; she can operate a vehicle and hasn't been involved in an accident recently. I'm grateful that Zoey has remained safe. Now that Zoey no longer requires a car seat and additional safety equipment, these matters weigh more heavily on my mind.

One of the more troubling aspects is that she has little awareness of when she is intoxicated and appears to be oblivious to her altered behavior. I am concerned that she may be on the road at times, bringing Zoey home while impaired to a level that she doesn't recognize. Her awareness of the road and surrounding traffic may be compromised in ways she can't perceive or chooses not to acknowledge. I remember several occasions when I had to alert her, saying, "That's a yellow light, that's red now, watch out for that car."

When it comes to the safety of people on the road, both for Anya and for senior citizens, I believe there should be mandatory retesting. If they are physically capable, cognitively sharp, and sufficiently aware to operate a vehicle safely, then they have proven that they belong on the road. But having a license for decades doesn't automatically qualify someone to continue holding it for another decade or another year.

The central issue is not whether one can operate a vehicle or possesses the technical skills to do so. It is a call to recognize how unawareness, fueled by denial, can shape much more than a single moment on the road. For those seeking to navigate life's blind spots, refusing to examine personal shortcomings can keep real growth out of reach and place others at unnecessary risk.

Closing Thought

Proper safety begins with honest awareness. Those who refuse to examine their blind spots can allow for shadows to grow, both in the rearview mirror and in their own reflection. With each avoided truth, the possibility of harm increases, affecting not only them but all who share the roads of their life.

CHAPTER 14.
Unexplained Secrecy and Its Unsettling Weight

Opening Thought

Precautions are reasonable. Security that spills over into unhealthy suspicion is not. When the effort to conceal reality appears disproportionate to its value, protection can become a desperate bid to control a narrative that has already begun to slip out of reach.

Strange behavior at airport security marked our first flight together, a minor preference that soon became part of a larger, more troubling pattern. We were flying out of an airport when Anya expressed strong reluctance to go through the metal detector. She insisted on being searched with a handheld wand and receiving a pat-down instead, making it clear that she would not walk through the standard security screening equipment.

Her stated reason was concern about radiation exposure. "You don't know what these machines are, these X-rays, or what they can do to you." I tried to explain that the radiation from airport security equipment was minimal compared with our daily exposure from other sources, and that these machines posed no significant health risk. She was not pregnant then, and she was bothered when they patted her down and searched her, though she was the one who had requested the alternative screening.

Her behavior caught the TSA agents' attention, which, in turn, made me question some of her motives. Her actions were disproportionate and puzzling.

I started to observe this tendency in other securityrelated situations. She was uncomfortable with certain types of screening or security checkpoints, which I found to be over-amplified. It wasn't about some hidden agenda, but it felt heightened beyond what I would consider regular caution. The same heightened response showed up with physical spam mail as well, blacking out addresses and then shredding bulk mailing items that did not have names on them, such as car insurance advertisement postcards. This came across to me as bizarre and unnecessary.

I came home one day to find her shredding a stack of documents. When I asked what they were, Anya became uncomfortable and emotional, but would not tell me what she was getting rid of.

This cycle of hiding and avoidance extended to many other areas, including her online presence. When I tried to look her up the day after we first met, I could not find much about her online. Her digital footprint had been scrubbed clean. I was curious about what had been taken down or what she might prefer to keep private.

> *"Covert actions that appeared strange at the outset evolved into concerning contradictions, leaving me to question not the conduct itself, but the impulse that fueled it."*

Later, I recognized that content had been removed from online platforms, including issues she had with a previous boyfriend who was involved in various questionable practices. To this day, I'm curious how much she may have been directly involved in those particular ventures with him. She slowly shared some details, like authorities showing up at her mother's house with firearms drawn. She was vague about why they kept coming, which had me questioning what else from her past she might be trying to hide.

The steps Anya took to hide information and her intense focus on concealment piqued my curiosity about what else might be undisclosed, and why such precautions seemed necessary for her. Early in our relationship, those mysterious elements intrigued me; they felt alluring and, to some degree, fascinating. Over time, that appeal diminished. I began to see these shifting concealment efforts as unsettling, problematic, and morally questionable.

I also paid closer attention to her lack of friends and social connections. When we discussed marriage, the idea of eloping or having a small wedding became much more appealing, since she appeared to have only one friend in the area and a second person introduced through that friend. If there were others, they were kept from me.

These two were drinking buddies; she did not spend meaningful time with anyone else. Despite my encouragement to socialize, she remained isolated in a way that went beyond normal solitude, introversion, or being a homebody. It felt suspicious, as if someone were knowingly avoiding social connections for reasons unrelated to personality preferences.

Covert actions that appeared strange at the outset evolved into concerning contradictions, leaving me to question not the conduct itself, but the impulse that fueled it. Each element reinforced the next: the secrecy around documents, her scrubbed online presence, the isolation from others, the vague past she would not discuss. These were not separate quirks; they formed a deliberate pattern.

Closing Thought

Intriguing at first, persistent secrecy exposed someone intent on hiding their authentic self. The consequence was not the mystery itself, but the web of distortions left behind. Real clarity comes from confronting what's been hidden, not from accepting silence as protection.

CHAPTER 15.
Resisting Pressure When Photos Became Battlegrounds

Opening Thought

Sharing a photo of a child shouldn't spark conflict. When that choice was met with a lawsuit warning, the issue was clear. This was not about the image. The response reveals a mindset where control is the only currency and any action outside that agenda can become an attack to neutralize.

Recording a podcast episode about Zoey's influence was not a marketing ploy, despite later claims. To me, it documented the importance of my daughter in my life and for Zoey herself, should she ever hear that show someday.

The episode explored how having Zoey has subtly evolved my approach to business and nurtured my personal growth. It was not intended as a pitch or a sales tool; I was not aiming to sway emotions or evoke sympathy. It was a tribute to my daughter and the profound significance she holds in my life, as well as the myriad ways she has shaped me without realizing it. The unintentional influence of my daughter and her profoundly positive effect on me are remarkable.

My daughter has been and continues to be the greatest blessing of my life.

I created this podcast episode with the hope that Zoey would eventually hear it. Most people who have heard or listened to my podcast understand it's not about marketing or selling products. Its purpose is to share beliefs, offer perspectives for consideration, explain my background, and present ideas using a positive, authentic, and transparent approach.

After finishing the podcast recording, I created a cover image and set up the webpage for the transcription. I decided to use a couple of photos of Zoey and me as the primary image. Since this would be displayed across multiple platforms, I took some precautions. I moved her image toward the background, added a watermark effect, and made it less clear for protection purposes.

Early in our separation, Anya and I agreed to keep pictures of Zoey off the web. We said we would revisit this decision over time, discussing when and where images of her might be appropriate to share. Still, as many choices and agreements changed after our separation, we didn't have a direct conversation to update this agreement. No moment occurred where we sat down and said, "Okay, now we're going to allow images online," or "We're maintaining the no-images policy." I decided, exercising my rights as a father and my rights to display those images, that they would be posted. That was the plan.

We'll be Right Back After This Message

There are photos of Zoey and me that hold deep meaning for me; images that I am preserving and making accessible to her. I insist that she can see our connection in ways that are not filtered through her mother's perspective.

I believe Anya has hidden many items from Zoey that were sent from or related to me. I've tracked packages, gifts, images, and audio messages that were sent but not received by Zoey. I can prove these items were delivered to the doorstep or handed directly to individuals. Still, being told later by Anya, "Oh, this didn't come." A personal and special gift was sent to Zoey, but it either got lost in the mail or was discarded. I am leaning toward believing it was tossed.

> *"Becoming so locked inside her own version of reality that when presented with facts, she can't accept them. If the truth doesn't fit what she wants to believe, she'll continue her attacks regardless of evidence."*

Having this podcast hosted on platforms that Anya cannot access, modify, or remove is imperative to me. I have also set up a file-sharing account and a website that contain videos, audio recordings, and images for Zoey to access in time. This way, she can see these materials and understand where I stand, what I stand for, and how I responded to what was presented to me, regardless of what Anya chose to share or conceal about me.

Because of my current situation, I've built in a series of protective redundancies. If these materials mysteriously get deleted, removed, or go unreceived, she'll have additional opportunities to access them through other channels.

And now, back to our regularly scheduled chapter...

After I posted the podcast transcription on my website, I added the cover image and a few images of Zoey and me. These photos hold a special place in my heart, as they reflect our extraordinary connection. Soon after the podcast went live and the images were online, I received a confrontational email stating, "This has to come down now, or I will bring an action against you."

I responded calmly but firmly. First, I told her that attacks do not work with me. Second, I explained that she had no legal grounds to file a claim. I have every right as Zoey's father to post these images. We don't have any written agreement specifically prohibiting these photos.

Her response exposed the disconnects and recurring tendencies I've been dealing with. Despite the many agreements we'd modified regarding Zoey over time, she suddenly decided this issue was set in stone. The images had to come down, or she would contact her lawyer and file a claim. This is her, and it's a common theme playing out again as she was becoming so locked inside her own version of reality that, when presented with facts, she can't accept them, and if the truth doesn't fit what she wants to believe, she'll continue her attacks regardless of evidence.

The confrontation escalated into a series of 19 emails exchanged between us. Then she shifted tactics, claiming, "You can't use her for marketing." She looked at the image and jumped to conclusions without listening to the podcast. This was a routine approach for Anya. She saw a photo that appeared to upset her, then focused on what it meant to her and what she wanted done about it, seemingly disregarding the whole picture and any discussion, cooperation, or compromise.

This highlights the type of person who takes immediate action based on minimal information and limited facts, the kind who reads a headline and claims to have the whole story within seconds.

No language in any form of that content indicated that Zoey was being used for marketing purposes, nor did it attempt to promote me through her image. After a few more emails, she denied ever making that claim, which I had documented from her earlier email. Wanting to call her out, I chose instead to offer a gentle reply.

"Please refer to your email from two messages ago, where that's exactly what you said." I stayed composed through this exchange for Zoey. I chose not to retaliate and not to stir her up to act worse or take some foolish action.

I offered to have an honest discussion about any valid concerns she had about Zoey, provided they weren't rooted in self-interest. I was clear that launching into accusations or putting pressure around the idea of filing a claim against me would not alter my stance. She continued sending lawsuit warnings in the emails, and I responded respectfully, continuing to try to de-escalate the situation and convey the reality and truth to her before it caused problems for her.

Beliefs That Could Cost Her

As the emails continued, I took a more assertive approach. I told Anya directly, "You will lose. Do not contact your lawyer about this. You will lose, it will cost you money, and I will not pay for your legal fees. You do not have the legal grounds to take the action you want. This is a fact. Go look it up for yourself. If you choose to pursue this and create problems over this misunderstanding on your part, that would be trivial, baseless, and foolish."

I continued, "If that is the game you want to play by coming after me for this, I will respond appropriately and within my rights. If your decision to proceed with this leads to any costs being incurred by me, those costs will become your responsibility. I will not escalate the situation, and given how you chose to attack me, I am still trying to help you avoid a costly mistake. Despite that, I won't allow you to mistreat my time or me. Please know, if you consulted your lawyer about this situation, they would recognize how out of line you are and see that no legal basis exists for your claims."

I stood my ground.

No, I would not take down these images.

No, they were not shared as promotion.

These photos express the bond I share with Zoey. I am within my rights to keep them visible. She has no legal grounds to demand their removal.

It would demonstrate progress if she could engage in a thoughtful discussion rather than confronting me with warnings, attacks, and claims about actions she was neither allowed to take, nor legally permitted to pursue.

Still, progress was not made that day.

She responded, "If that is how you want to handle this, I will talk to my lawyer." I let it go and told her, "You do what you're going to do regardless, but you're going to find that what I've shared is accurate."

That statement holds for many situations involving Anya. The issue disappeared. Her lawyer did not bring an action or serve any papers because, under the law, her claim could not gain a footing. Still, her approach and the intensity of her stance, which appeared to be preparation for conflict, focused solely on her perspective of the situation. She was not open to considering any view other than her own, including laws and documentation in the parenting plan that contradicted what she hoped was true.

This incident highlights a mind that may be fixed on a specific perspective, which can lead to multiple levels of misrepresentation. It appears to allow her to present her version of preferences and events in a way that might cast me in an unfavorable light, while also avoiding accountability for what she shares. The entire situation comes across as one-sided, disappointing, and fundamentally wrong.

Closing Thought

Reasoning with a mind that rejects reality leads nowhere. When legal claims proved baseless, recourse was clear. Standing firm and preserving a real, documented connection with my daughter beyond her mother's reach or control became a part of the approach I will continue to stand on and stand by.

CHAPTER 16.
Strategic Silence Disguised Behind a Forgotten Device

Opening Thought

Receiving silence, partial information, and a lack of effort to connect with my daughter painted a clear picture of unreasonable resentment and selfishness. This pattern shows a repeated choice to ignore reasonable questions, creating a communication blackout that serves one parent's agenda while harming a father's ability to connect with his daughter.

Elements of anger continued to surface and intensify, highlighted by a simple request to be filled in about a schedule change and whether the iPad would be going with Zoey. It felt as though she was informing me of what she wanted, in the way she wanted, using silence and vagueness to maintain control rather than offering straightforward cooperation.

I asked a reasonable question: Could she fill me in on when Zoey would be brought to Anya's mother's house, considering the change in the calendar, and share the dates and times for travel to and from that house?

I had a right to this information, and to ensure that the iPad would accompany her so I could maintain contact during the seven to eight days she would be away, and our parenting plan required her to share it.

She responded to only one of my questions over a day later, breaking our parenting plan, which requires responses within twenty-four hours. She did not address the timeline in her response and answered selectively, saying, "I'm going to pick her up after camp, and we're going straight from there."

I replied, "Okay, can you ensure that the iPad goes with her? I would appreciate it so I can be in contact with Zoey."

She responded with a double-standard approach, saying, "Okay, well, I'm not going to take care of this, and I don't have to; I'm only going to remind her about the iPad." This pattern has become routine. She does as little as possible or finds ways to avoid responsibility altogether to achieve results that serve her.

I shared that, "I'd appreciate having contact with Zoey. Can you please make this happen? Thank you." My goal is for our interactions to be respectful, honorable, and kind, including during disagreements.

> *"Packing an iPad so my daughter and I can stay connected takes seconds, but after asking many times, her refusal or flat-out ignoring my requests reveals her true priorities."*

I believe that, amid Anya's anger, distorted views, and constant editing of the truth, it would likely please her if the iPad were forgotten, offering another way to disconnect me from Zoey. That email chain indicated that this simple task, ensuring that an iPad is packed, apparently cannot be accomplished or honored.

I talked to Zoey in the days leading up to the trip so she would remember. I have also seen many instances of how Anya seems to distract Zoey in ways that lead her to forget the iPad, which has further distanced me from her at times. It has also upset Zoey when she has cried, saying that she forgot and how mommy packed all the other items she had to have, but not the iPad.

One infuriating part of this situation is the simplicity of the request itself. Packing an iPad so my daughter and I can stay connected takes seconds, but after asking many times, her refusal or flat-out ignoring my requests reveals her true priorities. It appears to be a clear signal that Anya's commitment to distancing me is greater than her commitment to supporting Zoey's connection with me.

Blocking Connection

I heard Zoey crying and saying the next day on a call regarding how hard the night before was. She said, "I told her I had to call you, but Mommy wouldn't let me," and "Mommy said it was only because I didn't want to go to bed." Zoey wants to talk to me at times, on her own initiative. She is not trying to avoid bedtime, as Anya claimed. Without clarity and cooperation regarding my rights, it seems to allow her to ignore and set aside my requests.

Considering the recurring themes, especially since she began working with her lawyer, I sense that several underlying issues are at work. Perhaps this is a way to undermine me by not giving Zoey the chance to connect and calm down when it would help her. It feels as if she wants to weaken that connection and replace it with herself.

I struggle to understand Anya's insistence on control and why the most straightforward task, such as ensuring a communication device is available for Zoey to connect, comes across as either a challenge for her or a way to weaken the connection. This leaves me feeling helpless and far away, unable to fix this issue or the chaos surrounding her behavior and her choices that keep Zoey from getting back to me.

Closing Thought

Continued efforts to disconnect me from my daughter remain visible. Navigating this struggle honorably, respectfully, and transparently remains my commitment, despite her determination not to. Her actions cannot be controlled, only prepared for. This reluctance to fulfill parental responsibilities confirms that these challenges will likely persist and compound.

CHAPTER 17.
Rejecting Her Drama When My Calm Was Judged as a Failure

Opening Thought

Questions arise when composed, rational responses are misjudged and met with accusations that you don't care. This is how a routine surgery became a loyalty test, a manufactured crisis in which my refusal to panic was seen as insufficient.

Information was shared with me in an email, not a phone call. Anya has shown herself to be too timid to communicate by phone for a long time. She sent an email stating that Zoey would require a simple dental surgery and that she was consulting with a surgeon about the situation.

It was a simple, concise email. I wouldn't call it cold, but it was factual and direct. My response was straightforward: "Okay, thank you for sharing this. Please keep me updated on what's happening, and we'll figure it out from there." That was fundamentally what I said, along with mentioning that I had that surgery when I was younger, too.

She shot back within minutes, referencing other issues and saying, "The lack of gravity in your response to this surgery is troubling.

This is major surgery." She went on to tell me my feelings about the surgery and how I didn't care.

It wasn't a major surgery, only major conclusions from Anya about my reactions.

I replied, "First off, you do not understand what I'm feeling." These types of responses were similar to those in past situations in which she implied that I did not love Zoey, and to an array of statements she felt were true, with no consideration beyond her own perspective. In this instance, failing to respond as she hoped meant I appeared to be treating the situation with insufficient importance. She seemed to judge my calm reaction as inadequate. My response became grounds for attack.

There are 10 years' worth of examples of her lack of response, respect, consideration, and attention to actual emergencies. Still, in this one instance, she chose to focus on my tone and her conclusions.

I responded, "I am concerned for how she is feeling and dealing with knowing this is coming. I had this same surgery when I was young, so I understand the situation." The idea of Zoey having surgery was hard for me, mainly because of how she was feeling about it and her concerns. I focused on explaining to Zoey that this procedure is routine for children her age. Many children undergo it, and I was one of them years back. I did not like how it affected her and her issues with the unknown, but I also was not concerned about the surgery itself.

Then Anya escalated. "She's going to go under anesthesia." Yes, she would be unconscious briefly while they performed the procedure, which would take maybe an hour. The actual surgical portion is less than an hour, with additional time for anesthesia and for recovery. But she was blowing this into a much more dramatic event than it had to be. Because I didn't join her in the panic and didn't match her reaction or unease, I was attacked for it.

I said, "I'm concerned for Zoey, but I am not overly concerned about a surgery like this. I will contribute my share of the cost. Have you talked to other specialists? Have you looked at referrals? Have you explored other options? I am happy to do research too if it would help." I was thinking about it from a practical standpoint. Anya's choice to make it into a bigger ordeal amplified Zoey's unease, which in turn created more tension.

Initially, she didn't seem troubled, but I felt that Anya's influence might be contributing to her unrest. I'm inclined to think that Anya is often unknowingly passing along her own issues, unease, and turmoil to Zoey. In my years of observing these behaviors, I have found that Anya appears to have difficulty managing situations calmly and coping with them effectively. I question how that may be influencing Zoey's emotional state at times.

> *"Failing to respond as she hoped meant I appeared to be treating the situation with insufficient importance. She seemed to judge my calm reaction as inadequate. My response became grounds for attack."*

Leading up to the surgery, I told Zoey I would be able to be there with her for the procedure. Many times, Zoey and I brought the discussion to a calmer place. Yes, Zoey was uneasy; it was understandable. We talked a great deal on FaceTime before the surgery and worked together to find calm again. "I feel better now," she expressed. "I'm concerned about this. I talked to Mommy about it, and it doesn't feel any better. I feel better talking to you."

I addressed her concerns calmly and with understanding. Observing how she settled when we talked and how our conversations brought her closer to calm, I knew I had to be there with her going into the procedure.

Zoey made herself clear before I arrived: "You take me to the surgery."

Getting to that point was a battle; being able to take her and have time with her before, during, and after felt like an all-out war of words. Leading up to the surgery involved a series of back-and-forth email exchanges that came across as vague, angry, and dismissive.

Initially, it was, "You can't bring her," and "You cannot see her right now." I had to gently remind her of the legal requirements. She has been able to get away with a great deal because I lacked legal representation. Despite disregarding the parenting plan and failing to adhere to agreements, she knew she could wield that power, and she continues to do so.

The volume and tone of the emails Anya sent were unhealthy. Eventually, I was able to see Zoey a couple of times before the surgery. I then asked, "I was hoping to be able to see her after the surgery. Can I come into her room? She has requested for me to come and see it. Can you honor her wish?"

"No, we don't want you here," Anya replied. Referring to her boyfriend and the household, she said, "We don't feel good about you being here."

I said, "Can I please come in for a moment? Or can she come with me?" I had booked an Airbnb nearby. When Zoey got up after resting for a few hours after the surgery, she wanted to see me. We spent that evening together, talking and hanging out in my rental car at a park near her house. The next day, she called, and we spent time hanging out in bed at the place I had rented, watching a few movies and some of her favorite shows she wanted to share with me.

All the while, I received over 20 texts saying, "She should come back. This isn't safe. She ought to be here. She ought to be resting." She was 17 minutes away, resting in a rented place with her father, calm and comfortable. She was curled up and happy. I asked to have Zoey with me until the evening. I told her she wants to be here. She has stated this several times.

Anya repeatedly resisted and opposed me on this. I broke down at that moment, knowing my rights but feeling powerless to enforce them. If I kept Zoey with me as she wanted and I had the right to do, I had no idea what might happen for the rest of my stay. I did not know how Anya might try to reduce my time with Zoey, as she had done in past visits. In the past, she would cut short the time or keep Zoey from me, breaking previous agreements for her to be with me during those days.

Zoey asked, "What's wrong?" I replied, "I'm sad about this situation." She said, "Well, let me stay here with you. I feel good. I'm resting. It feels good to be here. It feels good to be snuggling with you. And when I go back, why can't you see my room?"

In what felt like another moment of Anya's games and control efforts, she would not let me in for a brief visit to see her room. She did not want me to spend time with Zoey in her new room, which Zoey had expressed a desire to share with me. During this time, she also preferred that the iPad stay behind. Zoey and I both asked several times, "Could you please send the iPad along?" I planned to check that the files I was trying to share with her were getting through, as specific graphics, videos, or audio files I sent were either not received or went missing.

But the response was, "I do not have to send that with her. You do not get to have the iPad with you. She does not have to be on the iPad while she is with you." It came across as a display of irrationality and anger, unsubstantiated and untethered.

For this particular series of events, it all started when I didn't react the "right way," or her preferred way, to the news about the surgery, and it went downhill from there.

Her lack of kindness and lack of ability to honor her daughter's wishes are often replaced with her avalanche of power plays attempting to control as much as she can in as many situations as possible.

Closing Thought

Carefully constructed performances focused on her conclusions about another person's feelings, without proof, continue to define these exchanges. When she loses the upper hand, texts are fired off at me, trying to reclaim control over situations she cannot dictate. One

*day, the facade she has constructed may crumble, and the troubling
reality beneath it will stand on its own.*

CHAPTER 18.
Objective Facts Confronting Her Subjective Feelings

Opening Thought

Overt control can manifest in repeated patterns of forgotten or ignored responsibilities. When someone routinely overlooks legally required details and answers only certain questions, the pattern suggests intentional influence rather than absent-mindedness. Reliability vanishes when convenient forgetfulness becomes the primary defense.

Accountability requires acknowledgment of the record. When documented proof is met with denial, selective responses, and claims of being attacked, responsibility disappears. The tendency becomes clear not in isolated moments, but in the repeated choice to treat objective evidence as personal criticism instead of as reality. Anya often provides minimal responses to the questions she selectively chooses to answer.

If three questions are sent and she wants to answer only one, that is all she will address.

It reached a point where I said, "Do we have to handle this through emails for a list of items that we discussed and agreed to, but that have since been forgotten because they were on a phone call? So many of the questions during our phone conversations were dismissed and ignored." I was thrown off by how much could be forgotten and how much was overlooked.

I understand there was an accident when she was younger that included a blow to the head, which she claims is not affecting her. Still, I have experienced her memory failing, and when presented with information right in front of her, it is often forgotten quickly. Another difficult part is that she becomes defensive when reminded of what she forgot, perceiving the mention of her oversight as an attack.

Documentation became ammunition.

This became a significant reason why, a few years ago, I began documenting all communications in emails. It wasn't my intention to come across as confrontational. Instead, I thought she could use the reminders: "I have this documented information here. I did state or write these points you claimed I didn't. Would you mind paying more attention to these emails? It would mean a great deal if you could take a closer look and address the questions."

A standard response set was, "You didn't say that. You didn't say that. You didn't say that."

When she appeared backed against a wall, she repeated phrases of denial and deflection as if to make them stronger or more accurate. Proof contradicting her claims became attacks in her eyes. Facts meant to ensure my daughter's stability were dismissed as attempts to control the narrative. Instead of discussing reality or considering the evidence, she insisted I was trying to make her look bad.

It's unnerving that she chooses to ignore these details and then insists, "No, that was not said."

When confronted a third time, she might concede, "Okay, it was said." But then it becomes, "You're talking down to me. You're being condescending."

No, I'm trying to highlight a pattern so we can address these issues and move toward a better place. Unfortunately, that recognition is lacking. Once again, it's about the details, the information that works for her. Those are the only ones she seems to care about.

In some of these communications, she forgot to address questions in numerous emails after I tried to emphasize key points by bolding, underlining, and increasing font sizes for specific headers and bullet points that were critical for clarity. This is a practice I have used for many others, and no issues were ever brought up. More often, the opposite was true. It helped with clarification, but not with her.

Her response was, "This is mean." I shared that was not my intention. I was only trying to present the email in a way that might be easier for her to read and address. I would receive responses regarding those questions in bold, stating, "Those are not important," or, "I'm not going to share that," or she would ignore the bold questions altogether. Anya seemed to shift from a defensive to a decisive stance regarding the format of my questions, then disregarded them because, in her opinion, they were not worth answering.

> *"Proof contradicting her claims became attacks in her eyes. Facts meant to ensure my daughter's stability were dismissed as attempts to control the narrative. Instead of discussing reality or considering the evidence, she insisted I was trying to make her look bad."*

Again, consistent with what I regularly experienced with her, Anya tends to decide which details are important. She decides what she should share and what she feels does not have to be shared, regardless of the parenting plan and the rules in place. In those details, through her ignorance, arrogance, and anger, she declares, "I don't have to share this with you." I then request that she please review the parenting plan, as sharing this is required under the agreement. Then, no response. It's as if she's backed into a corner, but her reaction is not, "Okay, I'm sorry. Okay, I forgot that. Okay, I didn't realize that." Instead, she ignores it.

On one occasion, she launched a diatribe-style response, saying, "I do not have to provide the name of where Zoey is spending the night. I don't have to share a cell phone number. Maybe I'll see if they're comfortable sharing that, but you have no choice in the matter." She appeared to make that choice because I had no lawyer. That gap gave her latitude to break the agreement without consequence.

If someone is not comfortable sharing the required information when my daughter is staying overnight somewhere, that is on them, not me. It's part of a court-ordered parenting plan that requires knowing where she will spend the night, who will be there, as well as contact numbers and who they belong to. Anya called it an unnecessary power play. Then, she continues to resist it and denies that she was responsible for following through on it.

To add to the information gaps with Anya, I noticed a theme. When she dislikes a particular detail or is required to share it, she includes vague or incomplete information and often delivers many of those elements with minor inaccuracies.

In one situation, I carefully drafted an email to point out incorrect information that had been sent. This matched what I had already been documenting. Anya would provide incorrect phone numbers and addresses by altering a digit here or there, allowing her to later claim, "Oh, it was a misspelling. It was a typo."

My first thought was to respond and call her out for the games she was playing. Instead, I kindly asked her to check more carefully for typos so I could know where Zoey is, who she is with, the required information about that location and the individuals that will be present or reside there. Knowing her common responses to inaccuracies and how far she will go to defend a false statement would only upset her and get me nowhere toward understanding or any greater resolve to move forward.

She remains unaware that I have been tracking these "typos." What I have documented is a woman who can be detailed when she chooses, but then has all sorts of issues sending correct phone numbers, addresses, and other information she does not want to send.

It is concerning to me how Anya navigates details, what she chooses to acknowledge, what she prefers to overlook, and how she decides to handle information. I've questioned how her formula, or maybe better to call it her criteria, works or is laid out for determining what is significant and what can be disregarded.

Anya's pursuit of total control may stem from a life that feels uncontrollable, whether in thoughts, circumstances, or willingness to change. Because of this, her power is exerted wherever she can, over me, over Zoey, over the schedule, and over any gaps in my current resources or representation.

Closing Thought

Limited transparency can undermine clear communication and stability, especially when key details are set aside. By maintaining a steady focus on what is documented and ongoing support for my daughter, I aim to create an environment where clarity and honest answers provide her with the security she deserves.

CHAPTER 19.
Preserving Truth as Messages Fade and Records Disappear

Opening Thought

Records worth reviewing accumulate when care and intention shape each message and reply. If my daughter chooses to see all of this one day, I believe it will offer her an unfiltered context to the limited story she has been told. Each text and email carries a legacy, reflecting my choices and intentions long after they are sent.

Curious questions are emerging as I watch Zoey notice signs in her mother's behavior. She brings up aspects of her mother that bother her, asking how she should handle certain situations, all without any prompting from me. Part of me finds this heartbreaking, knowing what she's starting to see. Still, perhaps Zoey could be a light that helps her mother recognize a perspective she couldn't see when I shared it with her.

Is Anya so self-absorbed that she doesn't recognize Zoey's intelligence? Zoey is, as I've jokingly referred to her before, like a mini detective, hungry for knowledge, eager to learn, and unwilling to accept all that much at face value. She is a read-more-than-the-headline type of girl, and I am proud of the intellect she possesses. Is Anya perceptive enough to realize that Zoey is already noticing her behavior and has started to ask questions, occasionally challenging what her mother says?

This is where I've experienced some of Anya's more arrogant, egotistical angles. When she shares her opinion on a topic or issue with Zoey, she frames it as the truth and expects it to be accepted as such.

Given how she has chosen to interact with and respond to me in emails and texts, does Anya not realize that these communications can demonstrate that she is misrepresenting facts and not being truthful with Zoey?

I understand that, given the current circumstances, I cannot share as much information about her mother with Zoey. Still, as I gather information from observations, experiences, and communications, my goal isn't to criticize her mother but to ensure Zoey can make informed decisions when she's old enough, with input from both sides.

When she is old enough, she will have access to select correspondence between her mother and me, along with this book. Over time, she can see for herself how communication was handled and how I carried myself through it. I recognize that this is a long journey toward the fullness of the story and the honesty she deserves.

Permanent records exist in every email and text. I write mine with the awareness that our daughter might one day be the audience. I question whether her mother ever considers this or if she is unintentionally creating a legacy of anger and insensitivity.

As a man, a father, a problem-solver, and a communicator, I take pride in who I am and who I strive to be.

Three Lines I Drew for Myself

I will not match... her anger, her ego, her inaccuracies, or her negative communication styles.

I will not respond in kind to... the attacks, the insults, the foolish conclusions, or the false claims.

I continue to see it from two perspectives... Anya is not worth it, Zoey is.

Every email or text from Anya, regardless of where she is mentally or emotionally in those moments and how she chooses to behave, will still be responded to with honor, faith, patience, and love.

Part of my calm and careful responses is centered on working to repair, resolve, or ease the situation. So, I respond to every email and text with a breath, with a pause, and with the thought, "What will she see in my words, my responses, and my interactions? How will she perceive my reactions?"

There have been moments when I've tried to remain careful, reframing and softening objective, substantiated statements with a more subjective delivery. I've expressed my feelings, choosing more subjective, less objective phrasing, such as, "This feels unrealistic, this feels difficult," as I carefully word it and do what I can to avoid using or implying insults.

I've aimed to present facts as facts and feelings as feelings.

Then I consider the other side and question, "How might Anya perceive this?" Whether it is fueled by ego, other issues, or a range of unhealthy behaviors and traits, her perspective continues to differ significantly from mine. And, is this the type of mother Anya wishes to present to Zoey through her words, which include harsh criticisms, insults, personal attacks, and a range of self-absorbed behaviors?

Is this the impression she wants Zoey to hold of her?

Or does this suggest a more complex, two-sided nature within her?

It seems to mix ignorance and arrogance, believing that Zoey will not recognize these patterns, see the truth, and realize what has been hidden in the shadows for so long.

> *"Permanent records exist in every email and text. I write mine with the awareness that our daughter might one day be the audience. I question whether her mother ever considers this."*

I know we're supposed to shield our children from specific conversations and information, and I understand that. The parenting plan states that I can't share certain matters, and I wish I could. Some details will have to wait until later.

I've sent numerous emails asking, "Why don't we talk? Why don't we go out for ice cream together when I'm visiting? Why don't we make the situation more comfortable for Zoey?" These requests are continually ignored.

This is not where I try to cast her in a bad light, but I am clear with Zoey in explaining that I am here to talk when her mother is ready. I will not let her hold a false idea that I am unwilling to communicate. Anya has avoided having conversations for years now. This points to a negative pattern that highlights her ongoing choice to avoid communication with me at all costs.

This also occurs when Zoey and I are on FaceTime and Anya walks into the room. Sometimes, she appears not to know that Zoey is talking to me, and other times, she is fully aware. Still, she ignores me and chooses not to respond with a simple "hello" or show any respectful engagement at all.

My focus on Anya and her future has shifted, but my concern for how this situation affects Zoey remains sincere. I hope that Anya will become a more stable, loving, healthy, and strong mother for Zoey. What continually challenges me is Anya's uncooperative attitude, especially regarding self-care and growth, and her apparent inability to adopt a healthier, broader perspective. I hope that, over time, she will do so for her own healing and well-being.

Closing Thought

Satisfaction comes from preserving this account for my daughter, knowing that if she chooses, she will be able to see the intentions and choices that shaped each moment. These types of digital footprints can influence how we are remembered, and show how we behaved in the good times and the hardest ones, too.

CHAPTER 20.
Recognition Denied When Facing Her Own Reflection

Opening Thought

Mirrors can reflect both turmoil and clarity for some, offering opportunities for growth if the lessons are accepted. But what happens when the person who inspired the reflection is the one who investigates it? I've found that a concerning test of denial isn't only ignoring the truth; it's looking directly at it and insisting you see a stranger's face.

Confrontational emails from Anya, combined with the signs of misperception she has exhibited, led me to reflect on what might happen if she were to read this book. I'm curious what her reaction would be.

I'm also cautious on this path because I don't want to create a situation where she could challenge me based on statements that might give her ammunition for an attack.

There will be a specific editing process, and some of these experiences will be altered. Names will not be used, and details that could serve as identifiers will be changed to sufficiently distance them from her, preventing her or her lawyer from having any power over me or this work. I figured out the logistics of this, particularly the liability aspect. "Okay, so I will change this. I will shift that. It will be more of a story, more of a fictional character setup… here is the dad, here is the mom, here is the daughter, here are the concerns, here is this and that."

Once the final version of the book is approved, protected, and reviewed by a lawyer, I've thought about the question, "What if she reads it?" I'm curious to see how she might react. Reading this might prompt her to recognize herself if she were open enough to see the similarities, or would she dismiss it, choosing her tendency toward denial over acceptance? I could see her dismissing this entirely, and not for a second thinking it was about her.

With the self-identifiers toned down, would her response be, "Well, she's a touch unpredictable and over the top?" This idea keeps raising questions about the stories and events people are willing or unwilling to acknowledge, especially when the details mirror their own behavior.

At one point, standing in front of her, instead of adopting a softer, walking-on-eggshells approach, I said, "I feel like these self-absorbed actions have to stop." She laughed and deflected, replying, "Oh, you think I'm self-absorbed? Who are you kidding? You're the self-absorbed one." Without being bothered by her apparent deflection or taking issue with it, I tried to share some traits and patterns that I believed indicated her behavior, but she seemed to overlook them entirely.

So, I shifted my questioning and asked, "How am I self-absorbed?" As she has many times before, when she deflects or works on a counterattack and is questioned directly, she tends to have no response. To me, this emphasized another deflection without any proof or evidence to support her claim, effectively cutting off a conversation she did not want to engage in.

Later, when we were communicating solely through email, I came across a term that seemed to line up with self-centered tendencies and shared it with her. I mentioned, "I've been looking into certain behaviors. I'm curious whether, among the array of symptoms I've noticed in you, you might see some of them too. Plus, it has a name, and there appear to be several ways to address it." Anya replied,

"Oh, well, I spoke with my mother and my sister. They said I don't have it."

I found this intriguing because, ten years ago, Anya described her mother and sister as these troubled, self-absorbed individuals. Several years later, she is asking these same individuals whether they noticed any signs of self-absorption in her.

Their answer was no, and that was good enough for Anya to defend her ground and conclude she did not have those traits, based solely on the people she chose to ask.

> *"Reading this might prompt her to recognize herself if she were open enough to see the similarities. Or would she dismiss it, choosing her tendency toward denial over acceptance?"*

She may have put aside the problems, denied them, or chosen to make them disappear once she acquired a support system for her viewpoints and beliefs. It feels as though she has flipped some wild switch, now asserting that those issues no longer exist for them and don't exist for her.

Back to the Mirror of the Book

If there is any sense of self-awareness, she might think, "Okay, this woman in the story seems pretty troubled." Or might she automatically respond "Oh, I don't see that"? My sense is that awareness isn't coming.

Anya may be the least aware person I have known, unable to see the world around her or her own reflection. I believe that if she read this, she wouldn't remotely recognize these crystal-clear traits or see herself in these pages. That only sheds more light on her lack of awareness and her inability to recognize the traits and choices she has made.

Closing Thought

Sound judgment often hinges on the willingness to see, hear, and confront uncomfortable truths. I've known people with failing eyesight who perceive the world with greater clarity than she does. Her blindness isn't physical; it's a fortress constructed to shield her from accountability. I've learned you cannot offer a true reflection to someone who has already deemed the mirror false.

CHAPTER 21.
Abandoned Follow-Through While Fully Committed to Quitting

Opening Thought

Honesty about limits can carry more weight than promises quickly abandoned. I learned that open sharing of limitations serves connection better than false ambitions. The constant cycle of promising change while quitting at the first sign of difficulty wore me down more than if she had shared a simple, transparent truth that this was who she was.

Quitting showed itself in Anya's choices long before I understood how deeply her abandoned commitments would shape our time together. Her lack of commitment to go the distance surfaced early, showing up in goals she named, changes she promised, and efforts she abandoned as soon as they became difficult. At times, the song 'The Distance' by Cake came to mind, not because it described her, but because it captured the opposite of what she chose.

The first few months were filled with conversations, during which I felt she presented herself as she wanted to be seen rather than as she was. There was a chameleon factor, where she shifted and adapted her persona based on what she thought she should present or how she wanted to appear. It wasn't authentically her at all.

In moments that called for honest commitment or brought up real problems, any illusion of harmony would quickly slip away. From the outset, it was key to make my intentions and expectations clear. Without authenticity, pursuing a genuine partnership would be pointless. I shared my communication style, set my boundaries, and made it clear where compromise was not possible.

To me, it meant prioritizing open conversation, working together through disagreements to avoid repeating old battles, and choosing honest openness over falling into defensiveness.

She agreed that when we commit to a task, a plan, a change, or a promise, we should follow through to the best of our ability.

But follow-through was rarely seen with Anya. She talked about wanting to change and expressed a desire to improve, which kept me believing there was hope. I would think, "Okay, I'm going to believe that you mean this." But the follow-through was not there. The gap between what she promised and what she delivered became undeniable. Deeds rarely followed the promises. Words came easily, but the actions to make them true were missing when it mattered.

Back when she first said she was going to find a job, she didn't. When she claimed she planned to pursue various goals, she didn't. There was endless talk but no real action or effort behind it.

Perceived Pressures

These types of problem-solving and follow-through traits are what I actively work on with Zoey, trying to teach and apply them in her life. I do not expect flawlessness from her and would not put that type of pressure on her.

Unfortunately, I do believe that at times, Anya has done precisely that. She makes it seem like the pressure comes from me in an unhealthy, pushy way. She shares statements with Zoey, such as

"Your daddy wants this" or "Your daddy expects that," which do not match what I have said to Zoey.

When I revisited any conversation regarding pressure with Zoey, I would ask where the pressure she said she felt came from. I would ask if I had said the words that were bothering her. In most cases, it felt as though Anya had said those words to her, and that they did not come from me. This also led me to tell Zoey that if she didn't hear it directly from me, she should either ask me or not conclude it was from me until she was sure it was the truth and that I said it.

Comfort Over Commitment

I have rarely seen someone give up as much as Anya did on several goals, aspirations, and changes she claimed to want. This led me to repeatedly tell Anya that it was fine if these goals were not what she wanted and if this was not who she genuinely was. I didn't want her to feel pressured or pushed to be someone she wasn't, nor to commit to change, promises, or claims she had no intention or desire to keep.

She seemed to recognize the issues when I brought up our communication problems. She often said, "Yes, I can see this is a problem." I tried to tread carefully, as I didn't want to push my vision of change upon her.

But she would insist otherwise, saying, "No, I see this. I'm identifying this as a problem for me. I am making it a priority to work on this," and when I asked how she planned to work on it or how it would become a priority for her, both the commitment and the claim would evaporate. Brief acknowledgments of problems often shifted back to dismissing concerns, echoing what I had already seen in earlier conflicts.

Occasionally, there would be one small step or two. "Oh, I got a book. Oh, I talked to somebody. Oh, I went to one online therapy session." These were occasional, singular efforts with no sustained follow-through.

I would come home and find her sitting on the couch reading one of these self-help books, and it began to feel staged, like a performance for my benefit. When I brought up what she had learned, taken away, or applied from the book, there was rarely an answer beyond motivation. She might mention reading about healthy communication or attending some online seminar or event about positive growth and change. Still, when I pressed on what actions she had taken based on what she learned, the conversation would stall.

Checking Boxes Without Real Change

I questioned whether she viewed her claims as little more than boxes she only felt she had to check off her list. Maybe Anya's thought process was this, "All right, this should improve. I'll check this off. I read the book. I made an attempt. Since I checked off the items on the list, it should be better between us."

As the situation remained the same, this cycle grew harder to ignore. There was a lack of accountability and responsibility for growing, changing, or improving, as she claimed she wanted to. When the lack of change or the issues persisted, she would go on the defensive, stating what she read, instead of exploring what it would take for lasting change or authentic improvement.

> *"Deeds rarely followed the promises. Words came easily, but the actions to make them true were missing when it mattered."*

I suggested we look for themes and signs, focusing on the positive reinforcement of good actions. None of these approaches took hold in our relationship. When a behavior or trait she said she wanted to change started to improve, briefly and for a moment, it was quickly halted and reverted to its previous state.

I hoped that these little upticks of change, growth, and perseverance would last, but most of the time, they were abandoned as soon as they became too difficult, required long-term commitment, or no longer held her attention or interest.

This repeated consistently across various areas where growth was lacking, including healthy communication, a strong intimate connection, personal development, and career planning. She would express interest in exploring options and ask what I thought she should do, but no concrete planning or commitment to next steps would ever follow.

When Zoey was napping and later, when she was old enough to play independently, in preschool and then kindergarten, those small windows of time were rarely used for personal development or for working toward the goals she expressed wanting. I'm not dismissing the efforts she made around the house or with childcare, but 10 or 15 minutes here and there could have been used to take steps toward the changes she said she wanted.

When we were apart, this became more apparent. She struggled to devote herself to pursuits that offered true significance. Still, when it came to mixing with the neighbors, especially during festive gatherings, she seemed to have boundless energy and dedication.

I'm not judging these neighbors; they all had jobs, worked hard, and, from what I observed, had much healthier relationships and lives. Still, the moment she could get away to join them, she was gone. The moment she could pick up a drink, she was drinking. The distance and commitment she couldn't muster for personal growth or our relationship, she could easily find for partying.

With her health issues, the same held true. She would identify a problem, get enthusiastic about exercise or wellness for a brief period, then let it fade away. When I asked about depression, given all the signs she was displaying, she insisted she wasn't depressed, but when I asked what she wanted from life, she couldn't answer. I did not see any commitment to personal growth of the kind I believe we all owe ourselves.

At one point, she acknowledged these family issues. Still, as soon as she could use those same family members as support, particularly when her sister paid for the divorce proceedings, the people she had described as "so terrible to her" became overnight allies.

She gave most of her commitment to what brought easy satisfaction, while giving little to the hard work of building a life or a relationship. That refusal to face challenging tasks became more than a quirk; it became a defining feature of how she approached our time together.

Closing Thought

Consequences in both emotions and daily life can grow when words and actions stay out of alignment. I would have preferred her direct truth to the endless claims she had no intention of keeping. Healthy relationships thrive on honest self-awareness and sustained effort, not on commitments quickly abandoned. That pattern of quitting now concerns me most for what Zoey may learn from watching her mother.

CHAPTER 22.
Using a Lawyer to Avoid Answering Reasonable Questions

Opening Thought

Legal representation can become a shield from accountability rather than a tool to address and resolve real concerns. When someone uses an attorney to block dialogue instead of answering reasonable questions, the intent becomes clear. Choosing to hide behind legal protection rather than engage directly confirmed my observation that she preferred control over clarity.

Tension in our communication had been building for a long time, but a turning point came in early summer when the conflict escalated sharply. Anya and I had been discussing for years when meaningful change would happen, when healthy communication would start, and when real actions would replace empty promises.

She was not going to change, get a job, or help find a way to contribute financially. So, with that, I had reached a point where, for financial reasons, I was considering moving both Anya and Zoey to where I was working with a larger client and spending more time. While not the ideal solution, it would at least save money, allowing me to keep Zoey close. Then Anya could keep caring for her, and we could greatly reduce our living expenses.

This wouldn't have been easy for Anya because it would have taken her away from the few friends she had made, the people she drank with, and the children Zoey played with. It wasn't my preference to take Zoey away from a place where she felt comfortable, but the lack of effort on Anya's part had created an unsustainable situation. Apparently, this possibility became part of the grounds for her decision to file for divorce.

When I returned from a work trip that had lasted several weeks, I sensed a shift in Anya's demeanor. I remember saying, "What's going on? What are you not telling me?" After a series of false statements and redirection, she finally responded with, "Well, I filed for divorce." When I asked why, she claimed it was to protect Zoey, though I believe she did so to defend her own lifestyle and comfort.

I thought I was prepared to deal with Anya, but I was unprepared for the challenge of facing both her and her lawyer. When her lawyer stepped in, it felt as if I was up against a clone of Anya, another person who seemed to mirror some of the same self-absorbed traits. I felt dismissed, faced with denial of facts, and a tone that was hard to navigate. The situation shifted from a personal conflict to what felt like a legal siege, with unhealthy tactics and poor communication delivered by her lawyer.

Our marriage had been over for years. Her choice, her timing, and her approach to handling the divorce filing felt selfish and subversive, ensuring she would not have to move and could maintain her living situation with no accountability or effort on her part. By filing for divorce, she ensured that no progress could be made during the ongoing proceedings.

I couldn't move her, alter the lifestyle she was leading, or implement any of the changes we had discussed. It was a sneaky, selfish move that allowed her to do as she wanted with no responsibility for the full situation.

This decision was one-sided and passive, reflecting her reluctance to face accountability for securing a job, getting her life on track, or honoring her commitments.

Anya's hesitation and focus on herself necessitated that I take on considerable additional work in response to her filing and prepare my own legal documents. Around this time, she finally landed a part-time job as a waitress and babysitter, and she was proud of these minimal efforts, though she claimed they were beneath her. She came to me saying, "This part-time service job, I'm so above this, but I'm doing it."

The ego in her claim was hard to process. She hadn't worked in several years, had made minimal effort beyond the occasional online job hunt, and took no steps to expand her skills or qualifications. So, when she claimed to be above this entry-level position and ready for a much better role, I told her the truth: she was not operating at that professional level. She should appreciate any job opportunity, given her extended absence from the workforce and her reluctance to learn new skills, despite ample time available.

I also questioned why she felt so deserving of more. Why had she not secured a job at the level and pay she claimed to deserve? She then said she had an opportunity for a high-paying job, and her chances were great; she was waiting to hear back. This sounded more like one of her unrealistic, unsubstantiated fantasies than an actual opportunity. Once again, when I asked for details, what she shared was vague, with no company name, job title, or concrete evidence to support it. When I followed up, she explained that she didn't get the position.

> ## *"Conversations stopped the moment her attorney provided cover to sidestep difficult discussions rather than navigate them."*

After the divorce was filed, it felt to me that she began using her lawyer as both a shield and an instrument of control. In conversations, the lawyer's tone came across as arrogant and dismissive. Several times, I explained that I had some understanding of legal processes, as my father was a lawyer, and I preferred not to be talked down to. I also conveyed that while I could appreciate her objective and that she was serving Anya, her client, it felt unnecessary for this attorney to speak to me in a dismissive manner.

In my limited experience with lawyers, the law, and challenging business negotiations, I have not been spoken to in the way Anya's lawyer addressed me.

I reiterated that I understood she was Anya's lawyer, as she had mentioned several times throughout our emails. I also explained that none of my words were ever intended to be attacking, as she could review the emails sent. I was communicating from a position of openness to compromise and cooperate for the best results, considering all parties.

Still, this did not seem to deter her tone or her jabs. I have avoided countering or responding in kind, but it has become increasingly frustrating, and it seems as though she is waiting for me to retaliate.

I won't do that...

I will neither give her any ammunition to use against me, nor will I return a wrong with a wrong.

Staying on track by tracking

I am tracking all communication to demonstrate my efforts, show how I have chosen to respond with respect, and continue doing so when faced with the opposite.

The lawyer made some confrontational and inaccurate claims, as if it were easier to do knowing I was currently without legal representation. I considered how her communication and tactics might have been different if I had a lawyer.

The first filing she was supposed to receive from me was apparently held by the post office for two months before being returned. The lawyer claimed she had not received it. I question what happened with that envelope during that time. The certified letter was returned with a stamp indicating it had been addressed to the wrong address, but it was the correct address, right down to the extended zip code. It was also sent electronically through the courts online system, and the court confirmed it had been emailed to her, but she claimed that didn't arrive either. This also repeated with Anya when physical documents were sent to her that she avoided and were later sent back to me.

I navigated this complicated situation, dealing with two individuals who exhibited similar defensive behavior and questionable ethics. The collaboration between Anya and her lawyer seemed to enhance and reinforce her negative actions, allowing her to avoid taking responsibility. Direct communication ceased.

We hadn't spoken on the phone in a long time; all communication had shifted to text and email, where she chose what to respond to and what to ignore. Once her lawyer became involved, the approach shifted more. Conversations stopped the moment her attorney provided cover to sidestep difficult discussions rather than navigate them. Relying on legal support that I am sure feels both comforting and protective, she continues to avoid accountability and transparency.

A Shield of Legal Protection

Anya began to send increasingly harsh emails. They made me question how she was thinking and responding, and whether this came from long-standing habits, from resentment, or from feeling backed by her lawyer. My initial reaction was to respond assertively to several of those emails and pose the questions:

Do you realize that I have kept the emails you sent?

Do you understand that they constitute evidence?

Do you recognize that the inaccuracies, contradictions, false statements, and empty claims that you write in resentment, anger, or arrogance in these emails can harm you more than help you?

Apparently not, as she continues to send harsh communications with little regard for the truth and a sole focus on the story she prefers, unaware of the potential consequences.

Is this how she wants to behave while a permanent record is being created?

In her emails, Anya claims she doesn't have to update me on various aspects of Zoey's life that the parenting plan requires her to share. It has also been difficult getting Anya to send pictures of Zoey. When I have requested more social updates or images of events, games, or parties, she ignores them. This is her legal right in those areas, but why? Why the preference to punish and distance me when it could be so simple to send a text or email?

And I hear from Zoey often, "I asked Mommy to send this; I asked Mommy to show you that… did you get it?" The answer, more often than not, is no.

With key safety updates and details, there is a considerable gap between what Anya feels she should do and what she is required to do. Under the current parenting plan, I have the right to be informed about Zoey's safety and well-being, both physically and mentally, and to know her whereabouts in all situations covered by that agreement. Many of those requirements are not being followed. My intention is not to exert control. I am asking for what is fair, what is required under the law, and clear assurance that Zoey is safe.

Since her lawyer came into the picture, she communicates only when she chooses, fully using my lack of legal counsel and my health challenges to her advantage.

Closing Thought

Painful chapters can show how far a person will go to escape responsibility once it feels inconvenient. Filing for divorce and enlisting hired counsel to obstruct contact while I faced severe health and financial challenges epitomizes kicking someone when they are down. To me, this demonstrates calculated tactics chosen to gain advantage rather than to seek an equitable outcome.

CHAPTER 23.
Patterns of Non-Response and Collisions with Communication

Opening Thought

Dialogue thrives when questions are acknowledged, and the exchange is direct and transparent. When silence replaces engagement, it can expose the character of the person avoiding the response, in both business and family life. Before this woman, I had not come across anyone so disengaged in their communication that they repeatedly left direct questions unanswered, replying only when and how they chose. From this experience, I learned that silence and selective omissions can become tools for obscuring the truth.

Exposure to a broad mix of people inside and outside entertainment put me in the middle of conversational styles ranging from grounded collaborators to challenging personalities with sharp egos and guarded responses. I often found ways to translate, clarify, or bridge gaps between those different approaches. As tensions with Anya grew, I began to recognize elements of the most difficult communicators I had encountered appearing together in one person. One of the clearest examples was the way she handled messages and questions, answering only the parts she chose while acting as though the rest were invisible, whether in a single email or across several exchanges.

Here was a grown woman who chose to act as though certain questions did not exist. In my business experience, when dealing with the most egotistical individuals, a question or issue raised was at least acknowledged. The response might be blunt, harsh, or dismissive, but the inquiry was not ignored. Someone might say, "I'm not going to talk about that," or "I don't want to answer that," but there would be some response indicating they had registered the inquiry, whether in an email or during a conversation.

With Anya, some questions were denied existence. What made this more unusual was the follow-up tendency. After receiving mainly vague, brief, and incomplete answers, I had to ask for more information because her responses were often ambiguous, empty, or redirecting. I would point out that I hadn't received a response to a particular question and ask her to address it. I would clarify that I was not trying to be difficult, as she might have chosen to perceive it, but was trying to be informed. Most of the time, no response followed.

"Are you going to answer this? Are you going to address this? This is a question I still have that you have not responded to that has to be resolved." Replies to my questions often came only after five or six detailed emails repeating the same points, and she still focused only on what she felt obligated to answer, leaving the rest without any response. When I did receive a response, which was inconsistent and brief, it might be a dismissive statement like, "Well, I'm not dealing with that," or "That's not important."

I was not accustomed to such poor communication, especially when a third party had established rules. These were supposed to be addressed within 24 hours, as outlined in our parenting plan, but she appeared to give them no thought. This disregard for the questions I had every right to ask shut down my efforts to stay informed because she did not feel I had to know, and she apparently decided she did not have to tell me.

Is this style of ignoring questions, avoiding accountability, and refusing to address issues being taught to or observed by Zoey?

With this concern on my mind, when I speak to Zoey via FaceTime, I emphasize how excellent our communication is, which is true, and she acknowledges it, too. We problem-solve together. We address issues directly. This is not about trying to one-up Anya. It is about impressing on Zoey that she can communicate this way not only with me but with others.

Facing an issue head on with Zoey

A couple of weeks earlier, Zoey brought an issue she was having with me to my attention directly. I told her that if she doesn't like an action, behavior, trait, or, in this case, a nickname, I insist she brings it up, so I'm aware of it, and we can address it then and there. This ensures it doesn't continue to be a problem for her.

She mentioned that a nickname I had called her when she was younger, which she had liked at one point, no longer appealed to her. I told her I didn't know she felt that way. The last time we discussed it, she said she liked the nicknames I used but didn't want them shared with other kids or friends. I remembered that conversation and had told her specifically that I didn't want to embarrass her and wouldn't use those names in front of anyone else.

When Zoey told me she didn't like certain nicknames at all anymore, I asked how long she had felt this way. She admitted it had been a while but said she didn't want to hurt my feelings. I didn't scold her or make her feel bad about not speaking up sooner. Instead, I explained that I love her and want to review and address concerns, changes in preference, and feelings that have grown or emerged over time.

I shared that I'm not concerned about her hurting my feelings, and that telling me the truth would not change that. I explained it is important for me to know how she feels, what concerns she may have at any given moment, and what she believes she wants to say and see changed, but might be apprehensive to ask for.

From there, I told Zoey we can address and resolve any issue together. I also explained that if I were to take issue with it, how could that trust and confidence grow? I saw it in her eyes, in her posture, and in her peace that she felt comforted, heard, and honored. I also stopped calling her by any of the nicknames she mentioned she didn't like. She said, "Oh, that's great. Oh yes, I'll do that, Daddy." It was beautiful to see and hear this from her.

> *"Replies to my questions often came only after five or six detailed emails repeating the same points, and she still focused only on what she felt obligated to answer, leaving the rest without any response."*

Unfortunately, her mother seems to have difficulty engaging in this type of healthy communication. It's concerning that addressing issues directly and working through problems together is such a foreign concept in her household, where unspoken matters are ignored or dismissed, and others are attacked with guilt.

Zoey has shared with me how she told Anya about certain feelings and preferences, only to receive responses that seemed selfish, including statements about how those feelings hurt Anya and expressions of confusion about how Zoey could feel that way.

How does this style of communication make a child feel safe to share, comfortable addressing issues, or hopeful about conflict resolution? When I addressed this via email, suggesting she consider it when talking to Zoey, Anya told me she had asked Zoey about it and said Zoey told her she didn't mean it that way.

This felt like pressure on Zoey to say what Anya wanted her to say, as I had been told the opposite: that Zoey did not feel comfortable telling her mother the truth. This denial from Anya sweeps the issue aside and ignores the reasons why Zoey is more open with me.

Closing Thought

Resolve strengthens when concerns are met with clear answers instead of avoidance or delay. Real understanding can grow when difficult topics are faced rather than sidestepped. The cost of that avoidance appears in strained relationships and missed lessons when honesty is postponed or buried instead of brought into the open.

CHAPTER 24.
Reflecting My Words Back While Remaining Empty Within

Opening Thought

Substance calls for honesty beneath the surface, not imitation or display. There are instances when a conversation feels fully reciprocal, only to emerge as an echo rather than a shared understanding. What seems like engaging presence can be your own language and energy cast back by someone playing a part for acceptance. When pretense replaces sincerity, it becomes harder to know who the other individual is, or whether they know themselves at all.

Mirroring has uncovered some of the more troubling mental and emotional signs I have seen up close. As I noted early on, Anya's mirroring first appeared in our earliest conversations and gradually evolved. What stands out most is the tendency to mimic another person's behavior. This imitation of what appears to be normal can create a sense of ease and, at times, be used to influence or mislead negatively.

Over time, I recognized that much of the way she presented herself lacked authenticity. We appeared to share the same political ideology, which felt comforting in that moment. I had met her in a context where I kept my political views quiet; they were not views I shared openly. As we talked, I did not recognize it as mirroring, but now I see it differently. She often rephrased my ideas, themes, and beliefs to reestablish a connection, but over time, it became clear those views had not originated with her.

As I hear stories from Zoey about her conversations with Anya and her observations of Anya with her new boyfriend, it becomes clear how differently they now approach politics from how Anya once said she felt when she shared her views with me.

They are now the exact opposite of what she had presented to me. It was more of the same unhealthy song, repeating, "Mirror, mirror on the wall, who is the person I have to agree with in the moment after all?"

The mirroring extended to her communication style as well. She would deflect, claim it wasn't her fault, and then suddenly insist it was all her fault. Anya could not acknowledge that I wasn't trying to place all the blame on her, nor could she recognize my intent to resolve the issues at hand.

Then, in an intense shift, she would mirror my desire to fix these issues, copying my communication style and claiming she wanted to handle matters the same way I did. These twists and turns resulted from what felt like an erratic way of thinking and communicating.

> *"Quiet moments leave me curious whether*
> *Anya has any idea who she is beneath*
> *all this behavior. Is there any steady*
> *foundation to this woman, or is she mostly*
> *a facsimile of the people around her, seeking*
> *their approval?"*

Anya's mirroring wove into many elements of our relationship, marked by complex forms of imitation and inventive presentation. Reflecting on it now, I feel like a fool for missing these signs. For many years, I had honed my ability to recognize such traits, observing someone and realizing, "I don't suspect that is their actual perspective; they are saying it to influence the situation." Still, while Anya displayed many of these traits, I did not catch it at first in how she demonstrated textbook mirroring behavior.

Quiet moments leave me curious whether Anya has any idea who she is beneath all this behavior. Is there any steady foundation to this woman, or is she mostly a facsimile of her friends and the people around her, seeking their approval?

I'm glad she has friends. My goal is still for her to be happy. I pray that she finds healing. Still, I think Anya's true self was rarely shown, and I perceived inconsistencies in her behavior that made authenticity feel elusive. What fascinates me is how often she hides behind mirroring, using it to connect with anyone she wants to. Over the years and through the pain, she appears to have forgotten, or perhaps been disconnected from, an authentic self-identity of her own.

Closing Thought

True connection depends on more than repeated agreement or hollow phrases. Real depth calls for transparency and authenticity, not a performance of borrowed traits. From this experience, I learned to pay closer attention when a relationship feels too easy and thin, and to ask whether I am meeting a person or mostly a shadow.

CHAPTER 25.
Rushing to Settle Before the Truth Could Be Revealed

Opening Thought

Urgency can expose priorities and true intentions in ways that are not immediately clear. The decision to address matters outside the courtroom highlighted where confidence lay and what remained unspoken. The sudden move to finalize, to drop their demands, and to correct the false details I had requested for months clarified who was uneasy about standing before a judge and what that meant for her case.

Pressure to close the divorce through a joint stipulation arrived without warning and carried a suspicious weight. Several months ago, a judge was scheduled to meet with us online to hear our case and assess its current status. That hearing was on the calendar, set, and ready to proceed.

Then, suddenly, this joint stipulation proposal emerged from her lawyer and Anya, suggesting that we should try to resolve all matters before the hearing. Prior to this unexpected development, I shared concerns about the parenting plan and communication issues. These were core matters I hoped to address.

I asked whether these issues should be handled before the divorce proceedings. The response was dismissive: "No, no, that can be taken care of after." Much of what I raised was being ignored. When I pressed for answers, I was told, "Well, you have to pay for that." Those questions were repeatedly ignored, left without a response on these critical issues. The attitude was, "We've got to get through this paperwork."

As they were filling out the paperwork, I reviewed it carefully. I felt torn, uncertain whether signing the document would best serve me, Zoey, and the broader situation. Finalizing the divorce would have been appealing. We had been apart for years, but would it provide the right form of closure for this chapter to be completed?

As I started to feel more at ease with the situation, I was taken aback. The stipulation included an alimony demand that I couldn't reconcile at all. I have tried to ensure that my child support payments were made while navigating my own health and financial challenges. Still, I also noted that Anya had moved in with her boyfriend, who appeared to be fully supporting her.

Considering my circumstances and Anya's seeming lack of effort throughout this process, I struggled to see how I could validate paying any further support beyond child support. It also appeared to me that she was in a stable financial situation. While I will meet all my child support obligations, I firmly believe that alimony is neither deserved nor legally required under Anya's circumstances. Given my clear rights in this situation, I chose not to agree to additional support.

The initial proposals felt preposterous, demanding a substantial amount of money for years and remaining unmodifiable. I researched situations comparable to my own, and every case I found indicated that such an arrangement was not warranted. So, I came back with a firm no. Then there appeared to be sudden urgency and a statement where I was told: "You do not want to be in front of this judge."

Part of me thought I should have waited to be heard by the judge before telling my story. Another part of me was concerned because I didn't have a lawyer. Anya's lawyer presented a variety of examples that raised ethical and moral concerns for me. It felt as though some tactics might be skirting the law. They seemed aimed at redirecting focus, using statements out of context, and taking advantage of my limited legal knowledge to undermine my credibility. I noticed several attempts to discredit or dismiss what I believe to be credible evidence, often through technical maneuvering or rhetorical misdirection.

This may reflect a response to the inconsistencies in Anya's case. Many of her claims are difficult to substantiate, and a closer examination showed gaps and narratives that did not line up with the facts. These tactics created an uneven playing field and seemed to confirm how fragile the foundation of their case was.

Weighing what felt like her selfishness and lack of cooperation against any realistic chance of reaching a balanced agreement, I held my position. The alimony demand fell to half the original amount, then to half the number of months. Still, I held my line in the sand. Nope, I wasn't going to do it.

Then she came back again. "You can't do zero. Will you agree to one dollar a month?" I told Anya I could. I didn't understand why zero couldn't be done legally, but one dollar a month was fine with me. I'd pay her one dollar a month for 96 months. Done, and I would continue to pay the child support and modify that amount as required.

That was another point of frustration. I sent child support faithfully, arranging help to ensure payments were made on time. I communicated that I was bedridden, not working, and in a great deal of pain, but every payment went out.

I could have contacted the courts about my medical situation, which could have allowed the payments to be frozen without putting me in legal trouble. I could verify the surgeries, the time spent bedridden, the medications, and the pain itself. Despite all of that, I still managed to make those payments happen with zero respect or gratitude for that effort.

"Apparent haste in pursuing the divorce
seemed to stem from a deep-seated

> *negativity, reflecting inconsistencies in her narrative that revealed more and more inaccuracies and a decreasing level of honesty."*

During that rush to finalize arrangements, there appeared to be concern on their part. If my story, the details I have collected, and the way I have handled myself under fire had been heard in court, perhaps the issues with the parenting plan could have been addressed sooner.

Anya focused on working with her lawyer to design the image she wanted to present and control how she was perceived. Given her reluctance and possible concern about transparency, keeping her actions and communications out of court would benefit her the most, allowing her facade and power to remain intact.

Still, I ended up allowing that rush to happen, and I go back and forth about whether it was the right decision. It felt good to be finally divorced. That said, I'm not entirely disconnected due to ongoing issues with the parenting plan, and I won't be fully clear of it until Zoey is 18. At least this primary stage is complete, and we are officially divorced.

The Issues Are Likely To Resurface The divorce is complete, but regarding the parenting plan, I have filed motions asking the court to address specific instances of noncompliance. It will take time; these concerns will not be resolved all at once. I will continue to pursue this until accountability and fairness are in place. I will bring the relevant evidence to the surface where it can be seen with full transparency and, hopefully, appropriately addressed for Zoey's benefit. I will not stop until respect is established for Zoey, for me, and for Anya as well.

Anya's apparent haste in pursuing the divorce seemed to stem from a deep-seated negativity, reflecting inconsistencies in her narrative that revealed more and more inaccuracies and a decreasing level of honesty. It appeared she was going to great lengths to conceal certain aspects of the truth and to shape a story that suited her preferences. If the whole story were to come to light, the result might be deeply unsettling for her and the weak narrative she has been leaning on for a long time.

Closing Thought

Outcomes shift when transparency guides how disputes are handled and decisions are reached. Careful documentation and steady preparation supported a clear path forward for me around her shifting statements, reinforcing the value of candor and persistence in a process seeking resolution. Her apprehension that the full record would come out in court seemed to outweigh any other factor.

CHAPTER 26.
Performing Politeness While Missing Authentic Gratitude

Opening Thought

Genuine appreciation expressed through a kind gesture is more than a mannerism to me. Teaching my daughter to value courtesy in routine exchanges anchors respect in practice and strengthens her character through the habits she forms. Instilling this core value in her is a priority for me, especially as I have noticed its consistent and troubling absence when I am not around.

Early on, I noticed how Anya often overlooked common consideration for those around her. I observed how she occasionally mirrored my behavior, becoming more courteous with certain staff when I pointed out actions that could be perceived as rude. She slipped back into the same dismissive tone when she thought I wasn't watching. This concerned me; it is an attribute Zoey is better off avoiding.

Working with my daughter on everyday behavior around gratitude has meant cultivating genuine kindness from the heart, not a performative politeness that shows up so often these days. No matter where Zoey finds herself or who surrounds her, I ask her to embody an authentic respect that stems from character, not circumstance.

I struggled to reconcile this with Anya's background in the food service industry. Having worked in the industry, one would expect her to understand the importance of treating service workers with respect. Still, I recall that before Zoey was born, she would place orders in a demanding way. There were times when she placed orders without much warmth in her voice or acknowledgment of the person serving her, beginning with a brisk "I'll have…" without the courtesy of a "please" or "thank you." When we dined out together, I often felt compelled to overcompensate for her perceived rudeness, going out of my way to be extra polite to the servers and staff.

I used to say that you can learn a great deal about someone by watching how they tip, how they order, and how they interact with service workers. These moments can bring out parts of a person's character that carefully curated conversations might hide. When I brought this up with her, she would temporarily alter her behavior. But I could see it was only surface-level compliance rather than true change. When repair technicians came to our door, or delivery people arrived, I witnessed a different version of her.

Still, she would sometimes swing to the opposite mood, becoming conspicuously bubbly and friendly, which felt more like a performance than a steady way of relating. During my visits with Zoey, I gently remind her about primary manners.

"Let's ask for what you would like nicely and lead with: 'May I please have?' These are little courtesies we will practice, and I expect you to practice them when I'm not around."

I feel strongly about being consistent with this.

Each visit since I've been away has included reminders about these habits. She's a kind-hearted girl and seems to make improvements easily when reminded, quickly returning to saying "please" and "thank you." As she grew, I taught her to look directly at people when speaking to them. She would order my coffee for me at cafes, and it became an adorable ritual in which she confidently engaged with the baristas. Anya seemed uncomfortable with this at times, but I have instilled in Zoey these steps, tips, and ideas to connect with people sincerely.

I hope Zoey understands the value of gratitude, knows how to show appreciation, and engages meaningfully with others who are kind and generous toward her.

Her friends may not practice these courtesies, but Zoey will. I've consistently emphasized this point, and she's started to see the results herself. "Wow, that was cool what they said about me being courteous," she'll observe, or "Oh, they gave me this little extra item, treat, or gift." I explained to her that "being kind is not only nice, but it often inspires people to go the extra mile. They do this with their efforts, engagement, and service and some will respond out of appreciation for that kindness and respect. Many servers spend a great deal of time on their shifts encountering those who aren't considerate, so you can be a welcome change."

This lack of gratitude remains a concern. I don't care how Anya behaves with her boyfriend or in her current situation; my focus is on ensuring Zoey develops sincere appreciation and respect for others.

> *"Working with my daughter on everyday behavior around gratitude has meant cultivating genuine kindness from the heart, not a performative politeness that shows up so often these days."*

The same issue emerged with tipping. I rely on a simple rule: take the total, move the decimal, and double it to ensure a 20% gratuity, increasing it further for outstanding service. Watching Anya treat these calculations as if they were a complex mathematical equation, and hearing her argue that certain standards did not apply at a bar, was frustrating. I believe in honoring a bartender who provides engaging conversation and true connection. When service is only adequate, I maintain a baseline of respect that she seemed unwilling to match.

Her Turning Tones

Several people, including my mother during times when our communication was more open, commented that Anya often seemed distant or guarded, quiet in ways that could come across as ungracious or withdrawn. I've noticed it as well. While she didn't initially direct that ungraciousness toward me, over time I began to experience a sharper tone and more tense exchanges in our messages and conversations. The tone I experience in her emails, texts, and responses has felt increasingly harsh. This wasn't common, but there was a subtle strain of unkindness that may have lingered beneath the surface for some time, perhaps dating back to before we were together.

When I was trying to get her involved in more social settings and introducing her to clients and new connections, several people commented, "That's who you are married to? I didn't expect that. You're engaging, outgoing, social." Still, Anya consistently appeared harsh, perpetually in a bad mood. There was a period when Zoey noticed, saying, "Mommy seems so angry. Mommy seems sad often." This harshness often showed on Anya's face, as if she had difficulty relaxing and sincerely engaging with people.

I didn't intend to change her fundamentally. That was not the goal at any point. I hoped to encourage connection, help her understand why some people might not be engaging with her, and identify reasons that could explain why she wasn't finding social interactions particularly fulfilling. Some of it seemed tied to the everyday ways we approached public interactions and common courtesy, where our habits and expectations did not line up. I noticed similar tension in her interactions with family, as she often described long-standing difficulties relating to her mother.

My focus remains on ensuring Zoey develops sincere gratitude. I hope she works in customer service at some point. I worked in convenience stores, delivered pizzas, worked in fast food, and stood behind burger counters. These experiences taught substantial lessons about social communication, gratitude, connection, engagement, eye contact, and appreciation.

No matter the career path Zoey chooses one day, these foundational skills will serve her throughout life. They will help her become a better person, engage more meaningfully with others, and grow into someone grounded in gratitude and respect.

Closing Thought

Decency shown in everyday actions, rather than in grand gestures, can expose a person's true heart. Honoring others in small ways creates a habit of kindness that my daughter can carry forward, building relationships with each sincere thank you. Acknowledging the humanity in those we meet is one of the most meaningful and lasting forms of respect we can offer.

CHAPTER 27.
Searching for Light in a Relationship Starved for Truth

Opening Thought

Positive moments can sometimes be found in challenging places. Seeking pieces of joy or truth in dark experiences can create memories that bring warmth when they matter most. Amidst the wreckage of a relationship built on falsehoods, finding positive memories was a struggle. It required effort to pull a small glimmer of light from the darkness and to salvage any moments worth holding on to.

Reflections on my relationship with Zoey's mother now center on the few meaningful memories I can share with Zoey in ways that might lift us both. Glimpses of the person I once believed I knew during our brief time together still surface. Finding good memories has been difficult. Much of what I believed about her turned out to be mirroring tactics and curated personas shaped to fit me, not a steady picture of who she was when she was not performing for others.

The other night, a question surfaced about what uplifting moments I could recall beyond my experiences with Anya's intense negativity, resentment, and recurring tendencies of self-focused behavior.

I've identified only two instances that stand out, separate from any that involved Zoey.

The first memory takes me back to that initial dinner party where we met. She had an uncommon way of eating corn on the cob. Rather than holding the cob and eating it, she would stand it upright and run a knife down it, slicing off the kernels in neat strips. I had not seen anyone take this approach with corn. I love corn, but sometimes struggle with kernels getting stuck in my teeth when biting it directly from the cob. Her method worked better. I could butter the corn more evenly, and it felt as though I was getting more of the actual corn. It's such a small detail, but it makes me smile because it was one of the few moments in our relationship that felt uncomplicated and true.

> *"Food has a remarkable way of anchoring how some remember certain relationships, preserving small, sincere moments regardless of how the larger story unfolded."*

The second memory also revolves around food and a specific dish I miss.

She could make this outstanding comfort food dish. It wasn't overwhelmingly spicy and balanced so well with precisely the right flavor profile. She also made this second appetizer dish that stands out in my memory. (I'll keep the specific dishes unnamed here.)

When I'd compliment them, she'd dismiss my praise with, "Oh, this is simple," but simple or not, they were extraordinary. It was another strange element of our interactions. When I praised her or tried to lift her with recognition and encouragement, she would deflect it immediately.

There's a part of me that wants to ask for those recipes, but based on our history, I suspect she might refuse out of resentment.

Food has a remarkable way of anchoring how some remember certain relationships, preserving small, sincere moments regardless of how the larger story unfolded. One of those food-type memories reminds me of another relationship from years earlier with a woman in the Northwest U.S. Although that relationship was much shorter, I have countless positive memories of her, including her intelligence, worldview, work ethic, the way she carried herself, and her sensuality. We weren't compatible in the long term, but I can still recall how special she was.

One of my strongest memories of her also involves food: a pasta dish she made that was outstanding. I lost touch with her, which I regret, because unlike Anya, that relationship ended on favorable terms with mutual respect and friendship. We were not compatible; we understood what the other wanted and did not want, and there was clarity about what each of us was and was not willing to change.

Still, I would be happy to get Anya's recipes. That would be excellent, for both nostalgia and the practical joy of making those dishes. It's sad to me that if I were to ask, it would likely be another request she would disregard.

Closing Thought

Memories tied to good food can provide a strange, hollow comfort. It was a taste of the real within a relationship otherwise starving for authenticity, a reminder of a connection that offered brief satisfaction but failed to nourish in any other way.

CHAPTER 28.
Breaking Through the Blockade of Her Exclusive Perspective

Opening Thought

Flexibility in weighing many angles builds a strong base for clarity. When receptivity to other views is missing, dialogue can stall and conflict may replace connection, like a conversation that collapses into a collision.

From our first meeting, early warning signs grew into major conflicts; her inability to consider another perspective was central, and she refused to entertain the possibility that her initial conclusion might be wrong. Once she decided what she wanted to believe, any further discussion was effectively over. Her refusal to consider that reality might differ from her preferred version became a central barrier. This rigidity was particularly challenging for me because seeing multiple viewpoints has been key to my career and relationships.

In entertainment, success hinged on flexibility. Early on I learned it wasn't about playing what I thought was right but about serving the song, the studio crew, the investors, the people footing the bill, and the person running the session. Whether in confidential or regular recordings, the creative work was secondary to the communication questions I asked.

Questions I posed: Who is in charge? What are they trying to achieve? Why am I here instead of the regular member? What went wrong before I was called?

If a member had been fired or temporarily replaced, I required the backstory. I weighed whether a returning musician could learn a new embellishment or whether simplifying my part would aid the track's clarity. This perspective proved indispensable for production communication.

During production planning when producing, I asked before the first note who I was producing for: the label, investors, band, or the member who controls most decisions. Understanding those relationships and adapting quickly was a cornerstone of my career.

This skill also extended to handling criticism. When someone said my playing "sucked," I didn't get defensive. Instead I asked, "Why do you think it sucks?" (or, with more arrogant clients, "Why does it suck?"). By understanding their perspective, I could often piece together what they were looking for and deliver it.

I tried to apply these same communication skills with Anya, but her views became so intense and immovable that she couldn't consider any alternative perspective. Often, she wouldn't share her viewpoint. Instead, she told me what I was feeling and doing. Her words carried the weight of what she considered the truth. If I made a statement or shared a thought that affected her negatively, regardless of my intention, she would immediately assert her own interpretation. She shut down further discussion and insisted her conclusion reflected my motives, without seeking confirmation or showing humility to consider another view.

Through my efforts, I sometimes found moments to gently encourage her. I'd suggest that her perception might not accurately reflect my intention. When she considered another view, if only for a moment, progress felt possible. Unfortunately, most of the time, bringing up the idea that I might not be doing what she claimed I was doing created a sudden shift in the atmosphere and led to a complete shutdown. She wasn't hearing me, or she was settling on her perception rather than considering my intention.

What followed felt like a workout to bring the tension down, lift up the calm, and convey that I was not attacking, insulting, or discrediting her feelings. Still, after reaching that calm understanding, she would quickly return to rigid thinking and conclusions that didn't consider other viewpoints. In select and brief moments early on, she opened enough to hear a different perspective without the walls, and the seeming requirement to defend or fire back.

This sparked hope in the few moments when we seemed able to connect and resolve issues respectfully. Still, while daydreaming that it could work, that it could improve over time, and that we could be together, the situation would shift back to a less effective, less productive style of communication. The counter-attacks, the shutting down, and the walls would grow, casting dark shadows and pulling the connection back to a challenging place. Navigating these emotional fluctuations left me feeling as if I had a broken compass and an outdated map, with no clear destination in sight.

In her narrative, I conclude that Anya sees me as the most awful person in the world. She has found a haven where her opinion is treated as fact; no one challenges her, and she dismisses any opposing view as inaccurate.

> *"Once she decided what she wanted*
> *to believe, any further discussion was*
> *effectively over. Her refusal to consider*
> *that reality might differ from her preferred*
> *version became a central barrier."*

This inability to see other viewpoints was one of the primary reasons I knew I couldn't continue the relationship. More concerning, it's a trait I do not want to see Zoey inherit. Small elements of this have surfaced sometimes. In certain moments, Zoey has made some rigid and linear statements, and I try to guide her gently, asking,

"Are you sure? What makes you see it that way? How did you come to that conclusion? Is it possible that the answer might be different from what you have shared?"

I walk this line carefully. Zoey deserves to feel heard while she develops the ability to consider multiple perspectives, so, I like to ask her, "How can we look at this differently? How can you see another view? How can you avoid concluding based on what you hope the answer could be, and instead take the time to find out what it looks like from a wider view?"

This is one of the key concerns I have about Zoey. She must not adopt the unhealthy traits associated with these combative, closed-minded communication skills. All I can do is continue talking with her.

Zoey deserves these positive skills for her relationships, her career, and her entire life. With this ability, she'll be happier, communicate better, understand more deeply, and develop greater wisdom. Zoey can also avoid finding herself trapped in the type of relationship I had with her mother.

Closing Thought

Openness to other perspectives can create understanding and mutual respect. I try to teach my daughter this skill daily, showing her how to examine multiple viewpoints and question her conclusions. She deserves a foundation built on adaptability and humility rather than the rigid, defensive, closed-minded thinking she has witnessed.

CHAPTER 29.
Frustrating Her Attempts to Bait Me into Reaction

Opening Thought

Silent conflict and immature tactics can unveil purpose more plainly than words ever could. Rather than waiting for a calm reply, she waited for an outburst she could use while sidestepping the issue. Steady restraint became my safeguard, letting me state my thoughts without exposing my emotions.

Signs pointed to a plan in motion, whether influenced by her lawyer or by her own approach. She appeared focused on drawing out a response she could later use to her advantage. Her dismissive tone and unwillingness to engage sincerely made her intent clear. Stirring conflict to later point to my words as proof of legal misconduct was the goal, not genuine dialogue. If facts no longer worked in her favor, encouraging a slip in my composure seemed to be the alternative.

She gives an impression that she has lost her footing and is trying to find any advantage she can, recognizing that a change in her approach is necessary. When agitating emails from her lawyer arrived, I learned to pause. I stopped letting frustration dominate, breathed, and reminded myself, "This person is being intentionally harsh, I will not respond in kind." My calm replies only intensified her irritation because I no longer took the bait. I responded with humility, strategy, and precise wording.

Questionable Lawyers that Bend and Twist

My father was a lawyer, and I sometimes struggle to hold many in the legal profession in high regard, despite knowing a few individuals who embody ethics, honor, and transparency; I believe they are a rare exception.

The law can be misused. Operating near the edge of legality, such tactics can infringe on rights, whether through filings, evidentiary presentation, or phrasing that turns a partially true statement into a misleading one.

It's hard to see some lawyers, especially those pursuing quick wins at any cost, prioritize narrative over truth and integrity. I see it as a significant moral, ethical, and honorable shortcoming in this profession. And this might be what is happening here.

Anya repeatedly tries to recast her choices, attitudes, personal struggles, and the inconsistencies I've witnessed, in ways that shift responsibility and reshape the story to work against me. If she were to consider the tendencies, history, and truth, it seems she might struggle to find a solid or healthy support system to keep her grounded, as the false elements that have served as her crutch for so long now appear to be slowly crumbling.

Since she may not have much to rely on, her strategy remains unclear. She has tried to get help from her lawyer to both cover up her inaccuracies and create a way for the truth to be lessened or not used against her.

Anya and her lawyer appear to be working to pressure me into feeling flustered when I discuss these uncomfortable truths. She might attempt to portray me as confrontational, perhaps by trying to bait me, encouraging me to react with anger, swearing, or using language that could be interpreted in a more negative light.

I once caught myself considering writing, "I can't wait until the day you are held fully accountable." It's a straightforward statement.

I am seeking legal accountability that yields fair and transparent arrangements for child custody and visitation.

But if I phrase it that way in an email, might it be perceived as a challenge? Could she or her lawyer interpret it in a more sinister light, as if I'm intending to take some adverse action against her? While that would not be my intention, given my experience communicating with them, they would likely choose to see it that way.

Strategic Precision in Every Word

This way of thinking often prompts me to pause and choose my words carefully. Presenting statements subjectively protects against distortion. I've been forming and sharing thoughts like "This feels misguided," "This appears to be problematic," or "This seems to be." When I am compelled to make objective statements, I verify whether I have access to emails, text messages, or documentation that could hold up in a more formal setting. This becomes especially important if the initial approach doesn't go as planned, if games are played, or if the context shifts.

Without proper legal knowledge of how to present information, my delivery could be distorted and countered. The depth of the information could be dismissed, regardless of having the facts on my side. If I can't verify the information with multiple sources, I express it in more subjective terms. When I do have solid documentation, I can make statements with a stronger, more direct tone, while still maintaining some subjectivity and humility to avoid potential backlash.

"Stirring conflict to later point to my words as proof of legal misconduct was the goal, not genuine dialogue. If facts no longer worked in her favor, encouraging a slip in my composure seemed to be the alternative."

Cautiously navigating this fine line likely frustrates her more, since I'm not providing the ammunition she might be seeking. I refuse to let her benefit from her own inaccuracies and destructive behavior to gain an advantage through legal technicalities. Many have seen instances where someone may have misspoken, mishandled evidence, or made procedural errors that allowed a party to escape accountability despite the underlying issues. It's difficult to accept how one mistake, or a series of them, can profoundly affect an entire case. I find this aspect of the legal system to be awful.

I believe the law should operate more like how it was written and intended to be practiced.

For me, the principle is simple: let people aim to be more like judges than lawyers.

It appears that lawyers can sometimes prioritize winning over honoring the facts and morals. This leads those types of lawyers to spin, mislead, or conceal the truth to present their case in a way that favors their client's victory. That perspective and approach conflict with honor and truth.

My father appeared to have no problem navigating those waters, but I cannot use those tactics while maintaining honor, morals, and truth. The lawyer that Anya has hired may be operating within legal bounds, carefully skirting the lines, but I could not live that way.

Stating Truth Carefully

This whole situation of her waiting for me to slip up has become extra motivation for me to be more careful. I focus on avoiding mistakes, watching what I say and write, and not giving her any ammunition to avoid taking responsibility for the harm she's caused.

My restraint might frustrate her, as she may realize she can't pressure or push me into reacting in a way that could be used against me. Specific points sometimes demand a direct response, but I'm trying to resist that temptation, not only for myself but also for Zoey.

Closing Thought

Careful communication and response strategies are being applied more for my daughter's benefit than for Anya's. I am choosing my words carefully because I refuse to let a legacy of negative influence and duplicity prevail, much less give Anya any more power to twist, redirect, or reshape my words away from the truth. Choosing words with strategic purpose and thoughtful restraint can enhance healthy communication and clarity, and I hope these choices inspire my daughter to respond, react, and resolve conflicts more effectively.

CHAPTER 30.
Refusing to Drown in the Waters of Her Resentment

Opening Thought

Trying to move forward with someone who has no intention of healing, growing, or learning is pointless. My final message to her, unspoken but deeply felt, is a declaration of my own survival. I refuse to drown alongside you.

Surviving resentment's undertow demanded deliberate strength and conscious direction. Under the weight of unresolved discord and lingering bitterness, I chose to stand firm in clarity and purpose. I refused to allow the turmoil between Anya and me to engulf my sense of self or diminish my dedication to Zoey's well-being. What follows is offered not to recount blame, but to provide transparency and a pathway forward built on respect and balance.

These words are for Anya to hear and to understand their intent.

The negativity between us is corrosive for both of us. The way you are handling this situation is not beneficial for you, me, or Zoey. The anger and dislike you present have not helped and are not helping us move forward in a healthy way. Can we please work on this for Zoey?

When I've shared this idea in the past, she responds with, "Oh, I don't dislike you." Still, it appears that she may hold a strong aversion towards me, as her actions often seem to suggest that. Then, the conversation shuts down.

When someone's dislike for you becomes their only strategy, the healthiest response is to refuse to participate. This is not about winning or losing anymore; it is about protecting your well-being from the malice and negativity of another person's unresolved pain.

Given the chance to speak directly to Anya, I would say, "I will not let your brokenness break me." Amid all your attacks, accusations, and attempts to undermine me, "I don't know if you love Zoey" stands as one of the harshest remarks you have ever said to me.

The more I considered it, the more I recognized that a statement without truth behind it only reflects sorrow for the person who utters it. Your hurt, avoidance, anger, and lack of respect become evident in comments like this, exposing the foolishness of someone unaware of the connection Zoey and I share.

I Tried with Anya

I made every effort to bring steady understanding and healing to the situation. Despite all attempts, I reached the same unyielding barrier and accepted that a path together was not possible.

The situation did not hinge on her meeting me halfway or achieving a resolution; what stood out to me was her reluctance to make small, consistent efforts. Attempts to engage, such as starting a self-help book, would quickly dissipate. Her lack of sustained engagement frustrated me, and I often found that the intensity of her attacks remained far out of proportion to the circumstances.

"Distortions and malice of the truth will be pulled out of the shadows where they have thrived, and she will be held accountable for her words, choices, and actions."

This persistent lack of accountability, along with a belief system she consistently treats as undebatable, where anyone who contradicts her is wrong, seems to portray her as viewing others as adversaries. The way she perceives every action I take as problematic reflects a sad outlook from someone unable to accept reality.

I'm not claiming to have handled each situation well. I know circumstances were far from ideal within our relationship. I reached a point where I was done. I wasn't going to continue this way. Maybe others could have persisted longer, but standing alone, it wasn't sustainable.

I will not descend to her level.

Her behaviors and actions deserve recognition for what they are. She must fulfill her responsibilities and be held accountable when she chooses not to. Fairness and balance matter when situations shift. I will not treat her the way she has treated me. Still, distortions and malice of the truth will be pulled out of the shadows where they have thrived, and she will be held accountable for her words, choices, and actions.

My focus will be on protecting Zoey and ensuring her safety. I will handle the situation differently from how Anya has. Bringing these issues to light matters, and I aim to do so with respect and care. I will continue to present matters in a way that, if Zoey sees them years later, she will understand that I approached each situation with compassion and understanding.

I know that, in writing this book, some parts are intense, but I'm being careful. When Zoey is old enough, she will be prepared to hear this. If she understands the intention of my heart, that this is more about documenting what I lived through than taking a mean, bullying, or demeaning approach to make her mother look bad, then I will have succeeded.

Closing Thought

Commitment to responsible decisions and transparent conduct builds the foundation this relationship deserves, rooted in dignity and balance. My daughter deserves to have a father who chooses love over disdain and integrity over retaliation, and I am committed to being that father. Practicing honest restraint daily ensures that these experiences offer lasting guidance, establishing the standards for healthy relationships and personal resolve for her future.

CHAPTER 31.
Conviction Became an Unwelcome Guest in Our Home

Opening Thought

Faith brought a quiet relief and a personal revelation that felt like coming home. This newfound peace became another barrier between us. Her aversion was immediate, a rejection not only of my journey but also of the person I was working to become.

Resistance to faith in our home was not a slow build. It was abrupt and direct. When we met, we both described ourselves as agnostics. We believed more lay beyond our physical reality, but we could not define what that might be. At least, that was what I understood, unless she had mirrored my description and did not believe that for herself. I grew up Jewish, had my bar mitzvah, but gradually drifted away from actively practicing any religion. Over time, Anya showed not only a simple disagreement but an active opposition to it.

As our relationship continued, I reflected on aspects that challenged my spiritual beliefs. When Zoey was born, I felt a significant shift within me. It was not solely the miracle of childbirth that moved me, but the realization that my life had appeared to be leading me toward her for a while, and what that might signify. During one of the more difficult periods with Anya, I experienced a profound sense of comfort, a whisper that reassured me, "It is about my daughter."

My devotion to faith and belief wasn't found in a church; it was forged on a back porch in the stillness of the morning, holding my daughter and whispering to a God I wasn't sure existed. It grew quietly and personally, but when it finally came into the light years later, it was met with a coldness that confirmed how little room there was for truth in her world.

I remember spending time on the long back porch of our home, holding Zoey in the early mornings, walking back and forth, sometimes singing, sometimes talking to myself, and eventually praying. I didn't know who I was praying to or whether anyone was listening. I did know I was in a state of giving thanks and seeking connection. I didn't fully understand what I was doing.

A series of seemingly coincidental events began guiding me toward deeper spiritual exploration. A church hired me to work on some of their public-facing communications. Initially, I thought this was a good fit; who better than a non-believer to help create messages that would resonate with skeptics and possibly open people's minds?

Through that work, I made connections that led to speaking at two more faith-based events. I was still maintaining distance from personal belief, but I enjoyed some of the people I met (while finding others to be precisely the reason I had avoided organized religion).

Then I was hired to speak on a Christian business cruise, where I was one of the few non-believers. It was there that I found a direct path to the faith I had slowly been drawn toward and shown over time.

Coming off that cruise, I felt an unexplainable calm and a new, more solid foundation I had not experienced before, a meaningful sense of relief. Aspects of faith, surrender, science, and strategy were all woven together. The person who served as my catalyst is someone I don't particularly respect as a person or in business, but he was still significant at the start of my spiritual journey.

Early on, before I learned more about him, our conversations felt different from the standard religious sales pitches I had avoided in the past. We discussed science, strategy, history, trends, and mathematics. It was more than making empty faith statements like, "This book is true because I say so." He kindly asked, "Have you noticed these details? Have you considered this? What are your most significant objections?" It was an honest two-way conversation, unlike the pushy, hype-filled approaches I had experienced in religious settings. I am grateful for him, and it taught me that sometimes it is not about the person sharing the Gospel, but about focusing on the Gospel itself.

> *"Devotion to faith and belief wasn't found in a church; it was forged on a back porch in the stillness of the morning, holding my daughter and whispering to a God I wasn't sure existed."*

One of the most critical moments in my life turned out to be a truth I could not share with the person I was living with. My turn toward faith was a journey I had to walk alone, met not with curiosity or questions, but with a grimace and a closed mind that shut me out of any conversation about it.

I initially kept my newfound faith private. A friend sent me a Bible, and I began reading and studying quietly. When Anya noticed the Bible, her reaction was sharp and dismissive. "What is that?" she asked with apparent disdain.

When she asked, "So what, are you going to start going to church?" I explained that I was not ready for that; I was exploring and reading. This led to arguments.

Over the next few years, I spent considerable time studying. I connected with someone I had met on the cruise and began working with him. Faith became integral to my life, and I started praying regularly. I didn't dive deep into biblical scholarship right away but progressed gradually. I watched documentaries, faith-based films, and slowly moved into expositional studies and more in-depth reading.

When I finally shared with Anya that I was embracing faith, her reaction spoke volumes. She showed no curiosity and did not engage in meaningful dialogue. Her immediate response was, "Well, I am not raising Zoey that way." I reminded her how Zoey is our daughter, not solely Anya's. Discussion was welcome, and decisions regarding our child's spiritual education require joint participation, not unilateral action, which she did not seem to understand.

It was not my intention to push my faith on anyone, especially not Zoey.

When I started attending church, I invited Zoey to join me rather than insisting she come along. I approached it with, "This is a path and a belief I am exploring. Would you like to come with me?" It was meant to be an invitation, not pressure.

I explored different churches, checking out their children's programs and asking Zoey if she would like to participate. Sometimes she wanted to come; sometimes she didn't. I was searching for the right fit and the right place to learn, grow, and trust. I was also differentiating between the people, the denomination, the types of churches, and what was in the Bible itself.

Zoey and I began reading the Bible together. When Anya would walk by during these sessions, her grimace was unmistakable. There were moments I bit my tongue and chose not to say, "It is fortunate Zoey is not seeing your judgment and closed-mindedness right now. Would you be making that same face if Zoey were turned around?" I was not pressuring Zoey to adopt my faith; I was inviting her to be curious alongside me. Sometimes Zoey would initiate our reading sessions and ask questions about the Bible and about God on her own.

When Anya saw me praying, I felt that look of disapproval again, the one she gave so often. No conversations, discussions, or curiosity, only the reaction of her seeing an action or activity she did not like and did not want around her or Zoey. I tried to engage her in some discussions about faith, but they went nowhere.

As I deepened my faith practice, I began working on forgiveness. To this day, I am still working on forgiving her actions and choices. I pray for her every morning and night, knowing this is what I am called to do, though I do not enjoy it.

I tried sharing resources with her, saying, "Read this or don't. Listen or don't." I found Chuck Missler, an extraordinary biblical expositor who had passed away some years earlier. His approach resonated with me because he incorporated science, strategy, and detailed analysis. He demonstrated the mathematical precision of biblical prophecy and structure, uncovering a depth of detail that could not have been invented or dismissed as coincidence.

Knowing that Anya leaned more toward atheism than agnosticism, I sent her some of Missler's shorter video presentations, followed by the longer ones. I shared a 24-hour series called "The Bible in 24 Hours" and suggested she listen in small segments of five or ten minutes. Her responses were dismissive. "I listened to it," she would say, but when I tried to engage her in conversation about the content, she would shut down entirely.

I kept trying to share ideas and perspectives that might prompt meaningful consideration and further discussion, had she been open to it. She claimed she was, but her responses did not reflect that. I wasn't trying to convert her, but I was hoping for dialogue.

I'm not making excuses for her behavior or her choices regarding communication with Zoey, her drinking, and her hiding. But I pray for her healing, and that she'll find what she desires to achieve true happiness with transparency, honor, and honesty someday. I don't think she is happy now, despite claiming to be "happier than ever." I think she is living in alcohol, denial, and a false reality where she is not being fully honest with herself or with Zoey.

I pray she'll grow stronger in love, find forgiveness, develop the ability to hear challenging truths, and change for the better, for herself, for Zoey, for her future.

Closing Thought

Prayer became part of my daily discipline. Despite her criticism and dismissal of both God and me, I still prayed for her. It was not an act of affection but of obedience and hope for her healing. I continue to pray that she finds the calm she so actively denied me, for her sake and for our daughter's.

CHAPTER 32.
Three Peas in the Same Pod and Warnings That Echoed

Opening Thought

Before I ever met her mother, Anya provided a script of sorts, outlining what to expect. She described a self-absorbed woman with harsh tendencies and a corrosive edge. While those descriptions contained elements of truth, they offered a telling glimpse into the complex interplay of personalities within her family and into Anya herself.

Caution signs surrounded me, but I did not recognize them. During our trip to meet Anya's mother, she repeatedly expressed her apprehensions about what lay ahead. Her concerns appeared to wash over her in waves during the flight and in the days leading up to it. Those waves were evident to me in the shifting tone of her voice, its volume, and her body language.

Anya seemed like a different person when discussing her mother, speaking with deep hurt and describing her as self-absorbed, subtly harsh, and sometimes outright insensitive. Anya also mentioned her mother could be pleasant at times. She asked me not to share too much or go too deep in conversation, which did not feel like a promising start to healthy communication.

She expressed that her sister would be picking us up at the airport along with their mom, which intensified her concerns. She explained that her sister exhibited many of the same traits Anya had attributed to their mother, along with questionable social habits and a track record of inconsistencies in her life and relationships.

"Don't judge me by them," she pleaded repeatedly.

"I'm not like this."

The harsh words Anya used to describe her mother and sister, including self-centered, angry, and misguided, among others, could be a warning sign. While many people have complicated relationships with their parents and siblings, the intensity in her voice as she spoke about her mother's character and her sister felt unsettling to me.

For many years, I had taken pride in reading people well. I knew when to speak up, when to stay quiet, when to listen, and when to share my thoughts. These skills had served me well in meeting the parents of previous girlfriends, but I was not prepared for the immediate coldness that greeted us at the airport.

The coldness and seeming initial judgments felt swift and undeserved. Here was a woman who didn't know me, but she had already decided who I was. The hour and 45-minute ride from the airport was less than fun. I tried to soften the situation with pleasant conversation, but her mother remained angry and disconnected from reality. Later, it became apparent that Anya, her mother, and her sister were not only three peas in a pod; they were a unified front defined by shared unhealthy issues, rigid views, and an inability to accept blame.

I believe Anya's mother's career working with younger children may have contributed to her limited healthy social skills with adults. I don't mean to question her abilities as an educator; she found her zone. I've seen some teachers who seem to struggle with social ease in adult relationships, finding comfort in roles where their limitations go unexamined. It seemed to create a protective bubble, and I sensed that her mother may have lived within one.

Like Anya, she often overindulged when it came to drinking, steadily refilling her fruity cocktails, though she maintained some level of control. Her house, though, was filthy. When we later brought Zoey there, I would help to clean key areas Zoey was in to achieve some level of safety. I was not demanding a spotless home, but the levels of dirt, dust, mold, and grime were considerable.

The Dog Incident

During one of our early visits, possibly around a holiday, Zoey was less than a year old. The dog, unprompted but perhaps overstimulated by the crowd, snapped at her. I quickly pulled Zoey away to ensure her safety. What bothered me wasn't the dog's reaction (animals can be unpredictable around babies), but the complete lack of acknowledgment from Anya and her family.

> *"Later, it became apparent that Anya, her mother, and her sister were not only three peas in a pod; they were a unified front defined by shared unhealthy issues, rigid views, and an inability to accept blame."*

I wasn't calling for the dog to be put down, but this animal wasn't prepared to be around babies, and the situation was unsafe. Had I not reacted quickly, I don't know how severe the bite may have been. When I brought up my concerns, Anya responded with a lackadaisical emptiness, which infuriated me.

"Look, I'm not saying get rid of the dog at all," I explained. "But could the dog go to another room for some period of time, be outside for a while, or what would you propose? Maybe visits with Zoey happen elsewhere. Let's address and try to problem-solve these issues because I'm concerned about Zoey's safety around the dog."

The response I was given? "You're blowing this out of proportion."

Given what I witnessed when a dog with no experience around children snapped at my infant daughter, this was not an overreaction. I was asking for safety, not punishment for the dog. When I addressed the issue with her mother, the real problems began to surface. She employed the same tactic Anya used in arguments, offering complete denial as if the incident had not happened.

I watched it unfold and felt an overwhelming unease for Zoey's safety. While I generally believe in allowing children to learn from minor bumps and bruises, to toughen up and grow through their experiences, I couldn't shake the feeling that this situation was different. I saw it as risky, and it seemed worse as I was trying to present and explore possible options to protect Zoey, but I felt I was being shut down altogether by Anya, her mother, and sister in harmony.

Anya's mother's reaction made me livid. "This is your granddaughter," I thought. "Is this how you're going to act?" I wasn't demanding they get rid of the dog, only that we implement some safety precautions, such as a dog gate, training, or another option or plan for when Zoey was there.

My concerns proved valid. A couple of years later, the dog snapped again and broke the skin near Zoey's nose. This time, Zoey had initiated contact, pulling at the dog, so the situation was different. Afterward, I was calming the animal, who appeared upset by what had happened. By then, after all our conversations, the dog had received some training. But those initial reactions confirmed troubling priorities within this family, along with a lack of problem-solving and consideration for what they perceived as unimportant.

The strangeness extended to how her mother engaged with Anya. I watched Anya, who rarely cried, become emotionally undone after conversations with her mother. She hid so much from her mother, keeping most of our relationship private. She didn't tell her mother for years that we had separated. Regardless of her reason, which I couldn't determine, the chemistry and the concealment were corrosive to both of them and it further made me question what was being hidden or kept from me.

Her mother shared the same brash voice when they both engaged each other and others in conflict. I noticed that Anya often appeared unaware of her volume, especially when she was with her mother or sister. They all seemed to compete subconsciously for false dominance and higher-volume status.

Anya routinely mirrored those around her, adapting to their tones and volumes. Still, in her mother's presence, she reflected someone struggling with various self-absorption issues, conflict, and difficulties in forming healthy relationships. I would gently bring up the volume, especially when Zoey was sleeping, but she would deny it altogether. When I asked, "May I record it?" it was not to belittle her but to illustrate a tendency I was experiencing. I had done it myself and found it useful. I hoped this might bring to her attention the volume jumps I was hearing. Without implying that she was doing it intentionally, she could listen to it as well.

The walls appeared to be up again, and the idea only seemed to upset and cause Anya discomfort. Anya then dismissed the behavior, the idea of addressing it, and any consideration of looking into it.

People are who they are, and I don't wish to change anyone. Still, I recognize the potential influence on Zoey. While I feel less concerned about Anya and her choices in the long run, I think about how this might influence Zoey during these critical years of development and connection.

Zoey must be strong enough to stand on her own foundation, one that is healthier than what she's currently witnessing with her mother, grandmother, and aunt at times. She deserves to grow in understanding and clarity, so she can recognize negative traits, and avoid carrying them forward into her own life and relationships. This cycle I saw running through Anya's family must break with Zoey. She deserves to be free from these types of issues and cycles for the rest of her life and for those who are a part of it.

Closing Thought

Guided by example and transparency, I aim to help my daughter identify and overcome destructive cycles. Zoey has the opportunity to build her own foundation rooted in honesty and positive growth, choosing a path distinct from what she has witnessed.

CHAPTER 33.
Enduring Illness Alone After Years of Caring for Her

Opening Thought

Human decency shouldn't be conditional. During a time of intense pain and weakness, the grace I had given without reservation was not returned. Her concern was not for my recovery, but for how being ill inconvenienced her.

Harshness directed my way during this time bothered me, especially given the care and support I had shown her through her frequent bouts of sickness while we were together and afterward. I saw how Anya regularly faced health challenges during the years I was around her, including colds, fevers, the flu, COVID-19, drinking-related issues, and complications during her pregnancy. It was hard to see her unwell so often, and I tried my best to care for her during those times.

During that period when she was ill, after we were no longer together, I still wanted to help, cleaning her sheets, bringing her food, and doing any task I could to support and expedite her recovery. Despite the complexities in our relationship, I didn't feel any resentment regarding her illness or toward her. Kindness remained my choice throughout her illnesses; I prayed for her well-being and did not once think she deserved to be sick.

When I became ill a couple of years ago, enduring significant pain without the means to cover medical expenses, I tried to cope. The lack of sensitivity I encountered felt off, and I knew it would have been worthless to say, "Look, I know we don't have a relationship anymore, but how about showing some kindness? Remember all the kindness I showed you during your many illnesses?" I also questioned if she had forgotten all those moments altogether, tied to her memory and cognitive issues.

After an emergency room visit, doctors removed a gallon and a half of urine from my bladder, confirming a critical bladder issue with consequences I will have to handle for the rest of my life. This seemed to start a cascade of health problems I had been experiencing for about four years.

I became bedbound, in considerable pain, unable to work, and struggling to be myself. Her response showed her common tendency to jump to conclusions without grasping the whole picture. She stated, "You haven't been that sick that long. You haven't done this. I don't know about this." Then came demands like "You have to tell me about this."

More concerning was the unease she appeared to instill in Zoey regarding my condition. "I have to be able to talk to Zoey about this," she insisted.

"No, you don't have to," I replied firmly. "I'm going to talk to her about it. I'm going to help her work through this with strength. We will communicate with care, comfort, and clarity. I will not let you be the person to discuss this with her. If you'd like to discuss it together, the three of us, I am open to that. For now, if she has questions, they come through me, so I can guide her through healthy communication, not a harsh, perception-based, inaccurate approach with limited information that I have heard you share with Zoey."

I added that we could also discuss this on the phone, rather than via email or text, as I was trying to create an opportunity for better communication and clarity. If she were willing to discuss and share with Zoey without jumping ahead or filling in what she thought was happening, I would be happy to share. So much has been taken out of context, and Anya often draws her own conclusions without all the details. I believed the best course of action was to speak directly with Zoey to ensure she received accurate information and the truth about what was going on.

"Kindness remained my choice throughout her illnesses; I prayed for her well-being and did not once think she deserved to be sick."

Right before a major surgery, I received emails demanding to know when I would be out of surgery, what was happening, and when upcoming events or decisions regarding my health would occur. After providing the information and emerging from surgery, barely half an hour into recovery, she was sending me bills for Zoey's summer camp that required immediate payment.

Could you wait a day or two?

Could you have brought this up earlier?

The lack of sympathy toward my health contrasted sharply with her expectations and requirements for care. I found the contradictory elements she seemed to exhibit to be crass.

While I was recovering, she had a surgery that she chose to keep from me, disregarding the parenting plan once again. I was supposed to know when she was unable to care for Zoey, or when someone else was providing care in her place. She was in the hospital but decided not to share this information. She knew she was going in; it was not an emergency surgery, but she chose to operate in a way that worked for her.

Despite her disregard for our agreement, my response was simple. I expressed hope that her surgery would go well, that she would feel better, and that her recovery would be swift. I let her know I was praying for her. Respectful gestures and kind words did not follow in return.

Setting aside our failed relationship, couldn't we maintain respect? I'm Zoey's father, and I have one of the strongest connections with her. Couldn't we honor that when either of us is facing surgery, or any hardship or challenge?

There appears to be a wall up in her mind, perhaps tied to her difficulty in remembering or her ability to overlook all that was done for her during pregnancy. This seems to make it difficult for her to express any amount of sympathy or honor.

Anya seems to struggle to take responsibility for her actions and for the choices she makes to conceal certain behaviors. While she may hide much of this from Zoey, I hope Anya would prefer that Zoey embody kindness, regardless of the circumstances. Traits like respect, transparency, and empathy matter deeply these days. I also hope Anya will do all she can to demonstrate those healthier behaviors, which could help her heal and grow as she models them for Zoey.

No matter how often kindness is overlooked or withheld from me, there remains an opportunity to show Zoey what real compassion looks like. The focus is to fill the gap by providing a living example that values and cultivates love, understanding, and empathy, regardless of what others may offer.

Closing Thought

Comprehending a mindset devoid of empathy remains difficult. Rather than dwelling on what I was denied, I hope to help my daughter learn to offer it openly, nurturing a loving legacy of compassion instead of apathy.

CHAPTER 34.
Offering Methods of Peace When a Child's Tensions Run High

Opening Thought

Emotional weight appears to transfer from mother to daughter, leaving my daughter overwhelmed and weighed down at times. When she reaches out, upset or unsettled, I try to help her problem-solve, calm down, and regain her footing.

Unease that begins with her mother too often ends up in Zoey's heart as tension she struggles to resolve, leaving her believing it's her fault. In our previous home, I was blamed for Zoey's discomfort, while Anya's influence went unacknowledged. Those patterns persisted. Zoey came to me for comfort, either in person or via FaceTime, when she felt uneasy. Each time she reached out, my role as her anchor became clear, and I provided guidance to help her regain composure and confidence as she grew.

When Zoey is uncomfortable or wound up, I have to calm her and alleviate pressures that seem influenced by her mother. On FaceTime, Zoey says, "I'm having bad thoughts; I'm feeling off." We work through it together, and most of those conversations end with her saying, "Thank you, I feel so much better. I love you, and I can be stronger." I know this is true, and I'm watching her grow in wisdom and strength from a distance every day.

I've realized there's a key difference between a parent who causes unease and one who calms it. I aim to be the latter for her. I believe a steady presence paired with gentle, practical steps helps my daughter loosen tight, negative thoughts and lift some of the weight she carries, so she can see herself, her situations, and her feelings in a better light, while taking small steps toward release, resolution, and peace.

While helping her settle and relax, I offer reassurance and comfort. "Okay, we can think about this. We can talk about this. Let's break this down. Let's breathe. Let's get a drink of water, or if you haven't eaten in a while, how about a snack?"

When she says, "I feel uneasy or tense," I ask her, "Are you drinking enough water? Are you breathing slowly?" Guiding her back to a calmer place leaves me questioning what support Zoey receives from her mother. That she confides in me means a great deal. Still, the lack of comfort Zoey seems to experience at times, and the tension that appears to stem from her mother, remains a concern.

I watch her piece together these bad thoughts, as she calls them, then help her take them apart, taking note of the patterns and seeing situations differently for the moment as well as for the future. Meanwhile, I aim to teach Zoey the importance of taking responsibility.

"Have you noticed that you feel more off, wound up, or have more negative thoughts when you're consuming too much sugar? Maybe we should cut back some. I'm not saying to avoid sugar entirely, but perhaps reduce it somewhat or have it earlier in the day. Maybe drink more water. Maybe read for a while before bed instead of watching one of your shows on your iPad."

> *"Steady presence paired with gentle,*
> *practical steps helps my daughter loosen*
> *tight, negative thoughts and lift some of the*
> *weight she carries, so she can see herself,*

her situations, and her feelings in a better light, while taking small steps toward release, resolution, and peace."

Zoey identified that pattern herself the other day when we spoke, saying, "I had a brownie pretty late, and then I had trouble sleeping." As we talked through it, Zoey said, "Maybe I should not have a brownie tonight."

The inability to problem-solve around her mother when feeling uneasy became evident when she said, "I'm concerned about going to this camp where there are no kids I know." I understand that trying new experiences and visiting new places can be tough for kids, but when she was with me, she seemed more social, braver, and more confident in facing unfamiliar places, people, and challenges.

I would have liked to know how this was handled and discussed before it reached me, and what her mother told her. Not to overstep, not to contradict, but to have a better grasp and be a greater support to her. We walked through it together on FaceTime. I shared my experiences from when I went to camp as a kid, about meeting new friends, and how she is the same age I was when I made a friend at camp who remained close for years.

Sitting with Zoey on FaceTime, gently guiding her through her unease, allowing her to explore her thoughts about trying new foods, meeting new people, and being open to new experiences seemed to center her. It built her confidence in this new camp and in other areas. I've noticed that Anya appears to grapple with this as well. Sometimes it feels like a recurring theme, and I question the effect Anya has had on Zoey when it comes to exploring new opportunities.

When we got off the call, she seemed more confident, ready to try, and less overwhelmed. She called the next day after camp and told me I was right and that she had a great time. It was another example of her mother amplifying concerns and me bringing her back to a place where she felt secure and confident. She is building a skill set that already appears stronger than her mother's.

That same steadiness carried into a phone call after her first dental surgery, when Zoey mentioned that another might be necessary. Her voice was higher, her words faster, and her tone was tense. I said, "Let's slow down, sweetheart. You've already been through a more involved surgery, and you handled it well. I know you felt uneasy about it, but much of the apprehension and discomfort stemmed from not knowing what it would be like or how it would feel afterward. You went through all of that, and now you might face a procedure you have already handled. The pain will be less because this is a lesser surgery, and you said you weren't in that much pain last time. Plus, we don't know if you have to go through it at all. Let's step back and see from a wider view."

I try to walk her through these moments with love and calmness, not oversimplifying but breathing together and communicating openly, allowing us to de-escalate any tensions and replace them with hope, love, and peace.

Closing Thought

Distance can keep me from seeing the whole picture, but when my daughter calls, feeling unsettled, I focus on steady reassurance. I do all I can to calm her, help her find clarity, and guide her toward peace. Each conversation becomes a small practice in patience and confidence, an exercise in self-control and self-soothing that I hope continues to grow with her, moment by moment.

CHAPTER 35.
Structure and Understanding Against Her Random Consequences

Opening Thought

Rules without honest self-reflection can twist into control instead of guidance. Anya has set rules for our daughter that overlook her own actions, behaviors, and traits, creating an environment where consequences can feel contradictory, inconsistent, and unpredictable.

Spanking became one of the first clear points of contention in our home after Zoey was a few years old. We chose not to spank, a choice about which I had reservations. Reflecting on my childhood, I remember being spanked, and I don't recall it feeling harsh later on. To me, it felt more like discipline than punishment, accompanied by conversations about why I was spanked, alternative actions, and future expectations.

Anya felt strongly opposed to spanking, and any conversation about it led to broad claims and accusations such as, "Oh, this is mistreatment." It seemed there was little room for differing viewpoints and no room for compromise. She mentioned that she had experienced mistreatment from her father when she was little. Whether she might be redirecting those unresolved issues toward me, perhaps perceiving me as someone who mistreats her, remains unclear, though I have not raised a hand to her or anyone else in my entire life.

Out of respect for her, I agreed, "No spanking."

I shared my position, "It's not about causing pain or punishment. I am not sure what happened to you, but here was my experience with spanking and why I found it beneficial."

But her mind was made up.

I recognized early on that I had to develop alternative discipline strategies to improve Zoey's behavior and teach her for the present and the future. I believe we could have achieved results faster with spanking, but I adapted. When I sent Zoey to her room, I set clear time frames and consistently followed up with a discussion to ensure she understood. Anya routinely sent Zoey to her room without any follow-up conversation, and when asked about it, she would often respond, "Because I told you so."

Years later, I still hear from Zoey saying, "Mommy sent me here and didn't talk to me like you do. Mommy was angry. I don't know what I did." Punishments in that home often lack structure, with no clear time frames, parameters, or resolution. She tells me stories over FaceTime about punishments that seem arbitrary, such as "The iPad's taken away" or "Go to your room," with no explanation or opportunity to learn.

Zoey told me she had to spend an entire day in her room, except for getting food and water. That was wrong. No effort to explain what she had done or how to improve. It was pure punishment without purpose. Zoey did not understand Anya's intention, and it only upset her rather than creating positive change.

I'm not advocating for spanking or harming children. Still, I see no issue with spanking when approached thoughtfully, from a healthy mindset, to encourage discipline and promote a clear understanding of cause and effect. The lack of clarity when punishing instead of disciplining is the larger issue. Dropping Zoey in her room with no time frame and no follow-up conversation is not discipline, and it leaves Zoey with no path forward.

> *"Punishments in that home often lack structure, with no clear time frames, parameters, or resolution."*

Despite my concerns, I'm glad that over time, though it seemed longer without spanking as an option, we reached a point where Zoey could recognize right from wrong. She understands that when I discipline her, it's to correct her behavior and prevent it from recurring. It's not about getting it right from the start. To me, it is about accountability and responsibility to strive to improve until the bad behavior is gone or changed.

A consistent tendency in Anya's approach has emerged. At times she drops a consequence on Zoey with no explanation or follow-up. At other times she walks it back entirely, letting Zoey push past limits she set moments before. Either way, Zoey is left without structure or clarity.

It seems she has shifted toward over-the-top permissiveness on multiple fronts, much like allowing recruits to call a timeout during boot camp. Is this the right approach for training soldiers, when I am relatively certain the opposition will not consider their feelings or offer a timeout during wartime? In a lesser circumstance, if we overly coddle, allow more than we should, and make excuses for conduct that should be addressed and changed, how much harder or longer will it take to make those changes?

Beyond that, having to remind Zoey not to spank her friends and to instruct her mother's boyfriend not to pat or jokingly spank her on the butt was troubling.

Anya seems to keep doing what best suits her, without accountability or consequences for those choices. While I eventually reached those discipline goals with Zoey through understanding and conversation, Anya still has not.

Closing Thought

Healthy discipline, rooted in clarity, transparency, and accountability, helps cultivate sound character. I know my daughter understands the reasons behind corrections and recognizes the difference between discipline and punishment. When her mother punishes without explanation, it leaves her confused about what she did wrong and without any direction. The random consequences fail to teach valuable lessons.

CHAPTER 36.
Monitored While I Talk Privately with My Own Daughter

Opening Thought

Love should free us, but for some, it becomes another form of control. Some of the most challenging conversations are the ones we cannot have because someone else has decided we are not allowed to have them.

Ongoing monitoring of the iPad remains a constant concern, highlighting Anya's tendency toward control. She has demonstrated the ability to track calls, texts, and connections on the iPad and, at times, appears to listen in on conversations, which is not allowed. I also believe that is why she will not let the iPad go with Zoey during my visits. Apparently, specific messages I have sent did not reach Zoey, which she says she does not remember receiving or cannot find.

I have also requested Anya to turn on the read receipts setting for over a year and a half to confirm delivery. Her response has been, "I am busy. I will get to that. I will set that up." A year and a half for a simple setting change. She continues to exhibit resentment, forgetfulness, and a lack of follow-through.

Revealing read receipts in the message logs would show that some messages were opened hours after our daughter's bedtime, a clear sign that Anya is monitoring our communications. Without read receipts turned on, she can review all correspondence while giving the impression that Zoey has not received specific messages. I am left trying to problem-solve the best ways for Zoey and me to communicate freely and, for that matter, privately. The same goes for the request to have her voicemail set up, which she continues to blatantly ignore, dodge, and avoid.

I have also seen a message answered as if it were from Zoey after her bedtime. When I raised this with Anya, she explained that it was not a problem and that she had written what Zoey wanted to say. She took no issue with it, which only deepened my concern about boundaries and the integrity of our communication.

Zoey has stated that she wants to share her thoughts with me, but only feels comfortable doing so when she knows her mother is not listening. Still, when it comes to some iPad text messages and FaceTime calls, Zoey feels pressured to share personal details with her mother, though she has said she would prefer to keep them private.

Zoey also feels more comfortable talking with me when she is outside the house. When she calls in the morning on the way to school, on her way home from school, or from her watch when she is out, she will often say she has to go because she is about to step inside and does not want us to be heard. At times, she will tell me that she is out of the house and wants to share more with me, which further suggests she senses monitoring in the home. She will also call in the mornings as soon as her mother leaves for work.

Both Zoey and I find ourselves navigating a situation where her mother tends to want to be the only manager of Zoey's schedule, layering on an approach that at times amplifies rather than resolves the issues. Anya appears to require oversight of many of our conversations, while overlooking the privacy and connection between Zoey and me that she has no right to intrude on.

"Revealing read receipts in the message logs would show that some messages were opened hours after our daughter's bedtime, a clear sign that Anya is monitoring our communications."

I've told Zoey she can share her thoughts and experiences with her mother; that is not my decision to make. But she should also be able to have personal moments privately with me if she chooses. Her mother's monitoring and push for her to share prevents that opportunity.

I asked months ago to set up a file-sharing platform account, offering to configure it myself during visits. The response? "She does not require the iPad when she is with you." This was another choice that should have included cooperation, collaboration, and compromise, rather than taking all the control over a decision that should have been shared. This is not only about how her one-sided decisions affect me, but also about their potential influence on Zoey.

When confronted, Anya's reply is often, "I check the iPad now and then to see what she is doing." That may not be the best approach. Why not focus on keeping an eye on her interactions with friends, the texts she sends, and the websites she explores? Why not allow her the space to have private conversations with her father, without anyone else listening or reading them? Instead, this tendency remains. Anya repeats, "I can do this," while ignoring my questions and disregarding my involvement.

My goal is to bring transparency and accountability to an aspect of communication that has become unclear and imbalanced, and that lacks the openness and privacy Zoey and I deserve during our conversations on the iPad.

Closing Thought

Control disguised as care can leave silent scars. Each attempt to monitor and restrict shows how a real connection can struggle to grow under constant observation. By working to protect my daughter's space for privacy, honesty, and trust, I aim to give her the freedom to feel seen, heard, and safe from a distance. Unhealthy monitoring and control cannot give her this.

CHAPTER 37.
Instructions Overlooked Despite Records and Clear Examples

Opening Thought

Clear intentions guided each attempt at connection and instruction, focused on substance rather than surface. You can lay out every detail and offer every example, and still watch someone attempt to rewrite the rules for their own comfort. Sometimes it is not the directions that get lost, but the willingness to follow them.

Core instruction-following was a persistent issue. Anya could be detailed when she chose to be, but only in areas that interested her. When she was a stay-at-home mom with Zoey, and I asked for help, which she had offered, the results were consistently problematic.

I would ask for computer assistance, and she would agree, claiming she could handle it. When she chose to pay attention to detail, she executed well. Still, most of the time, her attention was selective, and her help often created more work for me.

This tendency extended into many areas. When updating information or providing details, she would include only what she deemed worth sharing, disregarding the rest. When I pointed out missing elements or asked her to address specific issues, the same defensive response emerged: "You did not tell me that."

I'd respond, "I shared that with you, and it is right here in the email."

"No, no, no, that is not there," would commonly follow as a reply.

Then it was tossed out, disregarded, and dismissed.

The resistance and redirection continued without pause. When Anya finally addressed what was requested or acknowledged a specific topic from an email, she shifted responsibility and responded with self-defeating remarks such as, "I can't do this right at all. I can't handle doing this for you." At other times, she referred to issues with her memory, bringing up the car accident, but later dismissed the existence of any such problems.

It was perplexing to watch someone cycle from "It is not there" or "You did not send that" to "I am not paying attention." That was the problem. She was not paying attention.

Defensiveness and deflection turned clear correction into conflict and self-criticism, rather than allowing instructions and lessons to be recognized and applied. At times, it seemed that she did not listen to the words themselves, but to how they landed on her triggers.

When I sent examples and screenshots with clear instructions, I would add, "If you have any questions, please ask me. Please do not hesitate to ask. This is about making this time you are helping me as effective as possible for the work and saving us both time."

It didn't seem to matter how I phrased my requests or laid out every detail as thoroughly as possible; she couldn't follow instructions well. The output was consistently messy, leading me to ask, "Could you have asked for clarification right then?"

> *"Defensiveness and deflection turned clear correction into conflict and self-criticism, rather than allowing instructions and lessons to be recognized and applied."*

The denial and instruction issues persisted. She would add details she wanted while avoiding specifics she had forgotten or did not want to address. When specific information was requested, if it wasn't what she wanted to discuss, she did not provide it.

When working together and reviewing her work, she asked, "Why do I have to be treated like a baby?" I shared, "I am not treating you like a baby. We have had some issues with specific tasks in the past. My intention is not to treat you like a baby or talk down to you. I intend to lay out the instructions in a detailed way that might be easier for you to understand and save us both time."

When she offered to help with website updates, the results were consistently incorrect. I would gently explain, "This keeps coming up. I am not attacking you. My goal is to ensure we are not wasting time or adding unnecessary work by having to go back over what was already done."

She would dismiss those ideas and quickly claim I was being mean to her. Some people have can have trouble differentiating what is mean and what is the truth. I was trying to offer clarity and direction, not cause hurt. I was deliberate and careful, but it seemed she took those moments as attacks.

Tasks were completed to her standard, regardless of whether that standard was accurate. When gently corrected, she got angry and defensive, blaming others. Eventually the time spent explaining, correcting, and circling back cost more than doing it myself. That became the clearest sign: the instructions were not the problem. The willingness was.

Closing Thought

Lessons drawn from repeated misunderstandings and ignored requests highlighted the limits of what she was prepared to take in, and what she chose to throw away. Lasting improvement becomes possible only when there is a willingness and humility to recognize oversight and engage with instruction.

CHAPTER 38.
Married While Isolated in a Relationship Without Balance

Opening Thought

Persistent focus guided each attempt to connect, choosing acceptance over expectation. I tried to love her for who she was, not for who she had shown me or who I hoped she would be. Still, every attempt I made was met with a wall, a fortress built from past pains and present excuses.

Throughout our relationship, I poured effort into a space that echoed back silence, walls, and excuses dressed as reasons. This is one of those parts I hope Zoey can someday read and understand. No one is flawless, and I am far from it. As I share the issues about Anya, I am not claiming to be without fault. I had plenty of my own problems.

I grew up in an unhealthy communication environment and worked hard to overcome those issues, determined not to repeat those cycles with a partner or child. My parents separated and reconciled multiple times, creating constant uncertainty at home. My brother struggled with countless issues from youth into adulthood. I observed this regularly throughout my childhood.

Despite my background, I sincerely wanted to invest fully in Anya and the relationship. Still, before she became pregnant, I noticed emerging challenges and began withdrawing. A part of me felt compelled to embrace a deep commitment, though I wasn't entirely sure why. Early warning signs that I had not fully recognized had left me on the fence, while another part of me believed I should do all I possibly could to make it work.

I have concluded that it was God's will and that this was the path I was to take for Zoey to come into my life. I also believe I was put on this journey to face experiences that would require me to grow in ways I wouldn't have otherwise. These lessons helped me become a better father, a better person, and a better man. It became clear that the push I felt to continue trying may have been less about the relationship and more about the daughter that would come from it.

I sensed her pain, her struggles with her mother and sister, and her limited memories of her father. I yearned for her circumstances to improve. I longed to love her fully. I hoped she would find friends, feel strong and confident, and grow beyond her limitations. She deserved the best, and I was drawn to that vision and that intention. But the conflicts kept coming. Relentless trying on my side to put in the effort, to make it work, to stay patient, to listen, and to speak couldn't move the wall she kept between us; her words claimed she wanted to change, but her lack of follow-through only strengthened that wall.

One of the strangest aspects of it was how my most loving gestures would be twisted and misinterpreted. I'd share my deepest care and affection, only to have her response push me further away. In moments when I pleaded with her, "I'm coming from love, not anger. I'm trying to create calm, not trepidation," I still experienced a deflective, shut-down response, as she appeared not to hear or believe a word.

When she became pregnant, the situation did not improve. Her moods and vulnerabilities seemed to multiply. She appeared less stable emotionally. That's when I watched negative and passive cycles take shape. I told myself it was the pregnancy, but deep down, I recognized these behaviors had shown up long before conception. The pregnancy seemed to grant her an excuse to act in ways that were less healthy, more challenging, and less engaged.

I tried to offer her help, affection, food, massages, or any item or action I thought might support her, doing my best to be there for her.

After Zoey was born, I questioned whether these troubling traits would manifest in Zoey. I continued trying to love her while simultaneously attempting to bring her to a calmer place. Her combativeness with her mother, her dramatic mood swings (one moment lively and up, the next seeming depressed and down) were exhausting to witness, especially because she did not seem able to see this happening or recognize what was occurring.

> *"Relentless trying on my side to put in the effort, to make it work, to stay patient, to listen, and to speak couldn't move the wall she kept between us; her words claimed she wanted to change, but her lack of follow-through only strengthened that wall."*

When I suggested she might be contending with depression or significant mood challenges, she brushed aside my concerns. I saw our relationship unraveling before the pregnancy and watched it deteriorate further as time went on. Still, I kept hoping we could work together to cultivate lasting happiness. I listened, tried to understand, and searched for common ground, but all my efforts failed.

Once Zoey arrived, I foolishly believed the baby might repair the divide between us. I knew you can't base a relationship on a child, but part of me hoped this would be the turning point, that it would improve our communication, deepen our love, and secure our future.

It was not reasonable, realistic, or intelligent of me.

I grew closer to Zoey while continuing to do all I could to support Anya's feelings and viewpoints, still hoping that at some point, she might see mine. But despite all my efforts to love her, to try to understand her, and to find new ways to communicate, I kept coming up against those same walls. It was a lonely effort that led me to realize you cannot build a future with someone who refuses to leave their past behind.

Anya seemed lost in her own thoughts, plans, and opinions, which she may have intentionally or unintentionally turned into objective facts to ease her discomfort. This outlook created a perspective that made any real connections feel beyond reach. In many instances, it didn't seem easy to have any meaningful conversation unless it closely reflected her views, desires, or beliefs.

When someone has walls up to deflect every gesture, how can you be seen, heard, or understood? Every gesture was either ignored, taken out of context, or blocked. After some time, it left me feeling lost and losing hope for a healthy, productive relationship with Anya. I gave up trying to break through to her, trying to reach her heart, trying to get her to consider another angle.

I couldn't commit my heart anymore. I couldn't commit my love. I couldn't keep trying. I gave all that I could for as long as I could, being as patient as I could, but it could not be repaired, and it was over.

I was married, but alone with someone who wouldn't try with me.

A great deal of my frustration and pain came from hearing someone repeatedly say how important it was to try, how much she claimed to want to communicate, how much she supposedly wanted to be better for herself and for me, and how much it meant to her.

These inaccuracies, repeated with no integrity or accountability, felt like a form of disregard. I allowed myself to be hurt by her neglect, her lack of belief, her refusal to try, her inability to hear me, and her failure to become who she claimed she wanted to be. It seemed that her version of reality focused solely on what she said, but none of her actions matched those words.

So, after giving as much as I could, trying as hard as I could, and regardless of the words, the claims, or the moments of trying for a second, I gave up on her and focused on Zoey. I continue to focus on Zoey.

Closing Thought

Certain truths are heartbreaking. Mine was accepting that I was married but utterly alone. My love couldn't heal her, and her walls kept me at a distance. Letting go of my attempts to reach Anya, I turned my focus to making sure my daughter remained within reach and felt comforted, supported, understood, and loved.

CHAPTER 39.
Warmer at Home and Ice Cold with Clients and Strangers

Opening Thought

Acting as both interpreter and apologist became routine as I tried to reassure others and smooth over uncomfortable interactions. I covered for the way she came across, trying to convince them that her coldness was not personal. Defending a partner who refused to see how her actions pushed so many people away, including me, became a draining role I did not want.

Socially, there was rarely a sense of comfort when Anya and I were out together, away from our home. She seldom wanted to go out. Although there was some semblance of connection behind closed doors, her mood, presence, and engagement in public felt off. A tension lingered, distorting what I felt should have been natural, and what she said she had no issue with. I hoped it would improve with time spent around others. Going places with Anya proved consistently tiring, requiring what seemed to be unnecessary effort.

I sometimes considered introducing her to some of my clients, particularly the local ones, but I hesitated. When we were first together, I would invite her to join me at the end of meetings, when I might be having a drink with clients, thinking we could spend time together afterward. For most clients in the area, I would hold informal, off-site meetings where Anya would sometimes join as we wrapped up business, and the majority of them would later ask the same question about her, "Does she like me?"

> *"Making excuses for her behavior, it often felt like living with someone whose choices in public kept putting me in the position of explaining and covering for them."*

I considered suggesting that she observe her expressions on her phone to see how others might interpret them. This could bring gentle awareness to the signals she may have been sending, as an invitation to notice how particular looks might come across. She chose not to. When I asked if she felt unwell, tired, or on edge, she replied that all was fine and that she was not giving any particular tone.

I spent considerable time writing my third book in various cafés, bars, and on the beach, getting to know bartenders and baristas along the way. Many of them would repeatedly comment, "She doesn't seem like the type of woman we would have expected to see you with. She doesn't seem like someone who fits you." Making excuses for her behavior, it often felt like living with someone whose choices in public kept putting me in the position of explaining and covering for them.

I questioned whether Anya was becoming increasingly withdrawn and whether she could recognize this or whether she would want to change it over time. She made it seem like she wasn't this way, claiming to be social, and still, this mixed, erratic, and ever-changing presence was how she consistently showed up.

I heard this from people who interacted with Anya. Comments included, "She seemed standoffish," "She appeared angry," and "She comes across as annoyed." The encounters felt awkward.

When I asked her, "Do you want to be out? Do you not want to meet these people?"

Her reply stayed the same: "No, I do. I do. I should be out more, and I should meet more people."

It was difficult to watch her react and carry herself in many social situations. She was much more comfortable in private. I kept asking whether we should limit our outings or avoid going out altogether. Most of the time, she gave the same denial and said, "No, I'm fine. You're reading too much into this."

But was I? I would repeatedly see these examples, and when I shared them with her, they would be immediately dismissed. I started to prefer more public situations without her. I actively limited our time out and her contact with those I worked with, given her poor communication skills with most people.

There were a few moments when Anya appeared to enjoy the company of others, particularly during gatherings with those who liked to drink. Once the liquor started to flow, Anya's demeanor shifted positively. It appeared that the only version of her that others seemed to warm to required alcohol to surface, and I was still the one left covering for her.

Closing Thought

Caretaker more than husband in public settings, my role became one of smoothing over unease and shielding others from her coldness. The ring on a finger served as a prop in a staged presentation, preserving appearances for her mother and those around us. What remained felt less like a shared relationship and more like a sustained performance.

CHAPTER 40.
Boundaries Built on Consistency, Not Rewards or Shortcuts

Opening Thought

Discipline is more like a metronome than a volume knob, because changing the volume rarely changes behavior for long. A steady tempo of calm clarity, real conversation, and clear expectations can build a more honest and trustworthy process for a child navigating distorted and noisy messages.

Differing views on discipline were a constant problem between us. Anya's approach to consequences with Zoey was so weak and inconsistent that it did not earn Zoey's respect or lead her to listen, whereas Zoey responded to me more consistently and much faster. It brought to mind the old cartoon where someone draws a line in the sand and says, "Cross this line and you'll be in trouble," then keeps stepping back, drawing new lines, and repeating the warning. Watching that moving line in real life, without a solid foundation, created inconsistency that undermined clear standards for Zoey.

Zoey could feel how uneven her mother's approach was. I watched how Zoey acted with both of us; when she knew she was out of line, she adjusted faster with me than with Anya. As our time living together wound down, Anya often sent Zoey to her room in frustration without explaining why or for how long. When I sent her to her room, I told her how long she would be there and that we would talk about what happened afterward.

My approach focused on helping Zoey understand what she did wrong and why it was not okay, so her behavior would change. I showed her the behaviors I expected from her and the limits that protected her and others. I explained how I would hold her accountable when she crossed those lines. She understood this approach, and she responded well to it.

Zoey once told me that my rules felt too strict. I asked which rules she meant, and we walked through them together. I reiterated the accountability I expected in how she treated her mother and me, in good moments and hard ones. I knew some of her friends' parents did not hold the same expectations, which made it harder, but I encouraged her to stay respectful wherever she was. I showed her how that standard of accountability could help her, and I still believe it fits who she is.

As she has grown older, my expectations for her behavior and accountability have increased, but we keep those expectations grounded in conversation. Recently, we have been working on her habit of waking during the night, struggling to settle, and having trouble calming herself again. I believe this tendency is tied to her mother not standing her ground, not holding Zoey accountable, and allowing expectations to slide. Zoey often tells me she feels calmer after we talk and that she sleeps better afterward. Hearing Zoey call me her comforter is a title I cherish, and my Hebrew name translates to that same meaning.

In dealing with her nighttime awakenings, I've been working with her over FaceTime, teaching her simple strategies she can use to calm herself and settle back down. I encourage her to move around her room, stretch, or read without leaving her space. When she told me she was concerned about being tired the next day, I reassured her that it's okay to feel tired sometimes and that getting up at night and going to have her mother tuck her in is not helping her resolve this issue for the long run.

My goal is to equip Zoey with healthy, positive problem-solving techniques she can use when I am not there.

I noticed that Anya's behavior and responses to Zoey, which often felt passive in some moments and then at others, overly commanding, may have been causing more negative results than she intends or realizes. Zoey has shared that her mother tends to take away the iPad as a form of discipline, but this approach has not led to any meaningful change. Anya also tried to implement a weak reward system for good behavior, which I find ineffective, as it has not yielded the results she appears to hope for.

I gently suggested to Zoey that while rewards can be motivating, they should not replace accountability for expected behavior. Still, without consistent, accountable, healthy disciplinary support from her mother, it has not helped so far. Anya tended to focus on immediate rewards or punishments without fully considering lasting consequences. I wish she were open to discussing this with me and collaborating to find a better way to support Zoey.

One evening, Zoey asked me why she had been doing this for four months. I held back from sharing that it might be due to her mother having overly high expectations and consistently poor follow-through. While Anya seemed to handle situations in the moment, I questioned how sustainable those efforts were and whether they supported positive, long-term change. I've tried to guide Zoey from a distance, but the permissive and lenient approaches of her mother may allow Zoey to hold back and hinder her ability to do her best and work through the challenges she faces.

Another morning, Zoey called and said, "Mommy says it should count as a full night because I slept better and it counted as staying in my room for the night," but then she told me she had not stayed in bed or in her room and went to her mother to get tucked in again. I felt it was important to clarify that it does not count. She replied, "Mommy said it was okay." I gently explained, "That might be okay with her, but it is not okay with me. Did you do what you said you would do? Did you stay in bed and your room the whole night?"

"Let's focus on you following through on what you are committed to doing. I do recognize the small steps you are taking, and I'm glad you got more sleep. Still, let's also avoid overly celebrating, making excuses, or claiming progress that didn't happen. When you stay in bed and in your room all night, you can celebrate it and then work toward doing it two nights in a row." I felt Zoey understood that better when I explained it that way. I tried to keep the focus on the positive and talked with her about creating a plan for the next night that would emphasize the proper steps instead of relying on shortcuts that Anya appears to use routinely.

Her mother introduced sleeping gummies, which I found concerning. I would prefer Zoey build the discipline to settle herself rather than rely on a supplement.

I feel for Zoey because, as she has shared with me in tears on certain mornings, on top of some of the less-than-healthy approaches used to try to keep her in bed, guilt and embarrassment tactics are also being applied at times by Anya and her boyfriend when she does not stay in bed the whole night.

> ### *"Hearing Zoey call me her comforter is a title I cherish, and my Hebrew name translates to that same meaning."*

I emphasized to Zoey that she is growing up and should be treated as such. I proposed that we focus on daily accountability rather than long-term rewards. We discussed the pitfalls of negativity and how overwhelming it can be, especially given Anya's influence. Zoey deserves to understand that her commitment to following through and choosing the right path should hinge on her own sense of responsibility, not small rewards. She says she likes it when we make plans, act, and set goals, unlike her mother, who repeatedly seems to choose either praise or punishment and then is careless about the outcomes, unable to see the long-term consequences.

At times, Zoey has said she feels caught in a tug-of-war between the messages she gets from her mom and me. Recently, while we were discussing sugar, Zoey recognized that it might be affecting her sleep. When I pointed out the connection in an email, Anya reacted defensively, accusing me of trying to make her look bad.

I encourage Zoey to continue observing her feelings and behaviors to develop effective strategies and solve problems. She demonstrates stronger self-awareness and problem-solving skills as a young girl than her mother does as an adult. I believe that as she experiences small successes from staying committed in the right way, she will grow stronger and be able to handle more challenges. I appreciate how Zoey reaches out to me to make plans, adapt, and work through what is not working as hoped or expected.

Closing Thought

Strong follow-through in healthy, understood discipline can build respect that is honorable and clear on both sides. When consequences are explained with purpose and forgiveness in the same conversation, a child can grow a sense of self-worth that understands what is wrong and why, what is right and why, and how to adjust decisions to make better choices in the present and the future.

CHAPTER 41.
Too Much Daddy on the Wall and Too Much Mommy in Her Head

Opening Thought

Detecting when my daughter's voice carries someone else's opinion has become second nature as her father. I listen to her cadence, word choice, and tone, distinguishing her own thoughts from what has been fed to her. A seemingly small comment about pictures in her room exposed a broader, more troubling presence of negative parental influence and control.

Planted opinions can signal a parent's choice to distort their child's own voice, pulling that child into an argument that should stay between the adults. I understand my former wife is angry with me, and it's her choice if she wants to engage in those kinds of games, but when she extends these questionable behaviors to involve Zoey, it disturbs me on an entirely different level.

I find it perplexing that, in her anger, she tries to influence or alter aspects affecting Zoey's feelings and experiences. It feels like a significant overstep. Still, resilience demonstrates my daughter's growing strength to separate outside noise from her own instincts and trust herself more quickly each time. This reassures me of

Zoey's awareness and comprehension of what happens around her.

Now and then, I mail printed photos of Zoey and me to her as she has requested. At one point, I had picture frames made through a service that prints photos and creates simple, mountable pieces that were easy to hang on walls. I didn't know what she'd do with them or if she'd want to display them. I told her with zero pressure, "If you want to put them up, go ahead. If you'd rather keep them stored somewhere, that's up to you."

When she received them, she was elated.

She put them up throughout her room. She was ecstatic to have these images in her space. She already had numerous photos and mementos from me and was actively searching for more items from her old room, belongings Anya had either not opened or knowingly left in boxes.

One evening, Zoey said to me, "I think I have too much of you on the walls." That comment hurt. I wasn't sure if it was her own feeling or if Anya had influenced it.

I responded with support and clarity. "If you want to take some down, you're welcome to. If you want to store a few in the closet, go for it. That is your space. Hang the pictures, posters, and frames you like, and remove those you no longer want up. The decision is yours. That choice won't diminish my feelings for you at all."

I continued, "Maybe it's a good reminder and a nice connector for us. But if that's not true for you, that's fine."

Zoey's response was immediate. "No. I like what I have up." I wasn't trying to sway her in any direction. I was giving her options and explaining my reasoning, sharing possibilities in case she might like having these reminders around, and suggesting practical solutions if she wanted to change her walls by adding more or taking some down.

"Resilience demonstrates my daughter's growing strength to separate outside noise from her own instincts and trust herself more quickly each time."

The way she responded to her initial comment felt like a suggestion from Anya, who wanted more of herself on Zoey's walls. Then I heard the real source. "Mommy says there's too much Daddy on the wall."

This is the unfortunate reality. Perhaps Anya doesn't want to walk into Zoey's room and see images of me or how happy Zoey looks in those images with me. Still, it would be healthy and loving to consider what Zoey wants and respect her preferences in the matter.

Having the mental strength and ability to recognize the difference between her own desires and what might be best for Zoey would be a more thoughtful approach. This situation goes beyond mutual respect; it's about what is best for Zoey. Unfortunately, that consideration often feels overlooked, and I am left out of the equation altogether.

This "too much daddy on the walls" incident reminds me of many other subtle, unhealthy influences Anya has used to push or pull me away from Zoey. I've heard Zoey express uncertainty with comments like "I don't know about this" or "I'm not sure about that," and I hear them in moments when her posture, tone, and voice change. I've learned to see when she seems to be sharing thoughts that did not come from her. I've noticed a clear difference between when these doubts stem from her own feelings versus those shaped by her mother's words and perspective.

In many situations, I've told Zoey, "If that's how you're feeling, that's great. Do what you want to do. But if someone else is feeling that for you, that's not so great. If someone is trying to push a feeling or idea on you, pause and see if it's right for you. Don't let anyone control your direction or what you want." By giving her that space and freedom, and by not imposing guilt or pressure, she relaxes into her own thoughts and can share her feelings without her mother's influence or the pressure she regularly faces.

Anya has made little effort to share photos, videos, or experiences, despite promising to do so. This may be an attempt to create more barriers that keep me, and the thought of me, away from Zoey. Despite numerous requests, she continues to ignore my emails asking for images or videos that Zoey has asked to have sent to me. Zoey has said she reminds her mother that she wants them sent to me, or at least to her iPad, so she can text them to me. I love her persistence and the way she pushes back against her mother to pull us closer.

Closing Thought

Hope lives in my daughter's growing clarity. She may lean toward her mother's influence at first, but she seems to see through it more quickly each time and steps back that much faster. My role is not opposing her mother, but strengthening our daughter's trust in her own voice, her own heart, and her own path forward.

CHAPTER 42.
Interrogation Disguised as Concern, Not Curiosity

Opening Thought

Private conversations between parent and child shouldn't require debriefing sessions with the other parent. When my daughter tells me she is asked to share what was discussed, and feels that if she does not share, her mother will be angry, it exposes interrogation disguised as interest. Her right to privacy with me is being systematically undermined by pressure and monitoring behaviors.

Raising a child to trust her own voice becomes harder when she returns home to answer for every word she shared with me. After calls and visits, she faces the same question: "What did you talk about?" She shouldn't feel obligated to report back, but she does. Her mother asks for specifics, details, and accounts of our time. This behavior creates pressure that makes Zoey feel she must comply or risk her mother's anger and disappointment. The conduct undermines trust and privacy, eroding Zoey's confidence in deciding what to discuss with her father.

I've consistently been the parent Zoey turns to for communication more than her mother. When there is a real problem, she tends to bring it up with me first. If there were any critical physical, mental, or safety concerns, I would share that information immediately with her mother and the appropriate professionals. I'm not trying to control what she shares or how she shares it, but both she and I have every right to private conversations. This right is stated in our parenting plan, but has been continually denied because Anya has been able to get away with not following it, pushing Zoey and not being held accountable for those actions.

When I've tried to explain to Zoey that it is acceptable to have conversations that remain between us, I sometimes sense a subtle, darker influence at play. Zoey tells me, "Mommy will get angry. Mommy will get sad. I do not want Mommy to be angry. I do not want Mommy to be sad. When she asks me, I have to tell her."

I've tried to explain to her, "No, you do not have to. I am your father. I know I am not with you every day right now, but I am as much your father as she is your mother. You have every right to share information, feelings, and thoughts with me and feel confident that if you want them to stay between us, they can stay between us and us only."

Her response breaks my heart as she tells me, "I don't think I can do that. It's going to make her angry. If I don't tell her, I'm going to get in trouble." The next moment, she will ask if she can share feelings, an event, or some experience, and she seems to want additional assurances that it is only for us.

Several layers of negative influence appear to be at play here. Anya appears to be navigating the legal system in a way that does not line up with our parenting plan. Pressing Zoey to share what we discuss burdens her with a guilt she shouldn't carry and consequences she shouldn't navigate.

My wish is for Zoey to understand these tendencies in a way that supports her growth, not her bitterness. With that awareness, she can make stronger, more informed decisions, recognize these traits when they surface, and learn to communicate with her mother more effectively than I was ever able to. All this, being tied to her right to her privacy.

"Pressing Zoey to share what we discuss burdens her with a guilt she shouldn't carry and consequences she shouldn't navigate."

There should be accountability for the time I should have with Zoey, time when she is not required to check in or report back, time when no monitoring device is being used, and our conversations are not tracked.

If Anya wants to monitor other aspects of Zoey's digital life or check what she is doing on her iPad, that is her parental prerogative, but also a topic for us to discuss for clarity. I see no benefit to Zoey and no defensible stance in her mother's decision to monitor my private conversations with Zoey.

I feel that the monitoring and the pressure on Zoey to share our discussions, along with the guilt I believe she experiences about her mother's potential anger or sadness, might be seen by some as mistreatment.

When a child feels compelled to act as a messenger, it can undermine the trust that should develop between a parent and a child. The burden these expectations place on Zoey builds tension and weakens her sense of personal safety and security. Ideally, Zoey should be able to find comfort in her own voice, knowing that her words are respected and not subject to judgment or unnecessary scrutiny.

While every interruption cannot be controlled at present, providing stability and reassurance can help reinforce Zoey's sense of well-being. She deserves the freedom to share her thoughts or keep them private, with the confidence that her love and privacy remain unconditional and respected.

Closing Thought

Present circumstances expose a system that fails to enforce agreements meant to protect us. Accountability will come. This is not about revenge; it is about protecting a child who is being taught that love is conditional and privacy can be revoked. Zoey deserves safety, consistency, and love she can count on.

CHAPTER 43.
Combative Postures Against My Constant Prayer for Peace

Opening Thought

Coexisting with this woman felt like walking on eggshells around a sleeping giant. I learned to read her posture from across the room, instantly knowing whether I would be met with calm or tension. My home became a place where I had to strategize for calm.

Specific behavioral, physical, and vocal signs began showing themselves as inconsistent and unusual. I watched for these shifts, particularly how they changed depending on who was present. She would phase out, looking detached or unresponsive to her surroundings at times.

While many people occasionally zone out, I noticed that her blank stares and disconnected episodes happened more often. I watched her get lost watching TV or suddenly stop mid-task in the kitchen, staring into space. I questioned whether she was lost in thought, whether it was tied to a cognitive issue, or whether she was temporarily shutting down.

Her volume control was another issue. She often matched her speaking volume to those around her, mirroring the crowd. When she left that environment, she would remain at that loud volume. I suspect this came from her mother, who has a loud, high-volume speaking style, perhaps from years of teaching, or maybe that's how she believes she's supposed to communicate. I observed and experienced these shifts in how Anya would emulate this behavior, including changes in volume and speaking style.

When I gently pointed it out, asking, "It feels like you're a touch louder right now than you were a few minutes ago. Are you okay?" she would immediately deny it and give it no further thought.

When bringing up an issue or addressing friction or a problem, looking for clarity and resolution, what was raised in a soft, non-attacking approach with no ulterior motives was taken as an insult. Any consideration of the issue was shut down instantly. I offered to record our conversation so she could hear herself.

The argumentative body language was equally telling. I could walk out of my room after praying in the morning, often asking for a peaceful morning, hoping for calm engagement, and immediately read her posture. I could tell right then from how she stood whether we would have a pleasant interaction or not. It wore me down some. Exhaustion came not from conflict itself but from the endless calculation of how to avoid it, reading her stance to gauge whether silence or retreat was safer. When I saw that combative, angry, or seemingly depressed stance, I knew to stay quiet if I desired peace and calm. Bringing up any issue while she was in one of those states was not worth it.

The similarities reminded me of a child living with someone struggling with alcohol problems, planning day after day how to avoid upsetting an unpredictable parent, and hoping to keep the peace. I would assess her mood and body language, knowing that if she was like that, no words from me could redirect the conversation away from negativity. The exhaustion became so intense that I sometimes retreated to my room immediately, feeling as if I had to hide in my own home to find the calm I sought.

Another issue I observed was an unawareness of timing and a tendency to push forward when she was ready to speak or when she had an issue or topic she wanted addressed, regardless of my capacity in that moment. I repeatedly asked her not to bring up significant problems or issues that would require extended discussions at the end of longer workdays.

"Could we talk in the morning? Can we find time tomorrow?" I worked hard to frame it positively, sharing, "I'll address what's on your mind, but could you please give me tonight and let me be at my best for you and for the topic you want to work through."

I asked that on days when I had a longer schedule or had been talking for the bulk of the day, if it was possible and not an emergency, if we could discuss it the next morning.

> *"Exhaustion came not from conflict itself but from the endless calculation of how to avoid it, reading her stance to gauge whether silence or retreat was safer."*

On those busier days when I had to resolve communication issues for specific clients, I did not want that to carry over after I stopped working for the day. I also explained how those types of conversations on longer days sometimes kept me from winding down, keeping me in a work mode I had to step away from. I tried to convey that I would be more focused, energized, and precise in discussing her concerns if we could wait till morning.

This appeared to be too difficult for her. Whether due to memory issues, another issue, or self-centeredness, she would bring up topics she was thinking about or wanted to discuss at a time that worked for her. One evening, I explained, "I got up early this morning, I've been on video calls for eight hours, and put in another five hours of work today. I'm fried at the moment, my back hurts, and I have a headache. Can we please discuss this in the morning? I will be in a better place, more attentive, and hopefully that much more helpful to figure out what is required."

Still, if it didn't fit her timeline or meet her current requirements, my requests were ignored. Then she would be upset that I was upset about her disregarding what I had asked for multiple times.

I saw this as the creation of another counterproductive communication habit, one that favored Anya's desires over collaborative problem-solving and compromise. When I offered the same consideration I was requesting, asking, "Are there times you don't want to discuss certain topics? Can we find better ways and times to approach our conversations for both of us?" My questions were ignored, as was my request.

The combination was concerning: the volume issues, drinking, combative postures, intense defensive responses, and what felt like deliberate instigation. Sometimes I think she knew exactly what she was doing, choosing to be argumentative for her own satisfaction.

I noticed additional signs of unhealthy self-absorption and negativity during calmer moments as well. It seemed that Anya struggled to leave situations as they were, perhaps due to cognitive challenges, her mental state, or a sense of malice that appeared often, making it more difficult for peaceful moments to remain calm and last.

Closing Thought

Unwelcome calm became the pattern. In moments of quiet, my former wife often seemed compelled to instigate, to poke and prod until the tranquility was compromised. I cannot say whether this stemmed from malice or inner turmoil, but the outcome was the same. My home lacked lasting peace, and when a hint of it emerged, my former wife seemed determined to dismantle it.

CHAPTER 44.
Fortifying False Beliefs on Foundations Made of Fiction

Opening Thought

Evidence holds no weight for those who have already decided what is true. When a person constructs their reality on inaccuracies and defends those distortions with fierce aggression, proof cannot penetrate. I have observed Anya create and uphold her own version of truth, aggressively dismissing facts that conflict with her narrative. The energy devoted to upholding fiction as fact leaves little room for healthy growth or honest connection.

Strangers sometimes see what we may refuse to recognize or are unable to see in the early moments. Years ago, a person I didn't know messaged me on Facebook asking if I was married to this woman, using her maiden name. When I confirmed, they launched into warnings, "She's not who you think she is. She is not who she seems and has a way of hiding details you might not be aware of."

I blocked that person immediately, dismissing their warnings as baseless attacks. Today, those exact phrases describe who she is. For Zoey's sake, I defended Anya. I wasn't entirely sure the warning was baseless, but the words and the way this stranger described her unsettled me. Part of that discomfort might have stemmed from the resonance of those statements, the possibility that this stranger was right, and I didn't know who Anya was.

Still, I became her defender, spending time trying to validate her behavior to clients, friends, and neighbors, "No, she's good. She's tired. She's shy sometimes." Validating her falsehoods made me part of the problem, defending behavior I should have questioned while the cycle continued unchecked.

I witnessed truth being omitted repeatedly, but what I found harder to reconcile was how convinced she seemed of her own inaccuracies. You could present proof, show contradictions and evidence, but she remained blind to them, or blinded herself. This disconnect from reality was difficult to watch, given the depth of apparent ignorance behind it.

In more than one situation, she would hold her position on an untrue statement after being confronted with contrary evidence, still pushing a false account.

> ## *"Validating her falsehoods made me part of the problem, defending behavior I should have questioned while the cycle continued unchecked."*

Perhaps that's who Anya is, or it may reflect the mentality of many in this generation: "Here's what I'm going to be, here's what I'm presenting, and I'll die on this hill regardless of whether it's true."

Still, reality does not negotiate, though she tried often to bend it in her favor.

Thinking of that message, I question if she uses my last name as she claims to have the same as Zoey's, or if it is one more tactical move to hide the past and present a face of herself that does not hold up. I wish Anya didn't carry my name. I recognize that thought may seem selfish. It feels like a persistent reminder that she might still be living behind a facade and that my last name has become part of her ongoing performance. A performance that closed every honest door I tried to open.

Closing Thought

Futility came with every attempt to reach my former wife once she had committed to a falsehood. The tragedy rests not only in the false beliefs she holds but in the unwavering grip with which she fortifies them. Sometimes, the only path forward is to step away, hoping that those left behind will find the humility and courage to set aside distortion and finally choose honesty.

CHAPTER 45.
Clarifying Rights Through Specific Language That Protects

Opening Thought

Vague agreements fail when one person interprets every loose term in their favor. The parenting plan I signed was a generic template with no teeth. It said both parents should be involved in decisions, but did not define what that meant or hold either party accountable when requirements were ignored.

Requests for modification can replace broad statements with enforceable standards. I am working to file documents with the goal of bringing clarity where ambiguity has thrived, defining responsibilities where vagueness has allowed avoidance, and attaching consequences to language that has let her act as she chooses without recourse. I would like shared decision-making to be defined by expanded, clear protocols with more detailed communication requirements. My goal for each requested adjustment is to protect both my daughter's right to a consistent connection and my right to be her father without interference or chosen ignorance of requirements.

I've noticed various behaviors, such as mental games, subtly confrontational conduct, regularly fluctuating emotional states, and other interactions I found troubling, including self-absorption and high levels of negativity. I call it a humble, long-game approach to documentation, emphasizing endurance and persistence. I've worked patiently to document these occurrences, saving the emails and texts, and writing down the issues in a way that can help down the line.

I strive to one day share my thoughts and present these observations in a calm, collected, and thoughtful manner, while considering how they might be perceived or challenged. Every step, every response, and every interaction is no longer about a moment for me. They are for the benefit and protection of Zoey.

The parenting plan I signed was a document I should not have agreed to. I felt blindsided during mediation without legal counsel. I reviewed it under pressure and thought that because it was court-sanctioned, it would be followed.

A signature made under duress and misleading beliefs can become a cage. I signed, believing it offered protection, only to find it used as an instrument of control. I had not fully considered how much she would twist this agreement to work in her favor. Anya understood I lacked legal counsel, which allowed her to disregard the majority of the elements without accountability.

> *"Enforcing shared decision-making, transparent communication, and consistent oversight protects my daughter's right to both parents following the same clear standards."*

As the divorce neared completion, I requested reviews of the parenting plan, focusing on what was not being honored and what changes could improve accountability. Each time, the same answer came back. Mediation would be required, payment expected. I composed a detailed letter outlining concerns, challenges, improvements, and areas for compromise. Her response did not shift.

Twelve proposed modifications focused on what Zoey deserves.

I attempted to request these changes through numerous emails, but was ignored or dismissed.

1. **Fair Time-Sharing Schedule**
   Creating a fair visitation schedule for when I'm in town so Zoey can spend quality time with me without constant changes or disputes.

2. **Regular Times to Talk with Zoey**
   Establishing regular times for me to chat with Zoey to strengthen our bond, while also allowing her to choose times that suit her availability.

3. **Shared Decision-Making Authority**
   Thoroughly outlining that both parents will be involved in important decisions about Zoey's education, health, and welfare.

4. **Information Sharing**
   Ensuring that both parents receive timely updates about significant events, health matters, school issues, and any other information the non-custodial parent should be aware of.

5. **Talking Before Booking Holidays**
   Requiring both parents to discuss and agree on holiday plans before making any bookings or scheduling without the other parent's knowledge.

6. **Approval of Shared Expenses**
   Both parents should approve any shared expenses in advance, especially for activities or potential required items related to Zoey.

7. **Co-Parenting Communication App Requirement**
   Using a court-approved co-parenting communication

app to track communications, schedules, and shared expenses for accountability and transparency.

8. **Clarify Communication Protocols**
   Defining how parents should communicate (via text, email, phone, or co-parenting app) to avoid misunderstandings and accommodate any memory or processing issues that might arise, ensuring we are in agreement regarding Zoey's communication with her father.

9. **Define Electronic Use of Zoey's iPad**
   Specifying what apps, contacts, and features Zoey can access on her iPad to maintain transparency and safety, and allow me to access them as well.

10. **Define iPad Access Times**
    Setting specific times for Zoey to use her iPad, ensuring consistency and parental oversight, with modifications for weekends, summer, vacations, and emergencies.

11. **Read Receipts On and Voicemail Set Up**
    Turning on read receipts for Zoey's iPad would confirm message delivery and maintain transparency about when messages are received. This would also include setting up her voicemail, another request that has been ignored since she got her iPad and iWatch.

12. **Accountability Steps**
    If these guidelines are not followed, clear accountability steps or actions should be in place to ensure the plan is respected, unlike what has occurred in the past, and structured in a way that prevents these elements (and others) from being ignored as they have been.

I'm not looking to win. I'm looking for fairness.

I haven't experienced fairness regarding so many aspects of the situation with Anya, and the truth has been hidden for a long time. This filing and these modifications can be the start of that accountability.

Closing Thought

Modifications outlined in these filings can replace vague language with enforceable terms. The goal is to add specifics that close gaps and attach consequences where none existed before. Each clarification can limit my former wife's ability to interpret commitments as she chooses while still claiming compliance. My daughter deserves both parents following the same clear standards, not one parent deciding what counts as cooperation.

CHAPTER 46.
Biting My Tongue When My Honesty Became Her Ammunition

Opening Thought

Direct communication and transparency built my career and shaped many of my healthiest relationships, defining who I was and how I engaged with others. When dealing with my former wife and her lawyer, I found the way I preferred to speak could be used against me. Speaking strategically instead of openly felt unnatural, but it helped stop my words from being twisted.

Keeping quiet has not been my strength, and I don't regret being straightforward, honest, and transparent. I struggle with those who choose not to confront issues directly, a trait I observed in the oversensitivity-amplified culture where I grew up. In my younger years, I noticed many people were willing to talk, but not necessarily to the individuals they should be talking to.

Many were quick to share their grievances and experiences but slow to confront the root of a problem, or avoided it altogether. Whether out of unease or avoidance, they often refrained from confronting the person with whom they had an issue. I took the opposite approach and looked for those who would communicate the same way.

Not Biting My Tongue in the Past. Pre-Anya and Pre-Bruising.

When problems arose with friends and later with those I worked with, I asked to be informed directly, eager to understand the issue and find a solution. When I noticed a problem, I brought it up soon after. This openness ended a few early relationships, as I made it clear from the start that if I had a concern, I would address it and hoped the other person would do the same. My perspective was that I would rather express my thoughts while they remained fresh, so the other person could understand my viewpoint while also being ready to hear how I might have misread or mistaken their intention.

Perhaps I was misperceiving the situation or the other person's meaning, but I preferred to tackle it head-on. Over time, I stepped back from those who said phrases like, "This has been bothering me for weeks." I didn't want to waste time, connection, and transparency with those who wanted to hang on to issues or were too apprehensive to bring them out in the open for resolution. I understood the idea of waiting to see if a behavior or trait would appear again, taking a patient approach to see if the issue was real, but at some point it should be brought up, and I would bring it up.

I preferred to hear about present issues directly, so we could address them and move on. Honesty about a problem gave me a place to start, a chance to adjust if I was unaware my behavior was causing friction, or to clarify my intentions if a situation had been misread. When someone stays silent while irritation, displeasure, or tension builds, that silence becomes its own choice. At some point, that person carries a share of responsibility for what the buildup becomes.

This approach helped me as I entered entertainment in the early 90s. Those times seemed to be the birth of this new level of sensitivity that goes too far. Back then, many were already becoming more hesitant to express their thoughts, especially if it could trouble another's perspective.

In my career, I made it clear that I would not be troubled by criticism or take it personally. I asked anyone I was working with to share any difficulties with my approach as I was doing it, so I could adjust or adapt to better fit the person or scenario, or take the time to discuss and analyze the situation together, explaining my reasons for what I was doing or the choices I was making for the product, the shoot, or the session.

I did not want to misuse hours of other people's money or, for that matter, the funds of executive producers or those who were paying the tab. I aimed to reach the point as quickly as possible in any conflicting scenario, to get clarity, get all involved in harmony, and get it done.

I watched many people in entertainment often saying, "Oh, let him or her keep going; let's see where it goes." They hesitate to voice concerns, thinking that it might trouble the performer and affect their performance for the rest of the session or the shoot. To me, if someone is that reactive, they may not be the ideal choice for a fast-paced, high-turnaround entertainment environment. Possibly, they would do better with a much higher budget, looser timelines, and fewer expectations. That was not the style I worked in. I didn't want to continue down a path that was not working or waste time and money that could be better used.

I would share with artists, "Stop me if you think what I am doing is wrong, and tell me what you do not like. From there, we can find a solution." I would tell them I could explain my reasoning for the part, the choice, or the approach if they wanted to hear it, and then ask them to explain their view. Sometimes, when someone would express their dislike by asking, "Why did you do that?" I would respond by sharing my perspective. I would say, "Based on my experience, if I do this, then this happens, and this is why I believe it would be effective." Sometimes, explaining my thought process led to a resolution, as they could see the larger picture I considered; other times, it helped me understand what they wanted done differently.

Conversely, if someone said, "I do not like that; change it," I would respond with, "Okay, here is my rationale. Please help me come up with another approach, or may we sit here for a few minutes and brainstorm some different ideas until we find a solution that works for you?" This collaborative spirit allowed me to complete my work and solve issues faster, adhere to budgets and timelines, while staying connected to the creative and artistic aspects.

This mindset extended to other areas of entertainment, strategy, and public speaking for me. I had no issue if someone disliked my ideas, performances, or products I was involved in. I welcomed constructive criticism and was not easily troubled if someone pointed out flaws or expressed discontent. In my environment, I saw no reason to hold back my thoughts, and I honored and expected the same from others. As I grew older, this openness carried into my relationships; I did not want to hold back.

Learning to Bite My Tongue, and the Frustration of It

As my relationship with Anya deteriorated, I expressed early on that I preferred to resolve issues sooner rather than later. I believed that openly addressing our issues was critical, especially considering Anya's background, as I learned about an array of unspoken tensions within her family.

Early on, she had expressed her love for my communication style, the concept of resolution, and the idea of finding common ground. She said it was so different from what she had experienced growing up, and she believed it was the right approach for her and for us.

When we argued early on, though, and no signs of agreement on these transparent concepts surfaced, I would say, "If this does not work for you, that's okay; this is how I operate, and if it's not for you, it's ok, but this type of communication, where feelings are held in, is not for me." This was one of my non-negotiables. I thought the relationship would not thrive if she chose to hide her feelings, conceal issues, or shove them under the rug, hoping they would disappear. Such behavior would not benefit either of us, nor would it encourage the preferred communication I envisioned in raising a strong, mentally healthy child.

As our problems continued to escalate, especially while Anya was pregnant and after Zoey was born, I began biting my tongue at times in an attempt to create a healthier environment for Zoey. Accountability and followthrough were at a bare minimum. I was watching Anya turn into her own mother, or at least show how close she was to those habits in her communication style.

I was trying to backburner what had been agreed upon regarding communication, hoping it might improve. It was a mistake that only allowed Anya to fall back into the habits that were easiest for her, without being held accountable for her actions, or lack thereof. I did not hold back entirely, but it was the beginning of biting my tongue and watching the honest Anya come forth.

I resented it.

It seemed disingenuous, and I was hiding my true feelings and preferred communication style while allowing this destructive approach to become the standard.

Times occurred when I pretended circumstances were better, telling myself that although I was not discussing certain topics, it was going to get better, that the words Anya claimed were true, but that she had to have more time to follow through the way she claimed she wanted to.

In the early stages of our relationship's decline, I was much more assertive in trying to resolve our issues. I was direct in my emails and assertive in my calls, desperately seeking answers and trying to understand how matters would proceed, especially regarding moving, separation, and the divorce.

I asked her if she was only saying the words she thought I would prefer to hear rather than the truth. She continued to answer, saying it was what she wanted. This showed up in her communication style, in how she claimed to be trying to find a job, and trying to improve our relationship as parents, though it had been over romantically for many years. I was shifting back toward not biting my tongue, addressing inaccuracies, false promises, empty claims, and flat-out laziness, but it didn't do any good.

The Lawyer, the Spin, and the Trap

Biting my tongue became harder when she hired her lawyer. She shifted into a state of agitation mixed with arrogance, hiding behind her lawyer and avoiding direct communication altogether. Previously, she had difficulty expressing herself, but now she had the means to send messages through her lawyer, further diminishing our ability to converse or resolve.

This situation pushed me to take my restraint to a greater degree, in a way that I found unhealthy. She was getting away with disrespect and inaccuracies, hiding the truth or sweeping it under the rug, with a lawyer who gave her the power to do so. Then, adding to that, the spin of being able to use my words against me. These words that were directly representing truth, if they were shared in the wrong order or the wrong way, they could now become ammunition for her and her lawyer.

> *"Calculated language replaced raw honesty, not to hide the truth, but to prevent my words from being used against me, ensuring what I say protects my position instead of undermining it."*

I believe there was a point, with a certain number of emails and a specific way she communicated, that she hoped would set me off and push me to respond in a way that would have played into their hands. A strategy seemed to be to agitate me, as if the goal was, "Let's see if we can instigate him and get him angry."

Exercising Restraint and How to Articulate in the Now

While it continues to be difficult for me to hold back my thoughts, this restraint has strengthened and organized my approach strategically, ensuring that my intentions are presented correctly and compliantly so they are less likely to be used against me. I may not have it all in the right order, and I'm no lawyer, but I have learned the importance of this strategic self-control.

In moments when I find it best to express my thoughts freely, while still within the confines of what may and may not be said in court, I use a series of AI tools to help me navigate and edit what I can say, formatted in a way that is permissible. I also uploaded specific emails and examples, as well as the compliance parameters, to clarify my intentions and document what I had observed. This helps me exercise restraint so that my voice can be heard without the message being silenced. This process has given me a new voice and a different way to communicate, not in the manner I prefer but in a way that conveys my story, my words, and the truth without anyone else obscuring them.

I know I've articulated some objective points poorly in the past, and it remains frustrating to approach these emails, Anya, and her lawyer this way. Still, I now possess a cautious, renewed confidence. Composure became the strategy. Holding my tongue, choosing my words, organizing what I say and how I say it. I believe that's how the truth gets heard. Not silenced. Not used against me. Heard.

Closing Thought

Speaking in court-friendly ways without losing my voice remains hard. The tools, the edits, the timing, all feel strange. But practicing strategic restraint and precise wording has helped to prevent my former wife and her lawyer from using my words as ammunition against me. One day, if my daughter reads these records, my hope is that she'll see a father who chose thoughtful response over reactive emotion.

CHAPTER 47.
Jabs Delivered Through Pettiness Disguised as Cooperation

Opening Thought

Zero interest in cooperation, but all the energy in the world for pettiness. Responding at precisely 23 hours and 59 minutes isn't time management; it is a calculated demonstration of control, turning required correspondence into performance art that serves no one but her ego.

Unhealthy communication operated as resistance disguised beneath compliance. It became, "I'm in control, and you are not." Regardless, these actions only resulted in wasted time. Over the years, numerous instances have occurred, but one of the more recent examples involved a reminder issued after a motion was filed. She was reminded that, according to the parenting plan, she was required to respond to emails within 24 hours and to participate in conversations and respond to questions sent.

This appeared to upset her and her sense of control. So, she chose a way to make it about her and to control the situation in her own style, while still following the instructions.

In one email about an upcoming visit, I made it clear that I did not agree to the use of a tracker placed on Zoey and emphasized that such actions are not allowed in Zoey's state of residence. The person who assisted me with drafting that email suggested including a point acknowledging her receipt and understanding of the message. This was not only to address the tracker issue directly, but to ensure she recognized that it had been brought to her attention. The email included a request for a reply within 24 hours, consistent with the expectations outlined in the parenting plan.

She replied exactly 23 hours and 59 minutes later with a rude response. Meanwhile, I had sent an email the day before, five minutes after my initial message. This follow-up email requested the contact information for Zoey's therapist, as I had been left entirely out of the loop with the previous therapist, which defies what is written in the parenting plan. I proposed a session with Zoey's therapist, Anya, and me to connect and communicate for Zoey's sake, but that suggestion was denied in a response that also came 23 hours and 59 minutes after being sent.

> *"Linear thinking, resentment, and corrosive reasoning fuel these actions, rather than any real attempt at being kind, respectful, or responsive."*

Initially, I gave her the benefit of the doubt, thinking she got to her emails the next day. Still, with each of those emails replied to under the one-minute mark of the stated requirement, it appeared intentional. The energy she invests in being confrontational and "fluffing her feathers," for lack of a better term, comes off as foolish, immature, and petty. Linear thinking, resentment, and corrosive reasoning fuel these actions, rather than any real attempt at being kind, respectful, or responsive.

This repeated itself several times in more recent emails. In her last message, part of me wanted to respond with, "How petty do you have to be to act this way?" Another part wanted to express concern that Zoey might learn these awful traits and tactics from her. I also considered asking, "How would you feel if Zooy knew you were treating me like this?" Instead, I chose a different approach. I replied, "Thank you for the information you sent. I don't understand why you feel the urge to send your emails when you do. I'm still praying for you. Praying for healing and happiness. I hope you are well."

The subtle anger and resentment she continually exhibits is astounding to me, highlighting her inability to commit to the positive changes she once professed to want for herself. Still, when it comes to actions that allow her to take a jab or feel victorious, she engages fully. These actions are a waste of her time, not mine.

Whether it's setting an alarm on her phone, scheduling an exact send time, or reminding herself to respond at a specific moment, the calculated effort shows what matters to her and what doesn't. Over the past two months alone, most of her responses followed this same cadence. Important questions receive slow responses or silence, while topics she controls or wants to control receive immediate replies. The more calculated her behavior becomes, the clearer the record gets. Her precision is working against her, not for her.

Closing Thought

X-rays capture what exists below the surface, but these behaviors require no special equipment to detect. Every carefully timed response, every deliberate delay builds a documented history of choices made. The record shows priorities with complete transparency about where attention goes, what gets addressed, and whether working together was ever the goal. The time my former wife spends engineering displays of bare minimum compliance doesn't erase itself. It accumulates into evidence of her intentions.

CHAPTER 48.
Legitimate Authority vs. Her Manufactured Obstruction

Opening Thought

Cooperation between co-parents requires honest, timely information about a child's location and caregivers. Repeated incorrect addresses, misspelled phone numbers, and sudden calendar changes aren't accidents. They read as tactics. When one parent systematically withholds or distorts required information, it signals a calculated attempt to maintain exclusive control while appearing compliant.

Knowing where my daughter is staying and who is supervising her during sleepovers is my right as her father, not a request requiring Anya's approval. Residential status does not determine what is owed to me under our agreement. I was given wrong addresses, disconnected phone numbers, and schedule updates announced after the events.

Each time, the same defense, "mere errors," but errors don't repeat on schedule. Before one sleepover, Anya wrote, "I don't know if I am going to give you this person's phone number. I don't know if they want their phone number given to you." I reminded her that the parenting plan requires that information be shared with me. Her hesitation confirmed the habit: withhold required details, then act like disclosure is optional.

Custody was reframed as ownership through her mother's repeated messaging. She told Zoey that the parent she lives with makes all decisions. That lesson didn't come from our parenting agreement but from systematic attempts to convince her that residential placement equals total authority. My daughter questioned it and knew better.

Anya failed to list locations, or provided them after the fact. During one New York trip, I had no way to reach Zoey at all, not for daily calls, not to send a note saying "I know that hotel," or "I worked near that area," the small connection she could read when she had time. That was taken from both of us.

When asked about missed updates, Anya's replies listed obstacles rather than providing the required details. They were running late... I cannot share that... Plans changed... Each response avoided the agreement while sounding compliant.

The Christmas Blockade

This type of obstruction carried over to the holidays and when I was in town to visit her. I asked repeatedly about their Christmas plans. No response. I asked to see Zoey for five minutes on Christmas Day to wish her Merry Christmas. First, no answer, then Anya wrote back, "We are going to my sister's, but I don't want you to show up." I said I would respect that and stay away. She went nowhere. She stayed home. The answer remained no. I could see Zoey the day after Christmas, not on Christmas.

I was staying at a place minutes from her house and wasn't asking to come inside. I suggested meeting at the front door for one moment to hug my daughter, give her a present, and honor her wish to see me on Christmas Day. Anya refused. That refusal wasn't about plans or logistics; it read as control.

The Disappearing Calendar Act

Calendar entries appeared, then disappeared. During one visit, I rushed Zoey back for a trip listed on the shared calendar, honoring that commitment. The trip didn't happen, and she didn't tell me it was canceled. I lost time with my daughter for a plan that didn't exist.

I asked to see Zoey for her birthday. Anya wrote back within minutes. "Well, I should get to celebrate her birthday too." How long I had been gone didn't matter. What Zoey wanted didn't matter. What mattered was what Anya wanted.

> *"Custody was reframed as ownership through her mother's repeated messaging. She told Zoey that the parent she lives with makes all decisions. That lesson didn't come from our parenting agreement but from systematic attempts to convince her that residential placement equals total authority. My daughter questioned it and knew better."*

When I was discussing trip arrangements with Zoey, she said, "Mommy says she is in charge because she is the one I live with." I explained that's not how it works. Her mother may have primary custody, but I'm still her father.

I have a right to be involved in decisions about her life. Anya has tried to remove me from decision-making, but those rights still exist and will be recognized and restored when accountability arrives.

More Aggressive Acts of False Control

Anya sent an email outlining her plan for iPad time. Her schedule. Her restrictions. She offered to draft a joint stipulation for the court to formalize it. I asked where the compromise was. Where the two-way conversation was. Her reply ignored every question.

Her approach was clear: present one-sided terms, involve counsel immediately, bypass discussion entirely. Her limited perspective and belief that she makes all decisions may not serve her well when that changes. What she believes about her authority does not change what I am to Zoey, or my rights as her father.

Closing Thought

Primary custody does not erase my rights as a father. Those rights exist whether my former wife acknowledges them or not. Her belief that residential placement grants total decision-making authority misreads both the agreement and the law. The documented record shows someone confusing custody with ownership. That confusion will meet correction when accountability arrives.

CHAPTER 49.
Creating Financial Crises and Deflecting Accountability

Opening Thought

Unscrupulous behavior in our finances did not stop at missing payments; it often involved decisions that created new debt and then shifted the burden elsewhere. When she tried to place all responsibility for the back rent on me, it echoed what I had seen before, a repeated sequence where a crisis appeared, and accountability was pushed away in resentment.

Centering on her effort to avoid moving from our shared residence, Anya quickly made clear through her divorce filing what she planned to do without informing me. The owner of the house we were renting was considering selling it, and once that was confirmed, I responded immediately with, "How can I help? When do you want us out?" The lease was due to end in a couple of months, and I hoped to set a plan in motion for the move and clarify timelines and expectations for those involved.

That summer, I encountered a difficult situation with a business venture that played a critical role in my finances. Some individuals when called out, acted suspiciously and stopped their payments, leaving the next expected payments outstanding. Despite a strong legal standing, their response was dismissive, amounting to, "Try to come after us." As a large and profitable company, they implied that they could prolong any legal battle beyond our means to sustain it. This experience created severe financial strain and presented a range of significant challenges.

In the middle of that financial crisis, Anya made brash and unsubstantiated claims, saying I was hiding money and that I had more than I was sharing. I responded by offering complete transparency. She could review my bank accounts for herself, notice that the money was not there, and verify the payments that had stopped coming in.

I began working on a plan for the next steps for all of us, not knowing where it would lead or whether she and Zoey would remain in one place while I was in another. Laying the groundwork for a selfish and one-sided strategy, she said she would handle the situation, kept me out of the details, and then tried to shift the obligation back onto me when it no longer worked in her favor.

Anya's response left little room for doubt, stating that she intended to stay and that my responsibility to pay remained. My ability to maintain this home had changed, making it necessary to take steps toward leaving. The lease was approaching its end. I shared that I would contact the landlord, outline the new circumstances, and, as plans for Anya and Zoey's next steps took shape, offer help preparing the house for its transition since the owner was no longer in the area.

Anya then said, "I'm going to take care of this. You don't have to." So I left for a place where I could stay for free while trying to focus on the best next steps to be effective and repair what had gone wrong, as well as figure out how to improve the situation for Anya and Zoey.

Anya stayed in the house for an extended period. When I asked her about the situation with the owner and how it was possible, she said she was "looking at options," and that if no other options materialized, she might move in with "the individual next door for a while." I suspected that was the plan all along, and it was a matter of timing.

Time continued to pass. She was still there, I was not being given any information, but she had claimed she had "handled it." During the divorce proceedings, when I asked about the situation, I did not get a response. I had no information on moving dates, what the owners had said, what was agreed upon, or what costs were still being accrued. All I got back was that she was handling it, and one day, many months later, Zoey called to say they had moved in next door.

Over a year later, an email arrived from the landlord addressed to Anya, stating that he wanted to discuss the unpaid balance. She replied to him and copied me: "Tell him to take care of it," shifting all responsibility onto me. Once again, her ability to invent, cover up, forget, and avoid accountability for her decisions was on full display. Now it was suddenly all my problem.

When I received that email, I felt it was important to respond to the landlord, as I had not been informed about this situation beforehand. I shared my experience regarding her moving out and her assurance that she would handle it. I mentioned that it might be best for him to discuss this with Anya and that once I had a clearer understanding of my potential responsibilities and the details, I would be open to discussing it further.

> *"Laying the groundwork for a selfish and one-sided strategy, she said she would handle the situation, kept me out of the details, and then tried to shift the obligation back onto me when it no longer worked in her favor."*

I received an email from Anya, which she sent to him while copying me. It felt harsh and seemed to highlight her memory issues and lack of accountability. She expressed a strong reaction, suggesting that he might consider legal action against me.

When she followed up with an email claiming I was "throwing this all on her," I replied, "No, I am not throwing it all on you. Go back and read the email. You took responsibility for this. You said you would handle it. This is where you decided to stay. You chose not to fill me in on what was going on."

I clarified that it was her responsibility to determine the actual costs and what was owed. What happened to the first month's rent, last month's rent, and the security deposit when she moved out? What agreement was in place for the extended time she stayed? What was the actual amount owed? Then, in the next email, Anya responded saying that she was "trying to find that out." It was frustrating how quickly she redirected the burden back to me, as if she expected me to handle the entire situation on my own, with no information about what had been agreed to in my absence.

No response came after that. I have not heard about the situation since. She provided one total but did not answer questions about other amounts or share any of the information I requested. I followed up once with an update request, but still no response came, as I was dismissed again.

This reflects the tendencies of a complex individual who perceives information through her own narrow perspective, quickly concluding what was said without considering that it might have a different intent or meaning. How she sees the world concerns me because, at times, Zoey witnesses and overhears these events. I hope Zoey does not come to see actions like these as acceptable. In my view, they are inappropriate, unhealthy, misleading, and disrespectful.

Closing Thought

Avoidance and redirecting in this situation made it clear that my former wife took control of the arrangement, shut me out of the decisions, and then tried to send the entire obligation back to me when the owner finally asked to be paid. It did not matter what she had said about handling it; once the situation became difficult and the questions closed in, she avoided explanation and reassigned blame, so the responsibility no longer sat with her.

CHAPTER 50.
Visits Contested Through Her Selfish Cycles of Revision

Opening Thought

Planning any visit seemed to invite obstacles, as simple logistics shifted into significant challenges before arrangements could settle. Many efforts at coordination became a calculated pushback. I reminded myself that staying calm and keeping a clear record can speak more powerfully than any reaction, both in the moment and in the future.

Managing visits with Zoey has required navigating Anya's deliberate obstruction at most turns. I've sent email after email, text after text, to negotiate times with her. The process is irrational and unreasonable. Negotiating with someone who thrives on control means every visit feels like a battlefield. Lines are redrawn daily, rules rewritten mid-play. The reward is not claiming victory but sharing rare moments of peace with the child I love, allowing time together to take precedence over conflict.

Anya sometimes declares, with no consideration or compromise, "I have to see her now, or she must be here right now. She will sleep here tonight." She appears to overlook that this is not a choice she can make on her own without my input. Still, she seemingly chooses to ignore those elements and take advantage of the situation, as I am currently unable to enforce accountability for her actions.

She has held my lack of representation, finances, and health over me, taking advantage of the situation. Zoey has brought it up, stating, "You are my parent, too. Mommy can't do this." I try to tread lightly and tell her it is wrong, but right now, I have to bend some to spend as much time with Zoey as possible.

Visitation planning often becomes an ongoing negotiation shaped by directives and changing requirements that reflect Anya's preferences. Requests arrive abruptly, insisting on new arrangements, announcing sudden trips, or seeking additional personal details without prior discussion. At one point, I was informed Zoey had to attend her therapy session during our scheduled time together, and I would be unable to attend it. Zoey mentioned sessions can easily be canceled or rescheduled, but I was not given that option. The same applied to her missing volleyball games. This came across as a double standard, denying me the chance to participate in decisions I have every right to be involved in.

A Volley of Texts and a Volleyball Game

A specific volleyball game became one more example of this common exertion of control. I was told Zoey had to be at this game during a time I was scheduled to be with her. I said it would be great to watch her play volleyball and then spend some time with her after the game. The response was, "Well, it's going to be late afterward, and I don't feel good about that."

I offered to bring her straight home from the game. I was not asking for an overnight visit that night, either. We spent 20 minutes negotiating by text while I sat in a store parking lot. The entire exchange was maddening.

The next morning, when I picked up Zoey to take her to school, she said, "Daddy, you're going to be unhappy." I didn't let on how unhappy I already was. I knew a plan had been put into motion to reduce the time we spent together. Instead, I said, "Well, what's going on? I'll be fine."

She explained her mother had given her a choice between attending a volleyball game or a small party with her friends. I understood a girl her age would choose the party with friends, not thinking about the limited time I was there. Still, her mother presented this new option after we had already agreed on the plans regarding that volleyball game. Anya disregarded the agreement made in that text exchange the day before, retook control, and did what she could to reduce my time with Zoey.

That time was mine, and it was a subversive tactic Anya applied, but I wasn't going to put any pressure on Zoey to change her mind. It made for a difficult last night of my trip. Still, I remained calm, acted honorably, and documented the experience thoroughly to highlight the patterns and actions that would be addressed in time and in court. To Zoey's credit, she recognized the situation later. "I should have gone to the volleyball game," she said. "I should have had more time with you."

I told Zoey, "No, you make the decisions you choose to make. There's no guilt with me or from me ever." I thought about identifying several of the guilt-trip tactics that originate from her mother, but I chose to refrain. I stayed positive and calm, sharing with her, "You make the decisions you have to make based on the choices presented to you. Next time, when you're considering any choices regarding time with me during a visit together, consider both the choice for the moment but also for the enduring moments later."

"If you are given a choice, remember I am only here for a limited time during these visits, but the other option might be available to you at any time or on any weekend. Regardless of whether it's a choice about time with me or any other choice, try to think past the moment and see if that choice will serve what you want for the longer term."

Loose Terms After Losing Teeth

We also had an understanding when I visited during Zoey's surgery. It was a loose understanding, and that is precisely the form of ambiguity Anya appears to thrive on. She uses it to her advantage, altering and rewriting facts into fiction for her own benefit, doing what she can to take control and reduce my contact with Zoey.

I wasn't allowed to see Zoey after the surgery, despite asking numerous times. "Can I come in and see Zoey after she gets back and settled?" The answer was repeatedly, "You're not allowed in here. No one in this household wants you here." No one in that house or that neighborhood previously had a problem with me. Still, Anya demonstrated one of her unhealthy power plays by creating a false conflict where none existed.

"Negotiating with someone who thrives on control means every visit feels like a battlefield. Lines are redrawn daily, rules rewritten mid-play. The reward is not claiming victory but sharing rare moments of peace with the child I love, allowing time together to take precedence over conflict."

Part of our agreement for that visit was that if Zoey wanted to see me or come with me, it would be her decision, and she could call. She did call, and she came back to where I was staying. It was her first surgery, not major, but significant for her. She was still recovering from the anesthesia.

We returned to my place and sat in bed, watching the movies she wanted to show me. We went out to get food she could eat, including Jell-O, pudding, and cheese sticks that we cut into small pieces. I was reviewing the recommended list of foods and considering what would be most comfortable for her. We were having a restful, simple day together, no unreasonable activity; instead, it was a quiet, connecting, relaxing, and healing time.

As Zoey rested during our visit, a steady stream of questions came through by text from her mother, checking on her well-being and requesting updates about our activities together. The medication sent with her allowed for only a limited duration of time. When I inquired about having Anya provide more so Zoey could extend her stay, the reply expressed hesitation about prolonging the visit, preferring that Zoey return sooner as she expressed concerns for Zoey's safety.

How is it not safe? I am more aware, more careful, and far more attentive to Zoey's care. From what I have observed, these details, awareness, and understanding are not as strong at times with Anya regarding Zoey. I hope it doesn't come across as misguided or irrational. I believe I provide a safer environment for Zoey, encompassing her physical health and emotional well-being.

After this extended barrage of messages and Anya's refusal to relent, I weighed the situation and decided to bring Zoey back. That moment clarified that significant changes must occur, including closer adherence and modifications to the parenting plan regarding my time with Zoey. I believe that building on truth and documented evidence will help correct past wrongs and set a better course for our visits in the near term and our time together over the long run.

Closing Thought

Coordinating visits exposed my former wife's obstruction between my daughter and me. I chose to respond with quiet focus and detailed documentation, trusting each verified fact would eventually confirm the truth. My focus remains on my daughter, knowing that time will soon be on my side and that love grounded in patience will endure longer than any attempt to interfere with it.

CHAPTER 51.
Laziness Modeled Through Shortcuts and Broken Commitments

Opening Thought

Watching comfort overshadow consistency showed how shortcuts replace commitment. I saw how "maybe" can become a permanent address for some individuals. My focus remained on being a healthy role model for my daughter, demonstrating what sustained effort and accountability look like.

Shortcuts taken, commitments broken, and promises abandoned represent what my daughter has witnessed repeatedly over the years. If there's a shortcut to take, Anya will take it. If there's an email, a text, or a request she can ignore, she will. If there's a behavior, trait, or action she doesn't want to face, confess to, or address, she will bury it and move on.

Anya's behavior is being modeled for Zoey, and that is concerning to me. I'm seeing minor, troubling signs now, and Zoey is adopting a few of these same behaviors, including an occasional lack of commitment, poor self-discipline, and, at times, accepting her mother's approach, giving up in a defeated manner when Zoey herself says, "It is too hard to do."

Ensuring my daughter doesn't inherit a lazy, lost approach built on cutting corners and broken promises is the goal. This purposeful work from afar models the commitment her mother has seemingly abandoned. It's a careful rebellion for my daughter's character, planting seeds of integrity in a field of complacency.

Each week, I send Zoey audio and video messages on Thursdays and Fridays, generally twominute recordings that sometimes extend to four or five minutes. I also send her daily graphics. During a recent conversation, she casually mentioned, "I'm sorry, I haven't been watching them at all."

I explained to her that these messages are my way of connecting with her and of parenting from a distance. Her response? "Well, when I'm on my iPad, it's a fun time, and I like to be entertained." When not under that influence, Zoey often expresses real longings, as I find in several texts from her stating, "I miss you so much. I have to see you now. Can you call me? I miss hugging you. I miss you holding me." This contradiction points to a more deliberate effort, Anya working to put distance between Zoey and me.

I encouraged her to review these brief messages as they arrived, noting the time added up to only a few minutes each week. The request was not a demand, only a suggestion to set aside a small amount of time when possible. Her response reflected a cautious approach, expressing openness to try the process and evaluate how it might fit into her routine. It sounded like her mother speaking. "Well, I'm not sure. Maybe I'll try this for a few days and see how it feels."

I was not happy, not with Zoey, but with recognizing some of the mental tactics and unhealthy games that seem to be embedded in how Zoey has learned to procrastinate. Still, I see Zoey following through and standing stronger as a child than her mother ever did as an adult.

Some Common Visiting Tactics

During one planned sleepover visit, Anya sent texts claiming, "Zoey doesn't know if she wants to sleep over. She has been upset and emotional about it and says she misses being with me. Zoey doesn't know if she wants to be with you or spend the night. She might have dinner with you." This sounded as if a narrative was being pushed on Zoey, possibly using guilt, which I'd seen Anya use in the past. I was not happy, but I also wanted to let Zoey take the lead and know she had the final choice whether to stay with me that night or go back home.

When Zoey got in the car, I turned around and asked, "Are you okay? Would you like to only have dinner with me? You don't have to stay over. I can bring you right back afterward." It broke my heart to say those words, but I would make the most of every precious minute I had with Zoey.

"What do you want to do?" I asked. "Maybe, we can find somewhere closer we can go to dinner, and I can bring you home after?" I was offering options without pressure and honoring my daughter. Zoey was in the car for less than a minute, no more than that. Her response? "No, take me back to your hotel. I am spending the night with you. I do want to stay with you tonight, Daddy."

According to what Anya told me, Zoey's feelings were a complete reversal, which leaves me with questions about what Zoey said or what Anya said to Zoey that seemed to cause interference. Fortunately, it didn't work, and we had a great evening and a fun time together.

"Ensuring my daughter doesn't inherit a lazy, lost approach built on cutting corners and broken promises is the goal. This purposeful work from afar models the commitment her mother has seemingly abandoned. It's a careful rebellion for my daughter's character, planting seeds of integrity in a field of complacency."

When Zoey finds herself in this bubble of persuasion, surrounded by messages like "you don't have to commit to this, you don't have to do that," I sense she carries a weight of uncertainty, pulled between what she knows is right and what requires the least effort. Still, when she's with me, I believe she experiences moments of liberation from that confinement, along with a stronger resolve to follow through.

Recently, during a reading challenge, her mother told her she could listen to the audio versions toward the end. She asked me if that was acceptable. I asked her: is this a reading challenge, or a listening challenge? She stood her ground and stated she would read without the audio supplement. When her mother pushed her to use the audio, she nodded politely and read every page herself. I was so proud of her follow-through, especially with her mother in her ear, offering shortcuts instead of supporting her to complete the task in full.

Making the Time

As far as those videos and audios are concerned, I don't want to create pressure, but I would like her to watch them, listen to them, and make time once a week to fit this in. This type of discipline might strengthen her follow-through, especially when surrounded by inconsistency.

These small commitments matter, like drinking more water (which her mother rarely encourages) and limiting candy consumption (while she sits there pounding candy because she has unlimited access and then can't comprehend why she feels terrible). There is little consistency being modeled.

Miles away from Zoey, I guide her through some fundamental self-care tips over FaceTime, encouraging her to drink more water and be mindful of her sugar intake. I point out how late-day sweets seem to affect her evenings. Zoey acknowledges noticing this and is aware of it. When she discusses it with Anya, Anya contradicts what I've shared, dismissing the precise observations Zoey has recognized in herself. This only amplifies the underlying issues of control that overshadow my efforts to support Zoey and work together in her best interest.

While I focus on gently reminding Zoey about healthy routines, Anya's approach appears to center on denial and redirection, motivated more by a desire to preserve her own viewpoint than by any desire to collaborate with me for Zoey's well-being.

My goal is for Zoey to develop a real dedication to completing small, daily habits, especially when Anya's encouragement is absent. I remind her that taking ownership of these choices is worthwhile, regardless of whether she receives reminders or support from her mother. This is particularly significant, given that Anya's consistency often appears conditional, evident only when convenient and withdrawn at the first sign of discomfort.

When challenges arise for Anya, her response tends to involve shifting focus, glossing over the problem, or offering explanations for her lack of persistence. These habits represent a blueprint for complacency that I hope Zoey learns to avoid.

Closing Thought

Hesitation replaced commitment as shortcuts became my former wife's default. My task now is to demonstrate consistency through example, transparency, and accountability. If complacency breeds confusion, then perhaps sustained action can restore trust. This unhealthy cycle can end when effort replaces delay, and that steady commitment is what I hope my daughter sees and will continue to see in me.

CHAPTER 52.
Words Withheld and Walls Built Around Her Silence

Opening Thought

Phone calls stopped once she filed, and repeated requests to resume speaking directly went ignored. I cannot make someone communicate with respect, but I can keep my own conduct grounded in calm truth. I keep tracking contradictions and questionable actions, creating a record that will hold her accountable when the time comes to present it all.

Evasive tactics became standard once litigation began, eliminating phone calls altogether, while email responses stayed vague, addressing only what she felt like sharing and when she felt like sharing it. From the start, I noticed that when she seemed bothered or tense, she would go silent instead of addressing it. I would ask, "What's going on?" and assured her I wouldn't get upset. I did not react with anger when she brought up what we had agreed to discuss, though many of our agreements became null and void as soon as they didn't suit her. I encouraged her to bring up what bothered her so we could solve problems and avoid repeating mistakes.

Anya explained how her family would let tension simmer until it erupted, creating a corrosive environment. Since we first separated, she has emulated those same habits of silence, and it still fascinates me. I once told her, "You can dislike me, and you can have your own perceptions or fantasies. But when it comes to talking about Zoey, it's not about me; it's about her. Please, let's be the best parents we can be and talk effectively for Zoey's sake."

She has chosen to remain silent.

It's been over two years since she last spoke to me. When I go to pick up Zoey on visits, I have said hello, but she looks at me without responding, and this has happened when Zoey is right there. I cherish the moments when Zoey runs to me and hugs me after our long separations. Still, it is concerning to me that during these encounters, her scowl or silence might unintentionally leave a negative impression on Zoey.

I've repeatedly emphasized in emails that we should engage better for Zoey's sake. She insists that she doesn't have to talk to me more than she already does, but she doesn't talk to me at all, and her emails address the bare minimum, generally only what she chooses to answer, and are often supplemented with digs or false claims.

Attempting to communicate with her about our daughter is viewed by her as an effort to exert control. She has stated this in texts. This irrational stance allows her to ignore the parenting plan, dismiss our daughter's well-being, and maintain complete control without accountability. My repeated requests to discuss Zoey's well-being and activities go unanswered, leaving Zoey caught in a tug-of-war. She feels torn when I share an idea, an approach, or a solution, and her mother says the exact opposite, creating confusion.

My goal is to ensure that Zoey has a stable environment. Given how much Zoey confides in me, wouldn't it make sense for Anya to share her observations and approaches regarding Zoey? Healthy dialogue would allow me to support her and Zoey better. It could lead to constructive discussions rather than conflict.

Whether through the courts or through problem-solving dialogue, this line in the parenting plan must emerge from the shadows:

"The child has the right to see his or her parents being courteous and respectful to and of each other."

> *"Attempting to communicate with her about our daughter is viewed by her as an effort to exert control. She has stated this in texts. This irrational stance allows her to ignore the parenting plan, dismiss our daughter's well-being, and maintain complete control without accountability."*

I pray that when this matter is brought before the court, a new level of healthy dialogue can be established. I hope Anya can find the strength to see that my intentions are not to attack or gain control, but rather to improve the situation for Zoey. My goal is to alleviate the tug-of-war Zoey feels and honor her requests for dialogue between her parents.

Zoey has asked for a FaceTime call with the three of us. When Zoey suggested we go to dinner or get ice cream, I told her I would be happy to, which made her light up. Unfortunately, when I sent these ideas to Anya, she remained silent. I emphasized and reiterated that this was for Zoey, and it would make her happy, but Anya continued to ignore my emails and requests.

A crushing part of this for me is that, in her apparent malice toward me, she seems to dismiss and ignore what Zoey wants. Her anger and feelings of vengeance toward me outweigh her wishes for Zoey. I tread carefully, expressing my willingness to cooperate with Anya when she's ready, while also encouraging Zoey to continue standing up for herself and asking for what she would like to see happen. I also work with her on how to continue to request what she wants respectfully when she is denied, to feel the confidence to ask why, and to be able to receive clear answers about requests she is left in the dark on, but has every right to understand.

Zoey deserves more than the overused "because I said so" response from Anya.

Despite my ongoing efforts, Anya has chosen, and continues to choose, not to engage. I hope the courts understand the complexity of this situation and the emotional challenges Zoey faces. If a court order is necessary to facilitate honest dialogue about Zoey's requirements and some of the present difficulties, I not only accept it but welcome it and will petition for it.

Closing Thought

Responding to walls constructed from silence meant maintaining steady, documented communication while refusing to escalate. I continued engaging professionally, creating a clear record of my attempts versus my former wife's avoidance. She chose silence as her strategy. I chose transparency as my defense, knowing the record will speak volumes when she won't whisper a word.

CHAPTER 53.
Persisting Through Rejections to Cancel a Hearing on Her Day

Opening Thought

Notice of a scheduled hearing arrived weeks before my visit, set for the only day I would have my daughter with mτe for the entire day. I cannot dictate how bureaucracy operates or what barriers appear before me, but I will not surrender without exhausting every available option. Two weeks of filings, corrections, and rejections became the price to protect what could not be compromised.

Traveling against medical advice, I planned a visit to be with my daughter on her birthday. She wanted me there, and I was going to find a way. I prayed for a positive outcome and trusted the rest would follow. I had a quiet, nagging feeling questioning whether Anya and her lawyer had any control over the situation. I had learned of contradictory elements where someone could suggest a schedule without consulting the other party, but others insisted that wasn't permissible. I found evidence for both sides of the situation and how it might be unfolding.

A few weeks before my planned visit to Zoey, I received a notice that a hearing had been scheduled regarding a motion filed asking the court to address specific instances of noncompliance with the parenting plan. This hearing was set for the same Tuesday I was supposed to be there. The notice stated that I was required to appear for the hearing, which was scheduled to last an hour and a half, and that I was not permitted to bring a child with me. If I failed to show up, I could face sanctions, including an arrest warrant and 48 hours in lockup.

Regardless of any potential foul play or whether someone may have orchestrated this situation, I was compelled to act. I reached out to a self-help lawyer in the county, who offered brief consultations for a small fee, and I began researching all the relevant information I could find about the district and the county. I filed a motion for continuance, but I soon learned that I had made an error. The judge's assistant informed me that my submission was incorrect, so I attempted to refile it as best as I could (unfortunately, it was denied).

A couple of days later, I checked in again with another self-help lawyer and was told, "It's your motion; you can cancel it." I had been trying hard to gather as much information as possible to make the most of those 15 minutes with the lawyer. Unfortunately, the information I received from the judge's assistant contradicted what the lawyer had advised and what I had found in my own research. Despite sending another letter insisting that my motion should be rescheduled, it was denied.

I then attempted to submit a notice of cancellation, which two different people had recommended. It was denied a few days later. I continued to dig for information and filed a motion to vacate the judgment. Then, I was told that wouldn't work either. Anya's lawyer then contacted me, claiming I was wasting the court's time and hers. She stated that she had spent an hour on my case and indicated she might file a claim for the time spent representing Anya. Suddenly, I was faced with the prospect of being charged for her time.

> *"Facing lockup was acceptable if it meant*
> *protecting every moment possible with*

*my daughter, to hold her, talk to her, and
express my love and commitment to her for
the short time I was able to be in town."*

Anya's lawyer seemed self-absorbed. I chose not to antagonize her. Instead of pointing out that I knew exactly what to file next or that pressuring someone without legal representation was inappropriate, I took a gentler approach and said, "I understand you will do what you decide to do."

Anya's lawyer insisted in her email, "Show up. It's not getting canceled." I had previously stated in my motions that I hadn't seen Zoey in a certain number of days, emphasizing the importance of this trip to me. I added that I was not well and heading back for a series of surgeries after this visit with my daughter. I also stated I was going to spend every moment of that short visit I could with Zoey.

The lawyer claimed I was wasting her time and said I was sending repetitive emails asking for the same request over and over. In my response, I outlined the different motions I had filed and the corrections I was advised to make. I insisted that I would continue working on this until it was resolved. I asked why this could not be considered on her part or Anya's as well. After that, Anya's lawyer stopped responding.

I submitted a notice of withdrawal and eventually received a note stating my withdrawal looked fine but lacked a specific case number. I had already included the case number in the subject line, the PDF, and the email body. I emailed the judge's assistant to ask whether I had missed any requirements or supplemental materials, and sent the number again. A day later, I received a confirmation acknowledging that the number was there on the original documents.

Then I got a change-of-address form, which I had already tried to update. I didn't understand why I was receiving it again, so I promptly sent it back. In that moment, I also submitted a motion for Anya to correct her address, as she had used an incorrect one.

I pointed out that her address, Zoey's birth date, and various other details were wrong in the filings Anya's lawyer had sent, which I thought should be brought to their attention.

And then I waited. The night before leaving for the visit had been rough, but I decided that, regardless of whether the hearing was canceled, I would spend that Tuesday with Zoey. I trusted that the right outcome would come to pass. The following day, I boarded the first of several flights to reach her. On the second plane, I received an email stating that the hearing had been canceled, three and a half hours before my arrival.

The motion was canceled, too, so I had to resubmit it at a later date and deal with new delays. Reflecting on this experience, I recognized the faith and determination that carried me through. I considered the possibility of refiling the motion with stronger terms and addressing additional matters that required attention. While this added significant time and effort, it was all about my daughter and the time with her. Facing lockup was acceptable if it meant protecting every moment possible with my daughter, to hold her, talk to her, and express my love and commitment to her for the short time I was able to be in town.

After we said our goodbyes on our last morning together for this visit, when I walked her to school, and shortly before I was supposed to fly, I received another court notice requiring me to appear in the courthouse for the case. It mentioned I was now ordered to be there two days earlier. Some uncertainty lingered over whether this was another mistake, a misfile, or an attempt to delay my departure. The contradiction of the ruling seemed to show up with weird timing.

A final concern arose as I headed to the airport. Was some form of an arrest warrant filed, and would it affect my ability to fly? Was this another attempt by Anya to influence the situation to her own benefit? During the visit, Anya made several less-than-respectful remarks, leading me to think more could come. It seemed to me that she believed she had endured a series of losses, in what I saw as compromises, and that the added pressure on my way out could serve her own satisfaction.

Despite these concerns, I made it through TSA, boarded my flight, and remained steadfast in my stance. Throughout the visit, before, during, and after, I remained humble, gentle, and resolute. I advocated in every way I could to ensure my time and connection with Zoey would happen. When I made mistakes in my filings before the trip, I did all I could to correct them.

When pressure came from the lawyer, I chose to respond appropriately and respectfully rather than mirror the unhealthy tactics used against me. From the initial roadblocks before the trip, presented in the form of a hearing on the one day I would have been with Zoey for the whole day, to my departure at the end of the visit, I was committed to maximizing my time with Zoey and addressing every issue that could prevent it.

I cherished every moment with my daughter during that visit. One day, I believe she will understand how much I worked to make it fair for us. Twenty emails across ten days, all to spend as much time as possible with her. When faced with the possibility of arrest and unfair financial penalties from her lawyer, my commitment to Zoey remained my sole focus. I would do it all again without hesitation. She is worth every filing, every rejection, every sleepless night.

Closing Thought

Cancellation of the hearing came through hours before I landed. Bureaucratic obstacles slowed the process, and opposing counsel made it harder instead of helping resolve the scheduling conflict. I was prepared to face any consequences that followed, but missing that day was not an option I would accept. Patient and persistent filings delivered the only outcome that mattered.

CHAPTER 54.
Daily Digital Messages Archived to Outlast Distance and Time

Opening Thought

Developing this archive began on the first day after our airport goodbye. I made one graphic for my daughter. The next day, I made another. That practice continued for more than 800 days, growing to include over 100 weekly audio messages and over 90 videos. Each piece was numbered, dated, and texted directly to her while also archived in file-sharing storage and published online. Separation could not stop these messages. Silence could not erase them. They exist as proof that I showed up for her every single day.

Bridging the distance between us required an approach that could survive separation, silence, and time. I began making and sharing small, consistent offerings, whether it was a note, an idea, a reflection, or a gentle word of encouragement. This became one way to keep care present and available for my daughter. Each message represents my attempt to hold a space where love can linger, where understanding is welcomed at all times, and where a father's voice can be heard nearby, if only quietly or with patient intention.

I've constructed a digital gift basket archive for my daughter, intended to provide comfort whether I'm present or not. She may one day cherish it. Should I pass away sooner than circumstances allow, it's also designed to prevent erasure of my presence from her life, a concern rooted in the considerable effort her mother has invested in distancing me from Zoey since this separation.

During my illness, as I faced medical and financial obstacles, my constant wish was for Zoey to know that I loved her and thought of her every day, regardless of my physical absence. An idea took form, with the intention of ensuring that my thoughts, words, love, and connection could continue reaching her, no matter the distance or my health circumstances. I sought a way to remind her of my love, my intentions, and the truth of what occurred.

The Daily Practice

From that first day gone, one graphic became the practice. I knew she would remember our last day together at the airport, where we ran around, talked, and shared both laughter and tears. I was compelled to make another graphic the next day to remind her that, though I wasn't there, I was thinking of her and loving her.

Initially, she didn't have access to her iPad, so I sent the graphics to her mother's phone and asked if she had seen them. Some she had seen, but others she hadn't, leading me to suggest she ask her mother, or I could resend them. Each graphic shared my love, thoughts, jokes, cute animal pictures, biblical quotes, and memories of us.

I also began recording weekly video messages for her to see my face and hear my voice, as well as short audios, while working through health challenges to maintain this connection.

When health kept me from making new content, I created a series of them at once, preloaded graphics, videos, and audios to ensure continuity, no matter my circumstances. The breadth of this archive shows up in daily graphics, weekly audio messages, and weekly videos. All three types exist in my personal file-sharing archive. All three types are also distributed across public platforms designed as redundant fail-safes. A complete inventory of these titles appears in Appendix I.

The Multi-Platform Strategy

This approach to distribution reflects part of my core principle: transparency over secrecy, structure over spin. I've added the audios to a podcast for her that is hosted on a podcast distribution platform and available across several networks. Every audio message lives there beyond only being heard when sent in a text. If the file-sharing platform becomes inaccessible, compromised, or deleted, these audios still live and can be found in these distributed locations.

I established a YouTube channel containing all the video messages as well. The same redundancy applies. Videos stored in multiple locations cannot all be erased simultaneously.

I created and maintain an X page featuring the entire graphic archive. Each daily graphic message is available there, dated and documented. If someone stumbles upon these pages and finds encouragement, inspiration, or hope, I welcome that. But the primary function serves as a page specifically for her and the protection and preservation of these images from being deleted elsewhere.

> *"Consistency can persevere through access restrictions and deletions. Presence can survive the time and distance. Multiple platforms can secure the content from calculated attempts to remove it."*

To me, this is responsible strategic planning. This is documentation. This is clarity over comfort.

When messages disappear, when gifts don't arrive, when letters vanish, when access is restricted, my only recourse is to ensure backup systems exist. The stakes are too high to rely on a single pathway.

The file-sharing platform archive is built into my legal will. Instructions specify that if I'm no longer present, this digital collection transfers to her through designated trustees, with follow-up notifications scheduled to ensure that not a single item is deleted, moved or blocked. She deserves access to these materials not because she might want them all now, but because someday, I believe she will.

The complete inventory of this digital archive appears in Appendix I, with every graphic, audio, and video listed by number and title. I'm not saying to read each one, but if a reader has an interest in the themes and topics to perhaps create this type of content for a child, they are available there.

The Resistance and Persistence

Not every day brought reception. At one point, when she asked me to stop sending graphics, I complied and paused direct texting to her, while continuing to make them and update the social sites, podcast, and file-sharing archive. When she asked them to resume, they resumed. I remained aware that external influences, particularly from her mother, were likely shaping those decisions.

And it wasn't three days before she said she missed them and wanted them sent again.

Faith as Foundation

What sustained this practice was faith. Not certainty, but a choice to believe that love persists at moments when it seems rejected. I've found that presence can exist without physical proximity, that God's design for fatherhood transcends circumstance.

I prayed over many of these messages. I prayed during the health challenges that made production difficult. I prayed that, despite the barriers and her mother's deliberate interference, she would recognize the consistency of a father's love. Prayer became the practice that held my intention steady when results seemed nonexistent.

Structure over Spin. Love over Anger.

These principles meant I didn't attack. I didn't retaliate when access was restricted by Anya. I didn't send any sad or guilt-inducing messages when Zoey was distant. I do not work that way, and I would not disrespect my daughter in that way. I made them. I sent them. I saved them. I persisted. I believe this is a persevering structure that contains a tone of consistent love instead of allowing anger to distort it.

A Direct Address to My Daughter

These messages, graphics, audios, and videos are one way our connection has been chronicled, both together and apart. They sit alongside the stories, records, and efforts described throughout this book, which were organized during illness, financial strain, and distance, all with the intention of protecting truth and keeping you close in the ways that were still available to me.

They do not claim to capture every part of our relationship; they exist to show that, every day, I reached out to you, to share a message that you could open in a single moment or return to later, and to hold a place where you could see that you remained part of my daily life, whether we spoke that day or not.

Should you read this when you're older, you may come to understand that the volume of messages is secondary to what they represent. I thought of you every single day. When distance or your schedule limited contact, when your mother restricted access, and when you felt unsure about wanting these messages, I continued creating and assembling this archive, not to demand appreciation, but to keep a steady line of connection available to you with messages made for a moment and shaped to remain accessible for years to come.

If I'm no longer here when you reach this part of the story, these materials are designed to become a voice that carries across time. They are intended to meet you on a day when you look for a reminder and also to give you many days to look back on when you want to see how steady this effort remained.

They include lessons meant for you to apply, jokes that will make you laugh, and memories shared to stir your heart. On some days, the pain of the distance, the situation, and the silence hurt, but this remained as a commitment for me to follow through for you, regardless of those conditions.

Take what is helpful to you and leave what is not. Know that they exist so you can see and hear that you were loved across distance and across the obstacles between us, and that your peace and future mattered more to me than my comfort in the present.

A Strategic Testimony

For fathers and mothers in similar circumstances, this practice may offer one possible path. A parent can choose a rhythm that matches personal capacity, a monthly graphic, a short weekly audio, or a simple video from time to time and still build a catalog of connection over the years. Each entry may become another reminder that care did not stop when contact seemed uncertain or limited.

For anyone feeling the ache of distance from someone they love, this digital gift basket may serve as a small reminder to start or to keep reaching out. I believe love does not require total access at all times. It does require consistency, though. It requires showing up on days when a response seems unlikely. For some, it may also mean building an archive across multiple platforms and preserving it in a legal will. Consistency can persevere through access restrictions and deletions. Presence can survive the time and distance. Multiple platforms can secure the content from calculated attempts to remove it.

Closing Thought

Across text messages sent daily, file-sharing archives, and multiple online platforms, more than one thousand pieces now exist, protected by redundancy and preserved in my legal will. My daughter can access any of them at any time, whether I am present or not. Her mother's interference failed to block them. Circumstances failed to stop them. They remain as permanent evidence that a father's love reached for his daughter every single day, regardless of barrier or response.

CHAPTER 55.
Sustained Peace Through Structure, Actions, and Patience

Opening Thought

Peace can gain more strength when it is applied in the middle of tension, distortion, and repeated denial, rather than only when life feels calm. It has a better chance of holding a steadier rhythm when it clears chaos, shows what is true, and guides healthier choices. This is the approach I am working to live out through words and deeds. It shapes my decisions, protects my daughter, and holds me to truth in the middle of the turmoil.

Growing awareness of the thoughts and words I wish Anya could hear has shaped how I see this season and the choices I have had to make. This story has formed over the past decade, with some material gathered and compiled over the past two years, put into book form over the past eight months, and organized as thoughtfully as possible. It had been challenging for me to envision a future with someone who tended to withdraw in the present.

I believe that those who are... unprepared to address difficult situations, unable to handle moments of tension and friction, unable to accept a view that is different from what they prefer, and not strong enough to face a problem straight on without redirection, deflection, denial, or hiding, will accomplish little, find limited happiness, and tend to feel unfulfilled.

I don't want to be unappreciated or disregarded, and I think few do. Still, standing strong and developing the strength to handle situations without requiring others to like, coddle, or agree can establish a sounder foundation for a person and their healthy growth.

As I look at Anya now, I see that the life she lives allows for a certain coddling, where her negative actions do not require addressing or repair. It seems this has given her the freedom to make her perception of reality feel more real than reality itself.

Small Incidents, Less Than Honorable Conduct

I've noted how Anya exerts unhealthy control over Zoey. At one point, during a visit, Zoey asked me, "Can I go into my home? Should I call? Should I go in because I have a key? Should I go in through the garage?" Her hesitations about accessing her own home gave me pause. There were also other incidents, such as criticizing the stethoscope.

After one of the surgeries, my doctors kindly sent Zoey a cute surgeon's outfit, complete with a gown, headpiece, and stethoscope. She declared herself Dr. Zoey, and for most of my surgeries, they would list Dr. Zoey on the surgery information boards at the hospital as one of the doctors. Zoey thought it was cool and it was one more way to connect while reducing her unrest about all the procedures I had to have.

After she got the care package with all the items, later that night on FaceTime, she shared that Anya had mentioned, while she was getting dressed up, "It's a cheap stethoscope." I do not understand why that had to be said, or what purpose such a comment served in Anya's mind. It baffled me that, in that moment of connection, she still seemed inclined to undermine it.

There was also an intriguing moment of passivity when I received a text early in the morning while I was visiting Zoey for her birthday, and when she was with me, asking, "Can you please wish Zoey a happy birthday and tell her I love her?" I questioned what might be preventing her from making a phone call or asking straight out, "Can you have her call me?" It seems there's a strange reluctance. Why not ask to speak with her? And I would not stop her from doing that, though the same can't be said for Anya. It was as if she wanted to use my not passing the phone to Zoey and only relaying the message as a potential rationale for her own future actions of blocking my access, mirroring her past behavior on holidays.

It felt as though she was playing another game, preferring to use this text to her advantage at a future date and giving her a reason for not connecting me to Zoey when I request to speak to her on holidays or special occasions. The approach came off as childish and awful to me. I handed the phone to Zoey and said, "Call your mother. She wants to say happy birthday." This was also the second year in a row that Anya chose this approach.

I refuse to participate in the ongoing behavior Anya seems to prefer, and I won't block her access to Zoey as she has blocked mine multiple times.

> *"Patience, for me, has become the work of deciding whether it is the best moment to speak up or the better moment to write it down, knowing that a clear record can do more than a heated exchange ever will."*

Often, it feels like Anya's thoughts and statements are shaped more by an unhealthy desire for control and the image she wishes to convey than by their effect on Zoey. Her handling of several situations seems more negative than helpful. She often carries substantial frustration and perhaps lacks wisdom in these moments, choosing anger and ego over kindness and consideration. I've been put in the position of defending some of Anya's actions to Zoey, including her forgetfulness and her tendencies to misstep and misremember when she's been drinking. She tells Zoey conflicting information, forgets promises she made, and then claims they were not made.

I've told Zoey, "If you're sure she said it, you can try to gently explain when she said it and see if you can jog her memory." Still, in certain circumstances, it may be best to let it go and accept that she may be pulling the "Mom card" and will not back down. I advise Zoey to assess each situation and work on improving her approach for now.

Sometimes, if she chooses to stand her ground, it may not help her and may result in punishment. These are the types of conversations and problem-solving tactics we have to discuss, as they seem to parallel those used with individuals grappling with alcohol or drug problems. This dance around Anya's denials and memory issues should not be one a child has to learn.

I've thought about the ideas I have shared with her about choosing the right moments to address an issue or concern and the best moments to let it go. My experience, particularly in a proving-ground approach while I was living with Anya and dealing with what was or wasn't said, what was or wasn't forgotten, and the contradictions, inaccuracies, and attacks, came down to an analysis of the situation, Anya's state at that moment, whether she had been drinking, her posture, tone, and presence, as well as the tempo, volume, choice and style of her words.

With all those elements in mind, for me, it came down to one question with two choices: **is it the right moment to speak up, or is it the right moment to write it down?**

I've also shared this approach with Zoey, not for her to track her mother, but for her to learn more about how her mother operates, allowing Zoey a better understanding of the most effective times to get her points, concerns, and wants across in a way that will be seen, heard, and considered.

I've also posed this second question for both myself and Zoey... Given the specific situation, issue, or person: **is it the best moment to be right, or is it the best moment to make it right?**

Stepping back has felt like extending undeserved grace to a woman who has not earned it and is not equipped to handle conflict, contradiction, or being caught sharing false statements. Still, choosing to improve the moment rather than press it, especially when Zoey is in the right, sometimes means setting aside what is deserved in favor of what will land best.

What good does it do for Zoey to try to make her case with someone who is in a state of denial or in a mode where she will not be contradicted by a child, especially if that child is right?

I've considered Zoey's patience and when it might be best for her to be quiet, give in for the time being, or listen to her mother's words, when they don't seem fair, are flat-out wrong, or contradict what she was told previously. I think about how this patience, endurance, and understanding might serve her later that day or the next as she tries to resolve the issue at hand.

Sometimes, it seems Anya's approach is less about nurturing a child and more about training for loyalty, disregarding Zoey's point of view, understanding, and intelligence, and pushing the pressure-laden message, "I am the mother, I am right, and I will not be argued with."

I have long believed that some of the unhealthiest communicators don't have regrets; they have explanations to support their views, without considering how their actions can harm others. I feel that she may not fully understand how her actions could affect Zoey, potentially harming her emotional growth and introducing unnecessary agitation and tension into her life.

Having to troubleshoot with her on FaceTime about options that focus on stepping back and assessing her mother's state and behaviors in that moment, to determine if Zoey can express her wants and feelings without concern for repercussions, is unfortunate and detrimental to her. She deserves so much more.

Love as a Decision, Not as a Feeling

We can either be bitter and broken, or we can choose to be better and blessed by doing the work that two healthy parents, focused on their daughter's best interests, should do. Communication can still improve. I would tell Anya, if she were reading this, that I still pray for you. I still love you because that is what I am commanded to do.

To be transparent, I will also state that I do not like your behavior. I do not like how you have treated me. I do not like how you treat Zoey. I do not like what you have denied. I do not like your drinking. I do not like your choice of lawyer. I do not like the unhealthy actions, attacks, behaviors, and traits you continue to display.

But I will love you for Zoey's sake, and I will love you with the hope that we can improve our communication for a better co-parenting situation and for Zoey to flourish.

This, in my view, falls into the 'write it down and not bring it up' category.

I believe that communication in this co-parenting situation can improve. Connection and understanding can improve. A healthy relationship between us can emerge from the smoke and dust of all of this. I wish that Anya could consider taking a small step in this direction.

Closing Thought

Actions speak. Structure and patience have done more for my peace than any apology or agreement I kept hoping would arrive. I continue to document what happens, guard my daughter's space, and stand on what can be shown, trusting that steady truth presented with care will carry more weight over time than the shifting stories around us.

CHAPTER 56.
Trust Deepened Through Grace and Compassionate Guidance

Opening Thought

Grace offered through clear, practical guidance can steady a child who is facing confusing topics alone. By answering direct questions about her body, explaining how new information can replace confusion, and showing her how to sort opinions, feelings, and facts, I aimed to replace silence and avoidance with understanding she can trust. The choices I made in these moments, explaining, listening, and preparing her for what others had left for later, became another record of how I protect her knowledge, her confidence, and her voice.

Compositions can change dramatically with the presence of a new note that alters an entire melody. The arrival of my daughter did the same for my life, reshaping my role and deepening my resonance as both a man and a father. Watching her grow and communicate, first as a nonverbal child expressing herself fully through her eyes, gestures, touch, and hugs, has made me feel especially blessed. The journey has had its difficulties, especially over the couple of years, due to the physical distance between us. During this most recent visit, I felt our connection deepen in ways I hadn't anticipated, which helped me feel closer to Zoey than ever.

                    Calling Out the Shadows

We shared so many beautiful moments. I had been present in Zoey's life every day for most of her life, until distance separated us. This visit felt particularly special and meant more to me. I arrived with some apprehension about the timing, as I had been told I had to be there by a specific time or she would be put to bed. After quickly getting off the plane, which arrived on time, and getting into the shuttle 20 minutes later, I arrived at the rental car and was on my way to Zoey within about half an hour of landing.

The hug we shared was filled with warmth and love. I could feel our connection; she melted into my arms, expressing concern for my health. It felt as if no time had passed at all. After we checked into our place for this visit together, she explored the space, and I shared some of her birthday gifts with her a couple of days early. We went to dinner, and our conversations moved effortlessly. She expressed how much she missed me and how happy she was to have me there. Then she began asking direct questions about topics that confused or concerned her. I was having an insightful conversation with my daughter, someone I love dearly, but also with a friend, an equal.

She is significantly articulate, empathetic, and aware for her age, a true problem solver, sharp, and bright. It was impressive to see how much she has observed and pieced together for herself, especially regarding the divorce and what she has figured out on her own without being told.

A Gift For Preparation

Whether it was Anya avoiding it, forgetting about it, or concluding that Zoey would have her first period much later, I disagreed with the "wait until later and shove it under the rug" approach.

As her pediatrician shared, many girls are getting their periods much earlier. I had done some research on the topic and read about several cases in which girls were not ready, embarrassed, unprepared, or unsure of what to do.

One of the gifts I had for her was a first-period bag, and I took the lead on discussing it since it hadn't been explained or talked about with her mother. We sat on the bed, and I explained that if it felt too awkward, she could take it to her mother to discuss.

She wanted to talk to me about it, and she said she felt comfortable discussing it with me. I showed her the contents of the bag, which included baby wipes, extra underwear, a plastic bag for the underwear she would have been wearing, liners, and pads. I explained what each item was for and reassured her that it was a regular part of life.

We discussed how it might feel, emphasizing that it might not hurt much but rather be uncomfortable and annoying, and that each woman's experience can differ. She was engaged and eager to learn more, appearing more relaxed about it. I showed her how to keep the bag in her backpack and what to say to a teacher or adult to be dismissed to use the bathroom, and how to handle the situation discreetly. I also encouraged her to discuss it with her mother, since she had experienced it firsthand, but she said she was happy to go over it with me again.

How Babies are Made and Communication

We also touched on how babies are made and how women get pregnant. A few weeks earlier, realizing it still hadn't been discussed, I decided to answer her directly via FaceTime. I was grateful we went over it together; it brought connection and clarity. I had previously taken a backseat, figuring Anya would have covered this by now, only to find it was another topic left for later or not discussed at all. This is far too common, and one cycle I intend to break to ensure Zoey knows what she should and how to get answers to her questions.

Our discussions then turned to communication and her mother. She started asking many questions, and I shared my observations and thoughts, explaining that sometimes we must navigate the situation at hand, carefully weighing the pros and cons of addressing potential problems and concerns. I emphasized the importance of knowing when to speak up and when to listen, and of distinguishing between opinions, feelings, and facts. It was a valuable experience for both of us, filled with clarity, sadness, and happiness. We connected on a new and deeper level.

> *"Conduct in difficult moments is what I hope my daughter observes, especially when I am faced with words or actions that present a challenge. May she notice that my responses are shaped by forgiveness and love."*

On her birthday, she expressed her wish to stay with me the next night. While she looked forward to her birthday dinner with her mother, she was also aware that I would soon be leaving for my flight back and upcoming surgeries. She wanted to find a way to stay connected with me as long as possible while I was there. She decided to ask Anya if she could come back after dinner and spend one more night with me, though that was not part of our scheduled visit.

I saw Zoey quickly tense up once she made the decision, from her posture to the tightness in her face, seemingly concerned that Anya might disagree and say no. I've seen that same strain on FaceTime many times, a shift in her voice and a change in her presence, especially when Anya's conflicting statements come up. Still, I reassured her that it wasn't about one-sided permission or the outcome, but about being open to hearing the answer. Then, Zoey could either accept the answer or decide on her next step.

The following morning, after Zoey's mother had texted me to tell Zoey happy birthday, I gave Zoey the phone to call her. The conversation quickly shifted to Zoey requesting another sleepover. I heard her frustration from the other room as her mother repeatedly denied her requests. Still, I was impressed by how Zoey stood her ground, trying to find solutions by suggesting alternatives, such as, "I can open the presents at my birthday party on Saturday," and "Daddy is only here until tomorrow; I have to spend as much time with him as I can." The response was a barrage of no after no from Anya.

After the call, I comforted Zoey and expressed my pride in her for standing up for herself. I offered to help her write an email to her mother and watched her become energized about the idea. We carefully composed it together, I explained what we hoped to accomplish and why approaching it this way would be considerate, and then we sent it.

An Additional Birthday Gift for us Both

After I brought her back home for dinner with her mother, I received an email from Anya stating she could spend an extra night with me. She explained that she didn't have to send Zoey with me and had sent my earlier email to her lawyer. Anya claimed she was giving more than she had to, allowing the arrangement only because Zoey had asked. If this were true, why had she turned down Zoey's requests that morning several times, only to change her mind after getting the email?

I was getting the extra night, and I wasn't going to risk a comment or question that might prompt Anya to pull some trick or questionable move at the last minute. She had done this before, so I went quiet. She has shown she doesn't respond well to being called out, and I had no idea what she might try.

Later that night, when I was getting ready to pick Zoey up, I reassured her that I would be ready as soon as she was. I parked down the street to avoid any conflict and sent her a text letting her know I was nearby and available. She had sent four messages asking where I was and wanting reassurance that, as soon as her mother allowed, I could pick her up without delay.

I arrived 10 seconds after Zoey texted, as I had promised her. She came running outside, beaming and full of joy for one more night together. Pride showed on her face as she got in the car. She stood her ground, and when that didn't work, we worked together to achieve the desired result. I explained how proud I was of her as we headed back to the rental.

After she filled me in on her birthday dinner and some of the gifts she received, she started to raise observations about her mother and asked direct questions, which I addressed with care.

She expressed concern about some of her mother's behavior, saying, "I think Mommy is mean to you and plays dirty, you should respond the same way. You don't have to be so nice." I told her I don't engage in those kinds of tactics, and that I don't want her to do so with anyone either. I explained that I try to write every email or text response to Anya with the understanding that she might see them one day.

Honorable conduct in difficult moments is what I hope my daughter observes, especially when I am faced with words or actions that present a challenge. May she notice that my responses are shaped by forgiveness and love. Above all, may she understand that she is my most significant influence, my greatest inspiration, and the heartbeat of all my words, intentions, and actions, both in spirit and in purpose.

The Next Morning

We talked, laughed, and cried together over breakfast before dropping her off at school and saying goodbye. I gave her one last kiss, feeling light and filled with hope and love despite the physical pain I was in. Watching her grow more assertive, more communicative, and resilient fills me with love, faith, and hope. She is an outstanding girl who becomes more remarkable with each passing day. In the middle of all these challenges, I see Zoey choosing a better path for communication, problem-solving, and resolving issues. I couldn't be prouder. She is becoming the example of what I have been trying to show her all along.

Closing Thought

Compassion can grow when patience works quietly beside structure. Each step I take, guided by honesty and calm focus, creates a foundation for lasting progress with my daughter. Rooted in integrity, grace, and consistency, these actions become more than a reflection. They become a living example of healthy strength shaped by truth and love that she witnesses daily.

CHAPTER 57.
Strategy Rebuilt Through Christmas Denial and Documentation

Opening Thought

Rulings delivered on Christmas Eve cut across months of work and exposed what had been buried beneath procedure and delay. The court's refusals of my motions carried a heavy weight in that moment and led me to examine the filings, the documented behaviors, and the contradictions already on record with greater focus. That pause in progress left more time and space to show what had been happening, to expand the exhibits, and to refine the response with greater detail and precision. Pain stayed present, but it began to share space with a better plan.

Positioned in a strong place, with filings that were detailed, honorable, ethical, legal, and fully compliant with the court's rules and procedures, I had done what was called for to present them in the strongest format possible. The short-term outcome fell short of what I had hoped. Games appeared to be in play, layered with what looked like misrepresentations, inaccuracies, and deliberate interference.

I was spending time with my daughter. We had a great sleepover the night before, and the connection was stronger than ever. Setting up this visit had presented challenges, but unlike the year before, when she was kept from me on Christmas Eve and Christmas Day, I was able to spend half of each of those days with her.

Late on Christmas Eve morning, I received an email from the courts while Zoey and I were getting a muffin and a drink at a local café. Waiting until after I returned my daughter to her mother before opening it would have been wiser.

In That Moment, Though, I Made a Different Choice.

I opened it. The email stated that my three motions, along with all the exhibits and requests I had submitted, were denied. The denial felt like a punch to the gut, to the face, to all of me. While staying engaged with my daughter as best I could, I continued reading portions of the decision.

Such disappointment arose in me, and I worked to conceal it. Still, my daughter noticed and asked what happened. She told me she could see the tension in me. At ten years old, she reads people well. I told her a significant matter I had been working on didn't turn out fairly.

After collecting myself, I let it go and refocused on her. Being with my daughter helped my mind, my heart, and my spirit. We had a great afternoon together, shared lunch, and did some shopping before I brought her back home for her Christmas Eve time with her mother.

Emotions erupted afterward. I got back to where I was staying and fell to my knees in prayer. Not some dramatic claim; I went to my knees and was weeping. I was crying out loud to God.

What is this? Why is this happening? Why are you allowing this?

The questions kept pouring out. It appeared in the moment to be my breaking point. This negativity was taking the wheel. I couldn't see a clear path forward in the moment, though I also knew that quitting was not an option I would consider. As the early evening progressed, a shift started to occur. What seemed like a breakdown began to energize and lift me up to new clarity.

I took some additional time and examined what had been denied, as well as why. I read the order carefully several times. I brought it into an AI model to analyze the document, cross-reference the citations, look up the definitions on the court web pages, and understand the specifics of the ruling and the reasoning behind it. I noted a change and a peace as my breathing slowed with my pulse, and questioning myself morphed into questions I started to write down, not the doubts about why this was happening anymore, but rather the questions about the next steps to take.

Initially, I questioned whether this was my fault. What had I done wrong? I took the time to analyze my approach. Did I miss this? Did I overlook that? What had escaped my attention? Where had I gone wrong with the research, the AI, the prompts, and the documentation I had created?

After spending that evening reviewing the order, I determined that morally, ethically, and legally, my filings were sound. The submissions, the process, and the tracking all seemed to have been handled correctly and compliantly. The incorrect part appeared to involve strategic maneuvering to delay and cause confusion. It seemed to come down to deliberate interference on the part of Anya and her lawyer.

The Denial Rested on Two Key Points

First, according to the denial, Anya was no longer working with this attorney and had not been since the divorce was finalized in the spring. This revelation confused me briefly. The order stated that she was not her attorney, which meant conversations should not have been happening, and that these filings should not have been sent to her lawyer. They should have been sent directly to Anya.

The second point concerned her address. I had been requesting an update to Anya's address several times because she continued to use the old one. I had asked for this information because I was shown, when troubleshooting earlier, that this could be an issue if not correctly addressed for filings.

I had sent previous communications about it to both Anya and her lawyer. I had referenced it in previous filings. I also submitted a supplemental statement stating that the court documents appeared to list one location, while the facts showed another.

This is where she was living. This is where I picked up and returned my daughter on the last four visits. This is where they no longer resided. This is where they had moved. This is where I was sending items to my daughter. The email evidence showed they were living at this new address.

The infuriating nature of these discrepancies began to bring an unexpected calm. I recognized the recurring behaviors Anya had used for an extended period.

I went to bed that night in the Airbnb I had rented while visiting my daughter. In my prayers, I asked for guidance. Do I leave this alone? Do I work on this? Do I lay out a response? What should I do? I would have my daughter at 3 p.m. the next day. I planned to make this Christmas Day special for her. What could I do to honor both priorities? That morning, I rose invigorated, inspired, and righteously upset. I made my plan of attack. I prepared breakfast, went to a café, and opened the denial order I had received.

Four Hours of Calm While Collecting and Organizing Information

On Christmas Day, for four hours straight in that café, I patiently prepared my counter-response. I studied more deeply than I had before. In this light, I began to see what she had done, what the attorney had done, which, from what I found, was unlawful.

What Anya's lawyer had done contradicted the court rules. I ran it through multiple AI models and cross-checked the denial against court laws, rules, and orders. This interpretation held.

This was the answer I had hoped for. It also appeared to be a common place where people make a significant error. They receive the answer they hoped for. They settle on that answer without digging deeper. My approach with the AI models was deliberate.

It was centered in humility and not trusting the first response I got because I liked it. It was about digging deeper and asking...

How could I misread this? How could I be mistaken about this? How could the AI model be mistaken about this? How could this be taken out of context? How could this come back and be used against me?

Each element and response came back confirming the same conclusion: that I was right.

The question then became, how do I correctly prove I'm right? How do I deliver these facts in the most effective way? My initial impulse was to work up the response, revamp the filings, and send them back on Christmas Day. That was my mind's desire in the moment. That was not a strategic or sound long-term plan.

Going through the logistics of what had happened and asking the deeper questions positioned me in a stronger place than before. The actions that led to these motions being denied were the same actions that would amplify some of the documented rule breaches I had already referenced in these motions.

The incidents. The infractions. The attempted delays. The inaccuracies. The games.

I looked at the bigger picture, and I thought about how I should respond with all that I had learned, as well as how it could best be seen by the court, and how someday it might be seen by Zoey.

So, instead of the instant gratification and immediate response, I listened to my heart. I thought about the strategy, the integrity, the steps to take, and how to take them. That led me to create an extensive AI prompt, the longest one I had built to date.

Rather than building the paperwork or editing the files, I took a different approach. I created a fresh prompt. I began finding additional reference material for the division, the district, and the county court to best position my next steps. I started putting together this new master prompt to rewrite, rebuild, and refile in the most responsible way. One that would show that I was not stepping down, not stepping back, and not allowing this to continue unchallenged, while also taking each step accountably and transparently. It became both an educational experience and an emotional one rooted in patience.

I began to examine a new method of sorts during these four hours and how to apply AI to assist me in a careful, extra-detailed way. This is how I will review each sheet that has to be refiled. This is how I'll build these additional exhibits on what had happened. In doing so, I was educating myself while reinforcing the evidence of the problems, the aspects of misrepresentation, and bringing to light some of the areas where I had long questioned Anya's attorney and where they showed up in this situation. I was able to put together a plan and a strategy. This wrapped up and established the baseline of my new prompt.

> *"Spotlighting the tactics behind these delays and stalls keep revealing more of her choices, the questionable actions, the inaccuracies, the contradictions, and the patterns she keeps trying to hide. Each one strengthens the record that shows how she chooses to operate."*

This prompt took into consideration all that had been created and filed before, but also drew from more documentation, proof, and emails that highlighted how this was wrong. I saw a new foundation to update, as well as to create and resubmit these motions and exhibits, with elements that highlight and prove more wrongs. I felt a great relief, along with a stronger foundation under my feet than I had when I filed over a month back.

I shut my computer down at about 20 minutes to three. I saved it. I backed it up. I set it aside. Christmas morning and the early afternoon felt that much more productive because I was in that much stronger of a position now.

I left to pick up my daughter. She and I had the remainder of Christmas Day and a few more days together after that. It was a complete focus on her. I would not refer back to the case, and if I received any other emails, I would not open them.

I focused on my daughter as I felt a new calm and a fresh hope. Four days of daddy-daughter bliss followed.

Back to Work and Back to a New Drawing Board

After I left Zoey at her mother's on Sunday evening and headed out on my flight, I got to it. For the next few days straight, I put together these files, proved the points I had to make, and highlighted the contradictions from the court's denials.

What was stated and what was true conflicted. The order from the judge stated that this attorney was no longer her attorney and was not acting as her attorney. The emails I had showed otherwise. The emails documented that she had a meet-and-confer with me. The emails showed her responding to the initial request when I sought to cancel that first hearing.

She was also responding with the courts, which she was not allowed to do, according to the denial. A document should have come from Anya or from the attorney stating that the attorney was continuing to work with her. That notice was supposed to be sent. It wasn't.

What was being done appeared to contradict court rules.

I also had to exercise patience to set it up correctly. Rather than stating what is wrong, misleading, or unlawful, I chose to present the facts as the court would like to see them.

Here is what I found. Here are the inconsistencies. Here is what occurred. Here is the proof of it.

It required going through files and the documentation I had in place, collecting and organizing the emails, and assembling the material I had gathered. This included a great deal of double-checking, cross-referencing, and auditing on my part, as well as with the AI models, too.

I completed the bulk of the work on New Year's Eve. I hoped to have it done before the stroke of midnight. By New Year's Eve at 11 o'clock, I had the refiling ready and a plan on how to do it.

In the middle of this, and based on some of the prompt outputs, I incorporated a wait period because the denial included a requirement that Anya update her address. She had five days from the order to do so. I added in the holiday of New Year's Day, let that pass, and observed whether she would follow through. As expected, she didn't.

I lined up the documents; I checked them a few times, and though I am sure some errors may still exist, I was confident in what I was preparing to file.

This new super prompt, used with the AI models to build the refiling as well as the additional documents and exhibits, advised me to submit a three-part filing online the next Monday, followed by a fourth physical mailer that same day.

The three-part filing consisted of refiling the motion with additional exhibits that presented more of the problems, as well as addressing the issues with the denial, along with new issues. The denied motion included the original past three years of incidents and infractions. Since filing that, the AI models have helped me develop an updated system for tracking and documenting issues.

I presented both options: the last three years and the last 30 days.

I added an updated incident report so they could see what had occurred. I included the elements about the attorney, the ways this attorney was still working and should not have been, and I showed through court records that this documentation regarding an address update did not come through.

I reinforced the filings. I updated the documents. I prepared the submissions.

That Monday morning, I was filing the motions simultaneously:

1. through the online e-file system for the court;
2. sending an email with a zip file of the motions and exhibits directly to Anya.

And at the same moment, with another email window open...

3. I filed a complaint against the attorney with the bar of
    that state to explain actions that appeared to contradict
    legal standards.

I intended a one, two, three sequence because part of what was being filed in the motions and sent to Anya would surely be sent to her attorney. The AI model advised me to set this up and release it in sequence: one, two, three, then the fourth step.

The fourth step was a physical delivery of the motions to two addresses. The idea was to send it to the address where she lives via certified mail and to the old address listed on the court documents. Two full files, certified mail, priority, sent out.

Two Envelopes, One Strategy

As part of the refiling strategy, the AI guidance recommended not only electronic filing through the court system and direct email to Anya, but also physical certified mail delivery. Given the confusion about her attorney's status and ongoing address discrepancies, the recommendation was to mail copies to both addresses, including the old address still listed with the court and the current address where she lives.

These motions, with cover pages and key exhibits, exceeded 600 pages in total. Printing and shipping two complete sets would cost more than I was prepared to spend. After reviewing what had to be included, I determined that I could send the three core motions along with the lead exhibits that referenced the remaining documentation. That reduced each mailing to approximately 100 pages, down from over 600.

More Denials, but This Time Helping My Case

I sent both packages via certified mail the same day, two hours after the online filings. One went to the old address listed in court documents (the one right next door to where Anya currently lives). The second went to her current address.

As anticipated, the package sent to the old address was returned with the mark "addressee unknown." According to the tracking information, it was delivered to that location but was denied. Those neighbors could have accepted it and brought it next door. I can't prove what happened, but I believe Anya told people in advance not to accept correspondence addressed to her at that location. As advised, I checked the box on both the certified mail packages so that anyone could sign for them.

The second package, sent to her current address, arrived when she was likely home, according to my daughter's schedule. According to the tracking, no one answered the door. A notice was left stating the package could be picked up at the post office within a certain timeframe.

I expected she would not pick it up. I expected it would be returned. This delay allowed Anya to avoid receiving the physically refiled motions while I waited patiently for the process to complete. She didn't respond to the email I sent with the attached motion either. The old address package was returned as undeliverable. The current address package was also returned. I received a text saying it was not picked up after numerous attempts to deliver it, and notices for her to have it either redelivered or to pick it up from the post office were ignored.

The Cost and the Purpose

Every step I take documents the delays and tactics that come into play with Anya. Every returned package, every ignored email, and every delay becomes one more exhibit demonstrating how she operates.

I am not trying to write a lengthy narrative to prove she is a bad person in the motions and exhibits. That is not the point. The goal is to document the themes and consistent actions that run counter to the parenting plan and to the court's requirements of her. By doing this correctly, compliantly, and patiently, I can continue to shine a brighter spotlight on how this woman chooses to operate.

Now, her games with these physical mailings provide one more piece of evidence of less-than-honorable behavior and her determination to avoid what she doesn't want to face.

This is not finished, but I am making sure my choices keep my daughter as my priority, not an option. Maybe I was not meant to be a boyfriend, a fiancé, or a husband, but I know I was meant to be a father, and more so, her father. And in that, I will act patiently, compliantly, and correctly, regardless of what gets thrown at me.

Closing Thought

Setbacks tied to that Christmas denial did not end this effort; they reshaped how I moved forward. Rebuilding the filings, organizing exhibits, documenting each delayed delivery, and filing a complaint with the bar turned those stalls into proof that showed more of what had been happening. The focus has not been on attacking character, but on recording repeated choices, documented conduct, and specific departures from required standards. That delay also created the space for more of my former wife's actions to be registered and recorded in the filings.

CHAPTER 58.
Praying She Recognizes Her Patterns Before It's Too Late

Opening Thought

Weighing what my daughter shared about her mother and their connection, I felt the weight of her words. She described distance, walls, and arguments that echoed what ended our marriage. Our daughter is now on the receiving end of what I once lived through, and seeing it reach her cuts deeper than it ever did with me. The behaviors are practically identical, and if they continue, the distance between them will keep growing. I can pray for her to change, but I cannot make someone see what they have spent years determined not to face.

Recalling the final moments of the most recent visit with my daughter, my heart was full. Our time together had been beautiful: real connection, effortless laughter, honest conversations, and so much love. Yes, court matters arose during the trip, but I addressed them when we were apart. Every moment with her was sacred. She deserved my full attention, my complete presence, all of me.

Throughout the visit, my daughter sought clarity about what was true and what wasn't. She asked questions. I provided answers in the gentlest way I could, presenting age-appropriate evidence to address her observations. She was the one asking and wanting more, wanting to see, wanting to understand.

It was hard at times to speak positively about a person who has been so ruthless. At certain moments, I was more straightforward based on what I knew my daughter could handle; at other times, I did sugarcoat some, not intending to mislead her, but not wanting to distance her from her mother.

On the final day of our visit, she struggled with conflicting emotions pulling her in different directions, not wanting to leave me, but also wanting to go home, then feeling bad for wanting to go home. In those emotionally complex moments, she began sharing more about her mother, opening up with far greater detail than she had throughout the rest of our time together.

A Ten-Year-Old's Observations

"I can't talk to her the way I talk to you," she said. "I don't feel close to her like I do with you. I don't think I could share the same way with her. She doesn't listen. She doesn't hear me. She won't hear me."

Zoey went on to describe so many barriers. Many sounded like the same walls, the same distance, and the same kinds of communication breakdowns I experienced. The unhealthy behaviors I had hoped were directed only at me are now affecting our daughter. She's being kept at arm's length by someone who should be drawing her closer.

"Repeated patterns that broke Anya and me apart are now showing up between her and our daughter, creating the same distance, the same walls, and the same communication breakdowns I experienced."

I told Zoey she may be able to help bring those walls down with her mother in time. I believe she might become a catalyst for her mother to learn better, healthier communication:

To connect by staying open.

To hear another perspective without deciding its intention and meaning first.

To listen before responding.

To choose connection over being right.

Zoey's clarity and introspection cut through as she continued to share. "I don't want another you. I don't want her to be exactly like you. She doesn't have to be exactly like you. But if she communicated like you, it could be so different and so much better."

At ten years old, she was already seeing the difference between communication that connects and communication that creates distance. She recognized and shared that many of our conversations remain peaceful, regardless of what we discuss, while a great many of her interactions with her mother quickly turn into arguments. She also shared a resentful response, saying she didn't want to listen because she doesn't feel heard.

Recognition Without Resolution

Zoey continued to talk about her issues and feelings of disconnection with her mother. She made clear this wasn't only about her not getting the time with me that her mother has denied, controlled, and reduced, and that it also wasn't about her own behavior. She stated that her mother requires a different approach when she tries to talk to her, and one she doesn't understand or like. Then she shifted. She asked, "Am I communicating the wrong way?"

"No," I told her. I suggested she organize her thoughts, perhaps write them down, and prepare them for a letter or a conversation when she's ready to share them. Not right away, but when the time comes that feels right for her. Perhaps it could be a segue so that if or when her mother asks her why she doesn't communicate, Zoey might have more clarity about what to say.

Zoey said she was uncomfortable with that. She explained that she has tried to bring up experiences, examples, and behaviors, including how she looks at specific events or incidents and how it feels to her when her mother says or responds as she does. Zoey went on to say that it feels too hard for her mother to consider her view and that her mother only sees what she wants to see.

Zoey explained that she does not feel seen, heard, or respected. It was heartbreaking to hear, not only because of what she is going through in the moment, but also because I know exactly what that feels like from her mother.

The difference, though, is that I could get away from it. I could distance myself from her. Zoey can't. It brought me to tears for her and for what she's going through, as well as realizing that her mother is now having this effect on our daughter, and if you asked her, she would deny it, as she denied so many of the same issues regarding communication I had with her.

I listened in total amazement as my daughter, this beautiful, intelligent girl, was identifying both healthy and unhealthy adult-level relationship behaviors. She also recognized her mother's jealousy of our bond. She has observed inconsistencies between her mother's words and actions. She's witnessing so many issues and unhealthy aspects while still developing strong communication skills, learning to identify problems, and deciding when to bring them up and when it's easier to stay quiet.

The Behaviors Repeating

I've heard some close to me share throughout this process that these circumstances would draw my daughter closer to me and push her farther from her mother. That prediction brought no satisfaction.

I don't desire her mother to hurt or lose connection. I desire accountability. I desire change. But I'm not pursuing harm.

I am not jealous of Anya's relationship with Zoey, and I am not trying to be the favorite.

I am praying that her mother can soften her heart, learn to communicate differently, and identify the problems that create this distance between her and Zoey. Repeated patterns that broke Anya and me apart are now showing up between her and our daughter, creating the same distance, the same walls, and the same communication breakdowns I experienced. I pray she finds humility and begins recognizing the behaviors she's denied, dismissed, and chosen not to acknowledge.

I'm less concerned about strengthening my own connection with Zoey. In this distance and in this struggle, what Zoey and I have is solid, stable, loving, and transparent. But I also desire my daughter to have a meaningful relationship with both parents. I believe that for my daughter's well-being, she requires healthy co-parenting examples from two positive models.

As for my former wife and the behaviors I've endured, I'm done.

I do not wish that disconnection on my daughter, though. Still, if her mother continues with a rigid, selfish, and unhealthy approach, an unwillingness to see her own behaviors, and this insistence on maintaining appearances rather than reality, she'll lose our daughter the way she lost me.

When Anya lost me, she could easily dismiss it, as she has dismissed so much that doesn't fit in her world. She could rewrite the narrative. With me being away physically, she could send me away in her mind and assign all the fault to me and elsewhere. But how could she do that with our daughter? Or perhaps she could. Perhaps the same mechanisms that allowed her to erase my perspective could also lead her to dismiss our daughter's voice.

I pray that doesn't happen. I pray she can wake up. I pray my daughter can present these observations in ways that invite dialogue and potentially lower the barriers her mother has constructed. If those walls can come down, my daughter's walls may be able to come down too, and Zoey can build the connection she desires with her mother.

If circumstances continue in this direction, I wouldn't fault my daughter for protecting herself, for raising her own walls higher, creating distance, and stepping back from someone who requires complete control, rejects different approaches, and is unable to hear another view that contradicts her narrative.

Leaving Out the Rest for Peace and Rest

There is far more I chose not to include. Much of it is far worse than what is in these pages.

Some of it would have felt good to write, but it would not have served the story. Some of it could have identified my former wife directly and without question. Some of it I set aside to protect my daughter, and the rest I have let go of for my peace.

Present Connection

Through all this, Zoey and I talk more by phone and FaceTime on any given week than many parents and children who live under the same roof. The conversations may be physically miles apart, but it often feels like she is right next to me. Some days she calls four or five times, with some talks running longer and others being quick hellos or small updates.

My commitment remains focused on getting back to her, being with her, and being there for her. I notice how she is listening more, understanding more, and seeing more, all without me sharing the details. She is seeing it on her own and increasingly questioning and unraveling inaccuracies.

She is holding herself to standards not set by her mother and working at a level of accountability that continues to impress me. While I still feel at times like I am failing and falling, at least I am falling forward, closer to getting back to her each day.

Closing Thought

Accepting that my purpose is greater than my comfort, I will work toward healing, whether my former wife's heart softens or not, whether she chooses repair or walks away from it. My daughter deserves parents who communicate, to be heard by both, and to see her well-being placed above all parental conflict, held in steady love and devoted presence.

CONCLUSION.
Standing on Truth, Love, Guidance, and Resolve

Opening Thought

New beginnings can arise from lessons fully absorbed, especially when gratitude is leading the way. Through these lessons, compassion can deepen, understanding can widen, and forgiveness can lift what conflict once buried. This moment does not mark an ending but a larger beginning shaped by gratitude, care, and a light I pray will continue forward.

Gratitude fills my thoughts as I complete these reflections. My path as a father has shown me that strength grows not from defiance but from humility, especially during uncertain times. In the shadows, I sought ways to nurture, forgive, and build a foundation that could endure beyond my own story.

As I conclude this book, I address my daughter, knowing it may be several years before she reads it in full. I also speak to all who may find comfort, guidance, or companionship in these pages.

I believe that by identifying patterns, traits, and challenges, we gain a healthier perspective instead of dissecting individuals. This allows us to clear away confusion and respond with greater care. We can learn what to carry with us now, what to set aside for later, and what to leave behind.

Within these pages, some stories may help readers recognize warning signs and choose new paths in communication and problem-solving, whether with family, friends, colleagues, or present and future partners.

I am grateful for the opportunity to share these thoughts, hoping they may one day provide help or clarity. Other readers may recognize patterns sooner, choose healthier paths and healthier relationships, or find comfort in knowing that survival and hope can coexist on complex journeys when challenging people remain present.

Reflections for Zoey

Remember that you are your own person. You have your mother, you have me, but you also have yourself. You are stronger, wiser, and more powerful than you may realize. You possess a strength rooted in understanding and awareness, with a heart overflowing with compassion and empathy. I encourage you to nurture your mind, heart, and strength every day. As you look ahead, know these words come from endless love, deep care, and a belief in who you are now and who you will become.

Reflections for Zoey about Anya

Please understand that this book aims not to diminish your mother but to share my experiences with honesty and in a context that supports healing and understanding. My relationship with your mother was challenging for me, though your relationship with her may differ. While I may not fully grasp the reasons behind her choices and actions, I hope you come to understand what happened more fully. This awareness may help you recognize warning signs and communicate more effectively when facing difficulties involving your mother or anyone else in your life.

If troubling traits emerge during conversations or confrontations with your mother, remember that they do not define you. They may originate from her, whether related to matters of heart, mind, or circumstance, but they do not diminish your character or identity. I hope this book can serve as a guide, a map, and a compass to help you navigate tense situations and confusing moments, whether with your mother or others you encounter in the world.

I hope the seeds of peace and healing reach Anya. I pray that humility helps her recognize her less-than-positive patterns and, in time, allows her to act with kindness and refrain from passing on some of those hardships to you. I pray that any pain within her may be eased, helping her grow into a loving and kind woman who shares honesty and warmth with each person she meets.

> *"Remember that you are your own person. You have your mother, you have me, but you also have yourself. You are stronger, wiser, and more powerful than you may realize."*

Despite her anger, distance, and the challenges of the past and present, I wish her healing, personal growth, and lasting happiness. No matter what she has done or continues to do, I pray for her peace and a healthy mind every morning and night. May she find a harmony that allows for honesty in her actions, words, and communication, marked by love and trustworthiness.

Reflections for Others

To those amidst chaos, dealing with erratically shifting individuals, I have some understanding. I may not know your exact situation, but if you relate to this story and the challenging person described, I can empathize with some of the chaos and strain you face. You may encounter those who appear one way but suddenly shift to anger, resentment, and negativity, seemingly turning into entirely different people. They often struggle to see perspectives beyond their own and cannot handle tension-filled situations. Cooperation, compromise, and consideration may be foreign to them.

I am sorry you are experiencing that.

I wish for your resolve, renewal, and release from the pain and pressures placed upon you. I also pray not only for those facing challenges but for those who may be the source of that difficulty.

I pray for those who act with malice, selfishness, or arrogance toward others facing similar or worse situations. This includes those who have tried to break, mislead, or harm others due to their own issues, sickness, or darkness.

May their hearts soften, the burdens they carry be lifted, and the shadows yield to truth, understanding, and light. I ask that they be held accountable and guided to honor the truth instead of trying to shape a narrative to fit their desires. I pray they are drawn toward healing and given opportunities to make amends and help restore peace to those they have hurt.

Two Sets of Requests

I offer two collections of requests for Zoey and others who may find them helpful:

The Twenty-Four Seeds of Guidance and The Principles of Authentic Connection and Character. Born from years of learning through grace and hardship, they aim to guide a strong and healthy way forward.

The Seeds focus on emotional grounding and enduring hope, encouraging personal responsibility to bring them to life. The Principles provide practical tools for cultivating integrity, creativity, genuine relationships, and the courage to stand on a foundation of truth and honor.

I divided the Principles into seven groups for clarity, making it easier to revisit them in daily life or during times of growth, change, calm, or challenge. Together, these lists aim to inspire emotional strength, meaningful connections, and personal growth, serving as a guide for living and relating authentically.

I began writing these lists as a letter to my daughter, meant to serve as a companion throughout her life. These are personal requests intended to guide reflection, encourage meaningful action, and nurture kindness, patience, and forgiveness. I hope she reads, applies, and returns to these requests often, finding meaning and direction in both peaceful and challenging times.

They are not for her alone.

I share them with anyone seeking to build, mend, or strengthen their foundations and relationships. May they bring clarity, understanding, and renewal through moments of change, uncertainty, or growth.

These lessons stem from years of conversations, observations, and experiences with people from various walks of life, as well as my personal journey with family and close relationships. They were shaped by both joy and hardship, by successes and mistakes, and by learning patience, empathy, and understanding through difficult moments.

These words are meant to be lived through consistent practice and follow-through, becoming wisdom in action rather than empty words of inspiration.

Rooted in humility, hope, and love, may these ideas nourish and strengthen character. May they light the way for an honest, open path forward through accountability, responsibility, and clarity.

Twenty-Four Seeds of Guidance

May these Twenty-Four Seeds of Guidance bring comfort, support, and clarity, leading all who read them toward love, resilience, and the continual awakening of light.

1. **May you find...** the courage to stand your ground when conversations become challenging.

2. **May you choose...** humility and patience to let certain matters ease for a moment, calming tensions, and

returning at the right time to address what was left unfinished.

3. **May you honor...** the difference between opinions and facts, remaining aware that the words you hear may not fully reflect the meaning intended by the speaker.

4. **May you ask...** for clarity, seeking understanding before forming conclusions.

5. **May you pursue...** open discussion that brings resolution or shared perspective, rather than focusing on winning a disagreement.

6. **May you recognize...** the qualities that define trustworthy companions, choosing to welcome those who demonstrate honor, humility, patience, and love through their actions.

7. **May you build...** relationships rooted in mutual encouragement, lifting each other up to create bonds of genuine support and shared strength.

8. **May you become...** someone who is counted on, matching every commitment made with action to follow through.

9. **May you act...** with conviction, allowing accountability and sincerity to guide your words and your actions.

10. **May you select...** roads that reflect your values, remaining steadfast when the journey is difficult or unpopular.

11. **May you focus...** on a path that highlights who you are, releasing the pressure to compete and choosing steady progress with each step.

12. **May you strive...** to reach beyond your expectations, honoring healthy boundaries while believing you are capable of more than you first imagined.

13. **May you discern...** and nurture the qualities, habits, and patterns that strengthen your life, while paying attention to those that require thoughtful care and extra time.

14. **May you establish...** a foundation of strong mental and emotional stability as you face each season of life.

15. **May you grant...** yourself time to process your thoughts, feelings, heart, and desires in healthy ways, and choose carefully whom to share them with or keep them from.

16. **May you address...** your emotions directly, allowing yourself to experience every joy and sorrow so that no feeling remains buried or unresolved.

17. **May you embrace...** forgiveness with faith and gentleness, letting go of anger and resentment so you can stand in the light despite any hardships that may come.

18. **May you observe...** how people, choices, experiences, and everyday details affect your mind, body, and spirit, helping you grow in wisdom, awareness, and compassion.

19. **May you recognize...** challenges that unsettle your heart, welcome the opportunity to reflect on them, and release what no longer serves you, finding peace through that growth.

20. **May you nourish...** your mind with curiosity, exploring books, music, poetry, food, and other discoveries. Embrace learning as a lifelong journey shaped by fascination rather than the pursuit of recognition.

21. **May you strengthen...** your connection with God, seeking comfort and wisdom through scripture, and finding renewal through heartfelt prayer and meditation.

22. **May you live...** in the light, guided by the radiance of love, choosing to remain beyond the shadows as you stay true to your path.

23. **May you love...** yourself wholeheartedly, recognizing the brilliance within, seeing how you shine brightly and bring warmth to those around you.

24. **May you feel...** comfort in the love I have for you and embrace the hopes and dreams that light your journey. Trust in the limitless good you bring, the fullness of who you are becoming, and the lives you will touch along the way.

Let these seeds continue to offer comfort, reassurance, and quiet wisdom. In times of challenge, when shadows fall, or moments feel unclear, consider returning to them for grounding, renewal, and the courage to stand in the light with hope.

Principles of Authentic Connection and Character

Following the seeds, I hope these principles offer a practical guide for honest living and genuine relationships. They are inspired by lessons learned and shared over time, as well as my studies in faith, communication, and philosophy. Each principle is intentionally added to help build clarity, integrity, and follow-through for wisdom, knowledge, and discernment.

Foundations of Character and Integrity

Demonstrate integrity and let it guide you. Stand firm on your principles, especially when no one is watching or offering praise.

Accept truth willingly. Embrace objective, substantiated, and well-vetted truth. Be known as one who doesn't waver from those facts in challenging times.

Allow truth to guide and shape you, instead of trying to control or redirect it to what you wish it to be.

Take full responsibility for your emotions and how you handle them. No one can make you feel a certain way unless you allow it. The choice is yours, so choose wisely.

Authentic Communication and Connection

Communicate mindfully, listening intently and caring for both words and the silences that follow them.

Share your feelings when issues arise to support positive engagement in problem solving for mutual resolution.

Honor your words. Be intentional, loving, and strategic, respecting their meanings while avoiding fillers and exaggeration.

Relationships, Boundaries, and Trust

Respect healthy boundaries, support your well-being, and honor others' limits.

Watch for inconsistency or insincerity. Build trust with those who match words with actions.

Value those who remain authentic and transparent, regardless of their surroundings.

Release relationships that do not support your growth or well-being. Make space for positive, genuine connections as you let go of those that no longer resonate.

Growth, Learning, and Curiosity

Cultivate creativity, welcome fresh ideas, and give new thoughts room to take shape and grow.

Seek companions who inspire curiosity, encourage exploration, and challenge your understanding.

Stay eager to learn. Approach every new experience as an opportunity for greater understanding.

Find fulfillment in both large and small efforts, bringing focus and dignity to each task.

Resilience, Presence, and Self-Care

Honor commitments and follow through. Speak up promptly if modifications become necessary.

Acknowledge your limits. Allow yourself to rest, reflect, or pause as appropriate.

Notice who remains steady in hardship. Appreciate the rare gift of reliable support during life's storms.

Let your presence radiate calm, patience, and peace, becoming a gentle influence and inspiration to those around you.

Discernment, Reflection, and Objectivity

Protect your emotional health by balancing openness with discernment, creating steady ground for your mind and heart.

Commit to periods of fasting, meditation, and silence. Unplug to renew and refocus. (Fasting includes more than food; consider electronics, people, etc.)

Prepare for being taken out of context. Organize your ideas and evidence with precision, anticipating situations where context and support may be required.

Be open to being an answer rather than claiming to be the answer. Remain humble and adaptable in your abilities and authority.

Question conclusions based on linear logic or popular opinion presented as fact; seek a fuller understanding with more evidence from a range of vetted sources.

Guard your wisdom and worldview. Be mindful of those who distort or omit objective information, while continuing to learn each day.

Recognize that expertise is a journey. One experience or success does not make someone an expert.

Personal Agency, Influence, and Self-Expression

Differentiate and prepare for when it's best to be right, or to make it right.

Focus on investing in information and education rather than chasing fleeting motivation or inspiration.

Shift your focus from dwelling on others' opinions to what brings you joy, peace, and fulfillment.

Take time to explore faith yourself without feeling pressured; approach it with an open mind to appreciate the richness that can be revealed if you are ready to see it.

I know there are more, but I will stop here.

Please keep these reminders close and revisit them as your journey unfolds. They can serve as markers for building a life of strength, connection, and kindness, regardless of how the road changes. Consider these seeds of guidance and principles as ideas that can grow stronger and more lasting over time, helping to shape the path ahead, and the light that reveals it.

By embracing these ideas and directions, you may find a clear path toward the life you wish to build and the people you want to welcome into it. Through reflection, I've found that some of the most meaningful results stem from small acts of patience, genuine listening, and choosing a steady path for love's sake.

In all of this, my hope is that love, presence, and faith continue to ripple outward, bringing light and a sense of belonging wherever your journey leads next.

Closing Thought

Resolution carries forward when truth, love, and clear intention remain at the center. That truth continues to guide me gently, and love leads each step with integrity. The lessons planted here are meant to grow through patient perseverance and commitment to clarity, transparency, structure, and love. These principles form the strongest foundation and the clearest light, guiding continuous progress in communication and relationships.

When resistance arises, strength and resolve can remain firm, grounded in the courage to stand against the comfort of laziness, the shadows of secrecy, the false allure of spin, and the corrosive pull of anger. I hope we all move forward with grace and consistency, honoring, healing, and nurturing all that endures as we walk in faith with hearts grounded in peace, hope, and love.

EPILOGUE.
Recasting Shadows to Protect Other Stories

Opening Thought

Awareness of how a personal letter to my daughter evolved into this book has shown me that vulnerability, humility, and mindful adaptation can transform pain into wisdom. What began as an effort to structure and protect my story gradually revealed the greater value in sharing this experience and its organization, which may help others protect, share, and reshape their own stories for release.

Initially conceived as a letter to my daughter, when I thought I might not be around much longer, this work evolved from a father's private words into a system others might use to protect and share their own stories. Through each challenge and revision, the process highlighted the importance of safeguarding both the storyteller and those whose lives intersect with the story. Developing methods to ensure clarity, compliance, and privacy became central to the work, not only for personal reasons, but to provide a path for those facing similar risks in their narratives.

I guided every word, decision, and change with intentional effort to ensure protection, minimize legal exposure, and maintain respect for all participants. Carefully vetted feedback, formal legal counsel, and input from a small group of trusted advisors helped shape my approach and became a core part of the protection strategy. By sharing some of these steps and choices, I hope to assist others who feel uncertain or apprehensive about telling their stories with honesty, protection, and care.

As this book progressed through later drafts, it became clear that my protection work does not end here. A significant part of this new mission is supporting others in similar situations who wish to share their stories, including those who have been concerned about repercussions for revealing issues that could benefit many others.

Through developing these new protection talks and strategy sessions, a focused aspect of my consulting and speaking, I have created a system to help others take the first steps and establish foundational elements for sharing difficult stories safely. This includes personalized blueprints and resources for individuals navigating their own journeys in this area of expression.

My experience has taught me the value of reviewing each word, framing statements with care, anticipating challenges, and seeking guidance from multiple perspectives.

Anyone considering creating, writing, recording, filming, or releasing a sensitive narrative may benefit from building a solid foundation in protection first. It is wise to seek input from trusted advisors, learn from legal and editorial professionals, and practice patience in rewriting or rephrasing any words or sections that may pose risks. Careful, strategic, and humble language selection not only serves the narrative, but can create space for healing, privacy, security, and growth.

This process requires putting ego aside and being humble enough to sanitize and neutralize elements that could lead to problems later.

Understanding the differences between intention and perception necessitates careful consideration. Some with the best intentions may wish to help, heal, and reveal in the most transparent and authentic ways. Still, they can sometimes overlook how their writing may be misunderstood or taken out of context.

This can deeply shape how their work is received. At times, some people may isolate particular words or sentences and turn those fragments against the author, creating obstacles and tension that make the person more hesitant to share.

Another sobering realization is that you could have all the facts, evidence, and truth on your side, objectively substantiated and organized. Still, those opposed to your story can find ways to cause problems.

Because of these risks, many choose not to share difficult experiences, despite the potential for positive change. Concerns about scrutiny, conflict, or consequences often keep these stories silent.

This silence may offer short-term protection but hinders resolution, understanding, and opportunities for progress. With proper safeguards and planning, those stories have a much better chance of emerging from the shadows, reaching the light, and being shared with intention, clarity, and confidence.

Opponents can create delays, make false claims, and embroil you in legal battles while draining your resources as you defend what is right. This is not meant to deter anyone from taking the next steps. Rather, it focuses attention on the stability, security, and humility of what you create to minimize risk while building a strong foundation to protect you and your work.

> *"With proper safeguards and planning, those stories have a much better chance of emerging from the shadows, reaching the light, and being shared with intention, clarity, and confidence."*

As I considered these elements, I worked to understand, strategize, and apply protection and humility to my story. While I dreamed of shouting the truth from the rooftops, I took a breath and recognized the potential consequences of not stepping back.

I saw how the story could be suppressed, my daughter could be prevented from seeing it, and legal opposition could arise. A range of issues, including legal, financial, and emotional ones, could have cost a fortune and kept this narrative in the shadows.

This is where the protection process and protection talks originated. After the first draft emerged with emotion, assertiveness, facts, and anger, I stepped back and began drafting a blueprint for sharing this with maximum protection, security, and stability. In response, the protection process and protection talks evolved into a subset of my speaking and consulting, which I call:

Protected Narrative Pathway Solutions

Clarity, Coverage, and Courage for Those Ready to Share.

This approach offers personalized blueprints and structured strategic planning to help individuals share their stories with security, humility, transparency, and authenticity. Guided by the lessons of my own experience, the book and these strategies invite both caution and confidence, honoring the nuances of each story brought to light.

I developed these strategies by consulting various professionals to test the foundation from different angles. I spoke with lawyers who understand intellectual property, media, and contracts, as well as editors and communication strategists. I consulted an insurance advisor, a digital security consultant, a risk management advisor, and a crisis communications group. I also spoke with a couple of psychiatrists who could identify the gaps I might miss. They all helped confirm the foundation and elements coming into place, while adding pieces to the puzzle I had not considered.

Many of these professionals want to help others protect their stories in the years ahead, and I hope to see that happen. I do not wish to be the sole source of this guidance. I hope this model will be adopted and expanded by professionals who can teach it as part of their work. As a network grows, more people may find support in sharing their stories so they are seen, heard, read, and understood.

This helped me strategize a broader plan for myself and others. The goal is to support a new sense of stability, security, and transparency while preparing to shift pieces for protection and inspire better amplification of those who have been pressured to keep the volume of their voices on the lowest settings.

While this approach is not foolproof, I aim to help others with the first steps and a blueprint they can start from so they can share their stories with greater confidence.

I hope my book and these ideas provide an example and source of encouragement for those ready to move past confusion, hesitation, or doubt. This process is not a limitation but an invitation to awareness, intended to inspire sound confidence to share, to be seen, heard, read, and to create positive change or reveal more of a story that has been kept in the dark.

May this concept open a door for others to ask questions, seek safety, and structure their stories with protection. I welcome anyone seeking guidance or partnership to connect. The future of healthy, protected storytelling relies on more individuals feeling prepared, informed, and supported with the proper protection, information, and guidance to stand strong before moving from the shadows to the light.

Closing Thought

Strength emerges when a story serves as both a reliable guide and a foundation for those who feel isolated in their pain or hesitant to share their experiences. This journey reminds me that sharing our stories is not solely about confrontation; it can also be about cultivation. May this work encourage others to share their own stories thoughtfully, openly, and safely. As you bring more honesty and clarity to your own story, may it emerge from the shadows into the light, bringing healing, forgiveness, awareness, and protection.

LETTER FROM DADDY.
Through the Shadows, Toward the Light

To my daughter, who stands at the center of every hope and prayer I hold.

I am not sure anyone will ever love you the way I have, the way I do, and the way I will continue to, for as long as I am here and after I am gone.

My love for you is limitless, reaching beyond space, time, matter, or circumstance.

It is a boundless love that grows in strength, compassion, and care every moment of every day.

I believe in you, trust you, hope for you, and think about you more than you know.

I admire your intellect, grace, curiosity, beauty, empathy, transparency, and the way you communicate.

One day, I hope you meet that special person who will treat you with the kindness, respect, and care you deserve, someone who will believe in you fully and love you in healthy, thoughtful, and beautiful ways.

I have not been the greatest dad, but you have received the best I could give in every effort, word, and deed. You come first.

You have had my full attention, effort, and heart since the moment I learned you were coming into this world.

You have defined and redefined the cornerstones of my life.

You have led me to faith, taught me how to love, shown me what it means to trust, and given me renewed hope, direction, and a determination to stand firm, accurate, and transparent.

You may not realize it, but you were the one who gave me all these gifts. It was you, it is you, and it will be you, for all time, and in all ways.

You are the greatest person I have ever known, and no one will ever come close to you.

I thank God for you every day and pray that the love and lessons I have shared and taught will grow within you, guiding you toward love, peace, happiness, and faith.

You are at the center of my hopes, my dreams, and my world, forever.

I love you.

Your Daddy

CODA.
Anchored in Truth, Love, and Faith

Being a loving father to an extraordinary daughter defines me above all else.

My faith is the second anchor of my life, rooted in my Jewish heritage and expressed through a Messianic walk centered on Christ.

The accolades, performances, productions, recordings, books, and talks are part of my past that guided me to my daughter and my faith, but they do not define who I am.

Later in my journey, I aimed to connect genuinely with the wisdom of every book in the Bible, combining scholarly study with prayer, meditation, and fasting.

As with my faith, my daughter's presence has shaped me, inspiring me to grow in patience, love, and humility.

Because of her, I found faith and learned what it means to love and trust.

In every situation, I learned to stand my ground while keeping my daughter's best interests in mind with every decision I made.

If any thought or strategy arose that I wouldn't want my daughter to know about, it confirmed that it was not the right step for me to take.

Every decision, interaction, or reaction was made with my daughter in mind.

I feel her beside me, watching and hearing it all unfold.

She has taught me to create, respond, and share from a place of love, humility, transparency, and stewardship at all times, in every place, and under every circumstance.

I hope that being her dad remains the greatest honor for which I am remembered.

She is the chapter I hold dearest.

My legacy lives in every moment I have shared with her, and in the love I pray reaches her across every tomorrow.

If the shadow of my journey has any purpose, let it remind her that love defines us, faith sustains us, and every day offers a new chance to walk in light.

APPENDIX A.
24 Deflective and Evasive Communication Patterns

Identifying Unhealthy Argument Tactics in Relationships

Communication patterns that block productive dialogue and prevent resolution appear repeatedly in this book. The following 24 patterns represent the common tactics I observed from Anya in conversations where she avoided accountability, transferred responsibility to me, or controlled the conversation altogether.

To me, a fallacy is a flawed pattern of reasoning that sounds convincing but lacks logical support. In unhealthy communication, I see these fallacies rooted in efforts to redirect healthy conversations down ineffective and negative paths. These patterns shift away from productive dialogue toward deflection, shifting responsibility, or avoiding resolution.

By learning to identify these patterns, I hope people can recognize when discussions are being diverted from truth, understanding, and resolution. This does not provide solutions, though understanding can be a first step for some readers.

These 24 fallacies are briefly defined by me, with examples.

These are not clinical definitions. They reflect how I have come to understand them through my experiences and observations.

I fully understand that additional patterns exist beyond these 24. These were the ones I noted and experienced firsthand.

Throughout the narrative chapters, I avoided certain restricted words and phrases. In this appendix, as in the other appendices, some restricted terms appear within definitions and examples where they are necessary for accuracy and clarity. This distinction allows technical terminology and conversational examples to reflect the communication patterns as they occurred.

1. **Ad Hominem**
   Attacking the person making an argument rather than addressing the argument itself.
   "You're too emotional to look at this with any balance."
   "What do you understand? You can't manage your own life."

2. **False Dichotomy**
   Presenting only two options when more alternatives exist, creating an either/or choice.
   "Either you trust me entirely, or you don't trust me at all."
   "If you loved me, you would do this."

3. **Red Herring**
   Introducing irrelevant information to distract from the actual issue being discussed.
   "Why are we talking about this when you forgot to get milk last week?"
   "I did that, but what about the time you did this?"

4. **Strawman Argument**
   Misrepresenting someone's position to make it easier to attack.
   "So you're saying I'm a terrible parent."
   "You think I contribute poorly around here."

5. **Appeal to Hypocrisy**
   Deflecting criticism by pointing out the other person's perceived hypocrisy.
   "You did the same action last month, so you have no

right to complain."
"You're not flawless either."

6. **False Cause**
Incorrectly claiming cause-and-effect relationships, often to shift blame.
"You made me act this way."
"If you hadn't said that, I wouldn't have done this."

7. **Burden of Proof**
Demanding unreasonable evidence from the other person while refusing accountability.
"If you can't present witnesses who were physically present for every single incident you're claiming happened, then none of it happened."
"Show me written documentation from a licensed professional that proves my behavior was problematic, otherwise you're wrong."

8. **Sunk Cost**
Defending continued behavior based on past investment of time or effort.
"We've been together this long, we can't give up now."
"After all I've done for you, is this how you repay me?"

9. **Appeal to Nature**
Arguing a behavior is acceptable because it is natural or biological.
"It's human nature to get jealous."
"People act this way when they're upset."

10. **Appeal to Ignorance**
Claiming a statement is true because it cannot be proven false.
"You can't prove I was misrepresenting the truth."
"If you don't have proof, then it didn't happen."

11. **DARVO**
Deny the behavior, attack the confronter, and reverse the roles of the victim and the offender.
"I didn't do that. You're making this up. You're trying

to destroy me."
"You're the one causing problems here, not me."

12. **Appeal to Emotion**
Targeting feelings rather than presenting logical arguments.
"How can you be so unkind to me?"
"Think about how this makes me feel."

13. **Moving the Goalposts**
Changing standards after they've been met to maintain dissatisfaction.
"That's not good enough anymore."
"Yes, you did that, but now you should do this."

14. **Gaslighting**
Denying reality to make the other person question their own perception or memory.
"That didn't happen."
"You're remembering it wrong."

15. **Appeal to Personal Incredulity**
Rejecting truth because it does not fit the narrative they insist on maintaining.
"I don't believe you would think that."
"That doesn't make sense to me, so it must be wrong."

16. **False Equivalence**
Treating vastly different situations as comparable.
"You got upset once, so we're both equally at fault."
"Raising your voice is as bad as what I did."

17. **Circular Reasoning**
Using the conclusion as the premise without providing actual evidence.
"I'm right because I'm correct about these matters."
"You're wrong because you don't understand."

18. **Slippery Slope**
Claiming that one action will inevitably lead to severe consequences without evidence.
"If you bring up the past once, you'll keep bringing it

up forever."
"Eventually, you won't let any issue go, and we'll be stuck in the past."

19. **Appeal to Tradition**
Defending behavior because it's been done this way historically.
"This is how my family handled matters."
"People have done it this way for generations."

20. **Projection**
Accusing others of behaviors, feelings, or thoughts that the person themself exhibits.
"You're the one who keeps misrepresenting the truth."
"You're trying to control me."

21. **Whataboutism**
Deflecting by pointing to others' faults instead of addressing the issue.
"What about when you acted in a similar way?"
"Other people do far worse. How can you question me for that?"

22. **Appeal to Pity**
Portraying oneself as wronged to gain sympathy and avoid accountability.
"I'm going through so much right now."
"The world is against me. I can't do a single thing right."

23. **Stonewalling**
Refusing to communicate or engage as a control tactic.
"I'm not discussing this."
"(silence...)"

24. **No True Scotsman**
Dismissing counterexamples by arbitrarily redefining terms.
"A genuine partner wouldn't question me."
"If you sincerely cared, you wouldn't bring this up."

When You Recognize These Patterns...

If you encounter these communication patterns in your relationships, naming them directly may escalate conflict rather than resolving it. That was my experience when I attempted to name them in my conversations, and it proved ineffective. A person applying these tactics in arguments will likely not recognize their own patterns when presented with proof, let alone accept that they are communicating this way. They will also feel attacked when confronted, leading to more defensive responses that make productive dialogue more difficult.

A change in another person cannot be authentically created by external pressure. Recognizing these patterns may help protect you from doubting yourself. This awareness can support better-informed decisions about how to proceed during conflict, or whether it's time to step away.

For some, this awareness may lead to healing when the other person becomes willing to recognize their own patterns. For others, it may clarify why a relationship cannot be sustained.

Consider focusing on your own response rather than their behavior.

Document conversations where appropriate and legal. Set boundaries about which discussions you will engage in, and which you will step away from when these patterns emerge.

APPENDIX B.
Traits Witnessed, Researched, and Alphabetized

Documenting Observed Patterns Through Research and Experience

Transparency requires stating upfront that I have no credentials as a psychologist, therapist, or trained mental health professional.

What follows is based on two main sources.

First, my firsthand experiences with my former wife.

Second, my sustained personal research over several years into narcissism and narcissistic personality disorder (NPD), particularly as it manifests in women. Many of the traits described in the following pages, I either experienced directly or researched to better understand them and present options for her to consider. Some traits emerged with immediate intensity, while others revealed themselves gradually over repeated interactions.

Throughout the front matter, narrative chapters, and closing sections of this book, I avoided certain words and phrases that could be perceived as accusatory, definitive, or libelous. This appendix takes a different approach from the narrative chapters. Here, some restricted terms are used to better describe and define narcissistic patterns observed and experienced in a specific relationship.

This distinction is important; the aim is to provide clearer language for recurring behaviors, not to escalate claims or declare judgments. For readers who want to understand the broader language framework that shaped the rest of the manuscript, please see Appendices G and H. These appendices outline the restricted language model, the guiding categories, and the full list of terms that were limited elsewhere in this book.

From both experience and study, certain patterns became hard to ignore. Some women described in the literature and accounts I reviewed, including my former wife, seemed to express narcissistic traits in quieter or more concealed ways than those commonly associated with male narcissism.

I also observed firsthand that behaviors such as grandiosity and a lack of empathy can strain relationships, exploit others, and often go unnoticed by broader social circles. These patterns may arise in the context of narcissistic personality disorder, but this appendix does not attempt to diagnose. Instead, it describes how these behaviors can manifest through tactics such as passive aggression, sabotage, manipulation, and a chameleon-like ability to present contrasting personas to different people.

The duality of persona was one of the most notable patterns. In my own situation, my former wife directed certain behaviors toward me with greater intensity, while different, more controlled versions appeared in other relationships. These patterns tended to remain hidden from friends, extended family, and community circles.

Some research and personal accounts exploring narcissism resonate with the theme of duality. I found that many individuals in their social circles reacted with disbelief when these hidden behaviors were revealed. This person, known to friends, may appear caring or present themselves as the wronged party, while more negative patterns are reserved for select relationships behind the scenes. For some, a central interest seems to be avoiding exposure of how they behave with particular people while maintaining a contrasting persona with others. In these situations, performance can serve as a form of protection.

As I compiled this list, I aimed to identify a defining attribute for each letter of the alphabet, A through Z, to organize these observations. Where multiple traits could fit a single letter, I selected the pattern that appeared most prominently in my experience or proved most distinctive in my research. A few traits inevitably overlap, and many other attributes could be added or named differently.

This appendix does not attempt to provide an exhaustive clinical taxonomy. It represents my effort to bring structure to lived experiences and sustained study.

One Size Does Not Fit All

No claim is made that every narcissist, regardless of gender, exhibits all of these traits.

Many self-proclaimed experts make broad statements such as "all narcissists do this" or "every narcissist does that," as if narcissism follows a universal script. My experience and research suggest otherwise. Some individuals may display many of the traits listed below, others may show only a few. Narcissism often appears in individualized patterns that do not conform to generalized proclamations. This appendix acknowledges that complexity rather than claiming certainty.

The alphabetized list that follows provides titles and definitions for patterns and traits drawn from my firsthand experiences, combined with observations from research and interviews about how narcissism can present in relational settings.

I was deliberate in using terms like "some," "may," "can," "can include," and "can involve" to avoid broad claims or overarching statements.

This perspective is shaped by experience and study and is offered with humility and awareness of my limited scope.

Arrogance

Arrogance can fuel a haughty attitude in those who belittle others, either subtly or overtly, in attempts to raise their own status. This behavior may manifest in condescending remarks to service workers, sarcastic comments about others' choices or intelligence, or a superior demeanor in social situations. Some dismiss others' opinions as uninformed while positioning themselves as experts on topics where they lack any genuine knowledge or experience.

Boundary Invasions

Boundary invasions occur through privacy violations such as monitoring communications, borrowing without permission, or intruding into personal affairs. This may include reading texts or emails without consent, listening in on calls, rummaging through belongings, showing up unannounced, or demanding details about conversations or relationships. Some rationalize these invasions as concern, claiming a right to know, while disregarding personal boundaries.

Competitiveness

Competitiveness can intensify in interactions where individuals compare themselves and strive to outshine others in areas like appearance, status, or success. This behavior includes turning casual conversations into competitions over achievements, reacting visibly when others receive attention or praise, or quickly attempting to one-up others' accomplishments. Some perceive other women as rivals rather than allies, continually comparing themselves to maintain a sense of superiority.

Dismissiveness

Dismissiveness can reveal a lack of empathy in those who disregard others' emotions and concerns to prioritize their own. This behavior may include interrupting or talking over others, shifting the subject back to themselves when someone expresses pain, or minimizing legitimate concerns with phrases like "you're overreacting" or "it's not that big of a deal." Some may roll their eyes, sigh dramatically, or show visible impatience when others seek emotional support or validation.

Exploitation

Exploitation involves taking advantage of others' vulnerabilities without remorse to fulfill personal desires. Exploitative patterns include using others' confidences or weaknesses against them for personal gain, extracting emotional or financial support without reciprocation, or identifying what someone values most and weaponizing it for control. Some focus on individuals going through difficult times, presenting themselves as helpful while draining resources, energy, or trust for their own benefit.

Façade Curation

Façade curation involves maintaining a controlled image and narrative to conceal vulnerabilities and truths. This effort may surface through selective sharing that controls what others see, constructed narratives that position them favorably while omitting contradictory facts, or defensive reactions when their story is questioned. Some manage their public persona across social media, work, and social circles with precision, ensuring different audiences receive varying versions of events that protect their constructed image.

Guilt-Tripping

Guilt-tripping exemplifies passive-aggressive behavior in individuals who use silent treatments or sulking to gain control indirectly. These tactics can include reminding others of past favors, bringing up old mistakes, acting hurt while denying problems, or making sarcastic comments. The aim is to elicit sympathy and compliance without openly communicating genuine concerns or feelings.

Hero-Victim Twisting

Hero-victim twisting involves projecting blame onto others while portraying oneself as either a hero or a victim to escape accountability. This narrative includes reframing situations where they caused harm as instances of being wronged, claiming they were "trying to help" when confronted about manipulation, or positioning themselves as martyrs who sacrificed greatly. Some alternate between these roles depending on which narrative elicits more sympathy or deflects responsibility most effectively.

Indifference to Others' Feelings

Indifference to others' feelings manifests as a consistent disregard for the harm caused. This pattern involves ignoring someone's pain, dismissing emotions as overdramatic or unimportant, or prioritizing personal wants without regard for their effects on others. Some rationalize this behavior as pragmatic or claim that others are too sensitive, appearing unable or unwilling to recognize the emotional toll their actions create.

Judgmentalism

Judgmentalism emerges through critical scrutiny of others, using perceived superiority to demean and control social interactions. This includes harsh criticism of others' choices, unsolicited opinions on how people should behave, or positioning oneself as the moral authority who determines what is acceptable. Some shame others for perceived flaws while believing their judgment is warranted and necessary.

Keeping Score Meticulously

Keeping score meticulously appears in those who track perceived wrongs with precision, building resentment and a one-sided quid pro quo mentality. This ledger-keeping style includes remembering favors given while forgetting those received, bringing up past mistakes during current conflicts, or maintaining a mental record weaponized against others. Some use this accounting to rationalize their behavior or remind others of debts owed, creating relationships where forgiveness cannot occur.

Lack of Remorse

Lack of remorse follows boundary violations in some, revealing no guilt over harm caused to others, lies told, or actions they knew were wrong but committed nonetheless. Remorseless patterns include denying wrongdoing, rationalizing their behavior as justified, or shifting blame to the victim. Some offer hollow apologies designed to avoid consequences rather than express genuine regret. When remorse does appear, it stems from how their actions affected them personally, such as a tarnished reputation, rather than concern for those they hurt.

Manipulation

Manipulation can target children or ex-spouses through tactics such as parental alienation. This may include badmouthing the other parent to distance or turn the child against them. It includes using children as pawns to punish or control the former spouse through custody battles or emotional blackmail. Other tactics include gaslighting family members to distort reality and maintain superiority, or undermining the other parent's authority by lying about their parenting or sharing false information to elicit sympathy and loyalty from the child.

Neediness

Neediness manifests as dependency on others for constant validation, masking deep insecurities with clingy or demanding behaviors. Needy individuals frequently seek reassurance, become anxious or angry when attention shifts away from them, or create crises to regain focus. Some alternate between appearing self-sufficient and suddenly becoming helpless, using vulnerability to keep others engaged. This dependency can coexist with superiority complexes, resulting in a contradictory pattern where they demand to be seen as superior while relying on others to support their fragile self-worth.

Obsession with Social Media

Obsession with social media is characterized by intense focus on likes, followers, and curated posts to boost self-image and status. This digital preoccupation includes compulsively checking validation metrics, crafting posts that present an idealized life, or spending hours scrolling through feeds while neglecting real-world responsibilities. Some assess their worth through online engagement, becoming anxious or irritable when posts fail to attract expected attention, or using social platforms to control narratives about themselves and others.

Preoccupation with Revenge

Preoccupation with revenge consumes some individuals, fixating on seeking vengeance for minor wrongs, making forgiveness impossible. This vengeful focus can extend to imagined offenses, where they construct faults and grievances that never occurred. Some become so entrenched in their invented narratives that they pursue retribution for perceived wrongs with the same intensity as real ones, blurring the line between memory and fiction.

Quarrelsomeness

Quarrelsomeness appears in those who provoke arguments over trivial matters, using conflict to assert dominance or deflect from their own issues. Combative patterns involve escalating disagreements without reason or creating drama to maintain control. Some thrive on tension, using arguments to shift blame or avoid accountability for their actions.

Resentment

Resentment arises from envy or unmet expectations, leading to bitter, withdrawn, or retaliatory responses toward others. Resentful behaviors manifest as silent grudges, passive-aggressive comments, or punishing perceived slights through coldness or sabotage. Some harbor resentment for years, allowing it to erode relationships while refusing to address issues directly or seeking resolution through honest communication.

Sabotage

Sabotage occurs when individuals target those they are angry with, using inappropriate flirting, undermining, or intentional interference to redirect focus. Tactics include damaging someone's reputation through gossip, interfering with relationships or opportunities, or positioning themselves as competition to provoke jealousy. Some sabotage subtly, making their actions appear accidental while strategically undermining their target's success or happiness.

Triangulation

Triangulation happens when someone pits specific individuals against each other to manipulate alliances and control their narrative within social circles. This behavior involves introducing a third party into conflicts to validate their perspective, comparing individuals to create competition or jealousy, or using others as messengers to avoid direct communication. Some invoke ex-partners, family members, or friends to make their target feel inadequate, isolated, or pressured to compete for approval.

Undermining

Undermining targets the achievements or self-worth of others to protect a superior self-image from being diminished. Methods include downplaying accomplishments with backhanded compliments, questioning decisions to sow doubt, or criticizing abilities in front of others. Some take credit for their target's work, spread damaging rumors, or offer unsolicited advice that implies inadequacy, all while maintaining a façade of support or concern.

Vanity

Vanity can manifest in a relentless pursuit of physical flawlessness through fitness regimens, restrictive dieting, or body-sculpting workouts, sometimes escalating to compulsive exercise. This may also include elective cosmetic surgeries. Many engage in vain behaviors, spending substantial time and money on their appearance, seeking continual compliments, or becoming upset over minor imperfections. Some harshly judge others based on appearance while using their own presentation as a standard of superiority or a tool for influence and control.

Withholding Affection or Support

Withholding affection or support appears in those who punish perceived disloyalty by using emotional distance as a control tactic. They may withdraw physical affection, refuse to communicate, or suddenly pull away without explanation. Some alternate between affection and coldness to keep others off balance, creating uncertainty and pressuring their targets to work harder to regain the approval or connection that was arbitrarily withdrawn.

Xenophobia-like Exclusion

Xenophobia-like exclusion is evident in those who dismiss individuals they deem unworthy, preferring to engage with elite circles or people who unquestioningly subscribe to their narratives, thus affirming their sense of exceptionalism. Exclusionary behaviors involve openly judging others based on status, income, appearance, or background and refusing to connect with anyone they consider beneath them. Some use exclusion to maintain power, surrounding themselves with people who validate their self-image without challenging their version of reality.

Yearning for Superiority

Yearning for superiority drives some to engage in constant comparison and one-upmanship across various aspects of life. These behaviors include striving to possess the best in all areas, boasting about their achievements while downplaying others' successes, or turning casual conversations into competitions. Some feel unsettled by anyone who appears more successful, attractive, or accomplished and respond by trying to diminish, criticize, or undermine those they see as challenges to their self-proclaimed superior status.

Zero Empathy

Zero empathy can lead some to show profound disregard for others' pain, viewing relationships solely through a self-serving lens. They may ignore visible suffering, dismiss legitimate concerns as dramatic overreactions, or cause harm without remorse. Some hear about others' hardships and redirect the conversation back to themselves or use vulnerable moments as opportunities for self-serving gains, instead of offering genuine support.

This alphabetical framework represents the patterns that appeared mfost consistently in the situations I encountered. Other traits exist, and different names could be applied, but these twenty-six capture what I observed, researched, and aimed to understand.

Again, I do not intend to diagnose or assert definitive authority over these behavioral patterns. My hope is that this appendix might serve as a helpful reference for those experiencing similar dynamics in their lives and seeking validation, clarity, recognition, or the courage to document their experiences more objectively.

I continue to learn, research, and refine my understanding of these patterns. What I have shared here reflects my current knowledge, shaped by my experiences, including patterns I observed in Anya, and by hours of research.

I hope what I have compiled provides some recognition for those navigating similar challenges. The traits listed here are based on firsthand experience and objective study, not clinical diagnoses or definitive declarations.

When you name patterns respectfully, you can frame them as observations rather than accusations. What you document can become your foundation when others deny what occurred. Trust your observations, record what repeats, and protect your clarity, especially when someone tries to rewrite the truth to fit their own narrative.

APPENDIX C.
Building Motions and Blueprints with AI Support

Organizing Chaos into Clear Strategic Documentation Systems

Order emerged from necessity during many months when recovery beds and court deadlines collided. During that period, a rushed motion sat before me that did not meet the standard I aimed to uphold in front of a judge. The pages that follow describe how that filing was dismantled and rebuilt into a motion of over 500 pages, and how that work became a structured way to track events, understand documents, write clearer emails, and respond with calm, consistent communication when tensions were high.

These sections focus more on process than on narrative. They cover timelines, tracking systems, email and message templates, response strategies, and careful use of AI to bring order to scattered records rather than to create drama or spin.

The goal is a specialized, repeatable approach to documentation, ensuring that facts, recurring issues, and court requirements stay central when emotions run high and capacity is low. This structure can help keep patterns visible in the record, particularly when faced with negative responses, attacks, or attempts to divert attention from core issues.

The emphasis here is less on the outcome of any single motion, email, exhibit, or log of an event, incident, or problem. It remains on the steps taken to build and tailor each piece to a specific situation, allowing others to adapt parts of this approach to their own tracking, communication, and organization of filings and documentation.

Reworking the Original Motion

This new motion arose from the cancellation of the first motion I filed. The hearing was set on the only full day I would have with my daughter during that visit, and although the filing was accurate in content, it was structurally weak and poorly organized. While recovering from surgery and under time pressure, I submitted the rushed forty-page motion.

Cancellation required me to rebuild from the ground up. I expanded the motion into a structured, 500-plus-page filing, split into nine documents, with clearer exhibits, stronger organization, and a more deliberate approach to how each piece would function in court.

Rebuilding from Chaos

The first document was a re-uploaded version of the existing parenting plan, used as an example. Next was the motion for enforcement, which served as the lead filing. This was followed by an exhibit containing an executive summary of the case and three exhibits, A1, A2, and A3, which provided chronological accounts of communication over the last three years.

Earlier in the book, there is a description of questionable actions involving Zoey's iPad. To address that, I filed a motion to inspect electronic devices. Lastly, I included a motion requesting a virtual appearance, sharing my compromised health status and physical distance.

Going from the original forty pages I filed in the summer to over five hundred pages in early winter was a significant increase in size and scope. I created shorter supplemental summaries to organize the material for quick review.

Training AI as a Strategic Partner

Drafting and submitting the new motion took weeks of gathering, verifying, and arranging records. I used AI cautiously, testing responses against court rules and multiple sources rather than accepting any single answer at face value.

With three years' worth of records, I organized them for proper use in the motion and supporting documents. My initial step in constructing the motion was to arrange the material so it could be understood and utilized effectively.

After the first series of passes, I learned how to prompt and train multiple AI models, developing prompts and methods to check, edit, subtract, and add pieces across different platforms. I worked with Gemini, Perplexity, GPT, and Kimi, as well as some legal AI systems. I conducted cross-referencing, asking various questions and exploring different angles. When answers contradicted each other, I looked for references, clear regulations, and laws on specific court websites.

Some of the court's own materials were confusing and occasionally contradictory, making it necessary to double-check AI outputs against the most current, official sources.

A seemingly straightforward question can lead a model to an answer that is popular but unreliable. This oversimplified example highlights a key point: no AI system automatically ensures the due diligence a person must apply to verify a response's accuracy. At times, AI may provide the most common response, fill in gaps, or generate plausible answers that simply do not hold up.

It became clear that the process was not about asking a question and expecting an instant, correct answer. It required more effort. For legal questions, I studied key sites, laws, requirements, and other resources related to the state where my motion would be filed. I researched where to find documentation for the state, county, district court, and the judge and magistrate involved in my case.

Creating the Master Prompt

I gathered a series of documents including…

- Administrative and Amending Orders Pertaining to the Court
- Court Guidelines
- Mediation Guidelines
- Hearing Settings
- Procedures for the Assigned Judge and Magistrate
- Division Procedures
- Existing Court Orders
- Family Court Rules of Procedure
- Circuit Filing Instructions
- Parenting Plan Templates
- Additional Court-Related Links
- Documentation of my last motion, which was disorganized and incorrect but essential for correcting the new motion.

I then outlined the situation, identified the problems, and noted the information I had at that moment. I specified what I would use to construct the motion and manage court and email communications from there. With those elements established, I proceeded to develop the prompt, detailing the relationship history, current parenting plan issues, and the desired outcomes for the motion.

I instructed the AI model to maintain a professional, respectful, compliant, and accurate tone, regardless of Anya or her lawyer's communications. I clarified that my aim was to create, respond to, and organize files, emails, and requests that represent my position and reflect Anya's actions and patterns. I emphasized that I was not seeking to retaliate but was committed to a long-term approach.

The initial responses I received helped me refine and enhance the master prompt.

The Elements of the Master Prompt Included...

- System Role and Scope

- Mission

- Complete Operational Rules and Zero-Assumption Protocols

- Reference Hierarchy

- Reference Datasets

- Modes of Operation (including accurate tracking of incident reports, outbound emails, and responses)

- Global Behavioral Rules

- Prohibited Language

- Mandatory Factual Purity Check

- A Final Checklist and Audit Before Delivering Output

This comprehensive prompt was incorporated before each inquiry regarding the motion, emails, incidents, and other relevant aspects related to the motion, court, Anya, or her lawyer.

With this master prompt and all gathered information and documents in one place, I would test and cross-examine the elements I was addressing. I utilized different models to ensure that the responses I received were consistent.

The focus was not merely on obtaining an answer but on receiving a well-grounded response, explaining its basis, and providing supporting reasons, references, and sources.

For those interested in the detailed structure and development of this master prompt, Appendix D contains the preliminary prompt preparation framework. This appendix outlines the specific components, training methods, and refinement process I employed to create a prompt system capable of handling complex legal documentation with accuracy and compliance. What I've shared here is the overview and application, while Appendix D provides the in-depth methodology for those wishing to build similar systems for their own circumstances.

Patience with Responses and Questioning Them

I questioned the AI models when the answers differed and reframed the questions in various ways. For specific elements, I asked how they could backfire, be misread, misrepresented, or provide ammunition for the other side.

After receiving a well-formatted, vetted response, I would ask, "Thank you for that answer, proof, and sources. How could this create problems for me, and how can I present it to avoid those issues?"

By taking extra time, reframing when appropriate, and leveraging the depth of the master prompt, I obtained results that helped establish a stronger foundation to build on.

Organizing Evidence Through CSV Files

To make the evidence usable, I converted unstructured emails, texts, and incident notes into structured spreadsheets. The final step was organizing years of tracked information. I asked the AI model, using the master prompt, how to best structure this material for better tracking and court use. It recommended a CSV file, a type of Excel format.

I used several applications to manage the emails. Over 800 emails were saved as a large PDF file, along with texts between Anya and me and between Zoey and me. I then categorized the emails by day, time, subject, body, attachments, and additional information.

The large multi-page emails and texts were consolidated into CSV files, making each email appear on a single line. This simplified loading those emails and texts into AI for review. As an extra security measure, I replaced Anya's and Zoey's names with "Petitioner" and "Minor Child" in the CSV versions of the emails and texts I uploaded to prompts, removing key identifiers.

When I tackled the extended and unorganized incident list I had created, these newly developed and searchable CSV files made it more efficient to find the days, times, and corresponding emails and texts for specific incidents.

Some entries were vague, lacked adequate backup, and included words that were discouraged. I used the master prompt to ask how to organize the information based on the emails, texts, and original incidents. The AI models helped me create a better, compliant way to format all the entries.

Looking Ahead

It also provided a structure for future texts, emails, and incidents and guided me on how to add each one for future filings. Since filing the updated motion, I have been using a solid template to track emails, texts, and incidents in compliance with the court's standards.

If my exhibits were excluded from the motion due to missing elements or an excess of pages, I could file the incidents and emails separately. I formatted them in the order and style preferred by the court.

While building the motion, I requested an analysis of my emails and texts, as well as Anya's. Initially, I focused solely on the motion to file it quickly, but I recognized this as an opportunity for both correction and instruction, learning a great deal about effective communication through this new filing and its aftermath.

In the analysis, I asked the AI model to identify content that could be taken out of context and used against me. The feedback indicated that frustrated language and reactive responses could negatively portray me, including when my concerns were valid.

In my conversation with this AI model, I sought the best approaches and suggestions for enhancing the existing master prompt regarding writing and responding to emails. This led back to some of the words and phrases included in Appendix H, which I have restricted from this book and from emails sent to her.

By asking questions and utilizing the previous CSV of old emails, along with daily updated versions of new emails sent since the filing, I learned effective tactics for writing and responding. I also learned to categorize emails within this new system, which includes the following sections.

My Email Communications Sheet Categories

- Email Number
- From
- To
- CC
- Date
- Time
- Subject
- Body
- Response Delay
- Tones/Actions
- Key Summary
- Issue Category
- Exhibit Status
- Action Item(s)

For each email sent or received, I can now use a prompt, enabling the AI model to help organize and track each aspect. I include in the prompt the information I wish to convey and the reason for sending it. This approach also applies to incident listings. The incident reporting sheet uses these categories so each event can be understood independently and within the broader thread of behavior.

My Incident Reporting Sheet Categories

- Incident Number
- Date
- Time
- Source

- Sender
- Recipient
- Issue Category
- Summary
- Full Content
- Parenting Plan Violation
- Tone or Pattern Observed
- Action(s) Taken
- Evidence File Name (if applicable)
- Minor Child's Input/Reaction
- Reference/Response or Follow-Up

With the AI models' assistance and adherence to the main prompt, each category gets filled in with the correct details. Each email and incident is tagged with the applicable issue categories, making it easier to cross-reference and identify recurring themes over time.

Issue Categories for Both Emails and Incidents

- Interference with Timesharing
- Electronic Communication Interference (iPad/Calls)
- Refusal to Co-Parent / Unilateral Decision Making
- Withholding Information (School/Medical/Safety)
- Denial of Right of First Refusal (if applicable)
- Disparagement / Alienating Behaviors
- Failure to Transport / Exchange Issues
- Financial Non-Compliance / Reimbursement Refusal
- Privacy Violation / Intrusion
- Hostile Communication / Harassment
- Medical Neglect / Failure to Notify
- Educational Interference / Exclusion

- Unauthorized Third-Party Care
- Legal Manipulation / False Allegations
- Gatekeeping / Rigid Adherence to Control

I have accepted the shift in tone I've been advised to adopt. It bothers me to bite my tongue, but I understand why I should do it, how to do it, and how it will benefit me in the short and long term.

Proactive engagement with the prompts shapes this process. Beyond the extensive master prompt added at the beginning, I also take the time to include my thoughts, the email as I believe it should be sent, and the ideas I'm trying to organize first. This is a better approach than asking simple questions and expecting complex, high-quality results that are copied and pasted without accountability. I am mindful of every word I send, whether it's my own or edits made by AI. I have closely examined and learned the reasons for the recommendations.

Time is taken to ask questions, rather than immediately sending back what I receive. With the prompt details and the AI's understanding of the case, I navigate a series of questions. In this active learning experience, each response I submit has proven stronger and more consistent, requiring fewer corrections and taking less time. Using AI as an educational tool with authenticity, accountability, and transparency can enhance knowledge, wisdom, and ability, unlike those who use it as a crutch, relying on quick fixes and forgetting, where little is learned.

The Filing Structure of 500+ Pages

A clear blueprint began to emerge. As I started organizing the format, it became clear there would be an exhibit section, followed by a first exhibit divided into three chronological parts. The sections were not going to be brief.

The Exhibit A summary was a little over twenty pages, with supplemental Exhibits A1, A2, and A3 adding well over two hundred additional pages spanning 2023 through 2025.

Accountability for what has not been honored in the existing parenting plan is the focus of this documentation. It calls for stronger language and clearer terms to eliminate misinterpretation. It seeks to establish real liability for my former wife when she fails to follow through, as this has been a recurring issue. Next are proposed additions that must be discussed and negotiated, but her track record of minimal contact, compromise, and consideration makes it necessary to present these matters to a judge or magistrate. This is detailed in Exhibit B, but before pursuing any remedy, the patterns, problems, themes, and documentation must be organized.

I do not expect her lawyer or the judge to read every line of the motion. As outlined earlier, the who, what, when, where, why, and how of each section are organized with summaries and key points for quick review. This effort aims to correct a flawed plan and hold a parent accountable for repeated power plays, attempts to control outcomes at any cost, and choices that undermine our daughter's stability and well-being.

These patterns indicate ongoing conflict, ineffective communication, and repeated violations of the parenting plan, which does not serve the child's best interest. The requested additions aim to create enforceable mechanisms that ensure both parents remain informed and involved in the child's life.

The 500-plus pages break down into five sections, A through E.

A. Electronic Communication Provisions

B. Information-Sharing Requirements

C. Time-Sharing and Visitation Provisions

D. Respectful Communication Provisions

E. Decision Making and Shared Parental Responsibility

My sections A, B, C, D, and E encompass the who, what, when, where, why, and how of the problems, proposed solutions, and established issues.

Each element corresponds to the reason for the motion, the requested changes, and the supporting rationale. The document also illustrates a pattern of how these requests were made and ignored. It tracks proposed changes, discussions of those changes, highlighted issues, and the numerous times my requests were discarded or dismissed.

The Page Count and the Filing Process

Exhibit B, the proposed modification and addition section, is over 160 pages. It is double-spaced, as required for filing, with wide margins and a large font. Learning the guidelines for headers, footers, spacing, margins, fonts, and font sizes lengthened a smaller document that contained significant detail. That is also why the full motion exceeded 500 pages.

This filing was structured around patterns, themes, and proof. It was built so that if one specific incident were dismissed, there were ten or more similar examples demonstrating the same behavior still on record. It was not created to frustrate the court or slow the process, but to ensure that actions did not slip through the cracks or get overlooked.

Pre-Filing Audit Process

As I finalized the documentation and prepared it for submission, I paused to ensure accuracy. I had written, edited, and organized the documents as best as I could, but this time, thoroughness was critical. I revisited the drawing board and established a series of new prompts.

These focused on auditing, formatting, creating correct file names, and addressing other potential concerns. I consulted various AI models about headers, footers, body layout, spacing, specific words to avoid, compliance, rules, and preferred elements for the court. I asked whether this could harm me, assist Anya's attorney, and what the pros and cons were of submitting a motion of this size.

Lastly, I inquired about immediate next steps, what to prepare for, interim actions, and what to expect. I also requested the system to review the documents again against the rules, laws, regulations, and requirements of the state, county, and district court to ensure compliance.

Mistakes may have been overlooked. I am not a lawyer. AI is not infallible, and while I could have spent weeks or months reviewing it in detail, I felt confident enough to submit it as is.

Taken together, the motions, exhibits, and 500-plus pages form a request for relief, revealing and addressing elements that are unclear or require modification. I am not seeking money, make-up time, or a lengthy list often offered in cases like these. I'm looking for fairness, accountability, transparency, and healthy communication regarding Zoey.

I also tested potential additions and removed any that the AI flagged as likely to weaken the motion, retaining only requests that aligned with documented patterns and the court's standards.

Post-Filing Experiences

Since filing, there have been delays and procedural steps, including a required meet-and-confer and reassignment of the case to a magistrate. During this period, I continued to track emails, texts, and incidents in the same system to document new developments in a consistent, court-ready format.

I also recognize the importance of a realistic long-term view. I expect there will be additional delays, attempts to reframe facts, and efforts to challenge or dismiss certain elements. My intent is not to rely on a single set of documents or a single hearing for a decisive outcome, but to remain steady and thorough in presenting the truth over time. With that in mind, I approach each motion and each appearance as one step in an ongoing process, rather than seeking an immediate, all-encompassing result.

The New Blueprint

Since I filed, communication has remained tense, but the blueprint continues to function effectively. Each new email or incident is added to the same tracking system, making it easier to document and present emerging issues and last-minute evasive responses.

While the AI models helped me organize my materials, I also asked for guidance on what to do next, what I should do differently from this point on, how I should track emails, texts, and incidents, and which categories would best highlight the actions, issues, and inaccuracies. I outlined some of the tracking elements I learned along the way. Right after it was filed and accepted, I took a breath, set up the tracking components, and started anew. This time, it would be a more accurate, stronger blueprint from the outset.

This new layout included a filing system for what I had compiled to date, detailing where to store it, how to name it, and improved methods for referencing the materials. I then prompted the AI model to help create an additional tracking system with clear instructions on saving emails, texts, and incidents, and categorizing them. This approach helps to surface trends, facilitates easier cross-referencing, and streamlines the presentation of data.

If the judge or magistrate deemed the exhibits too lengthy or numerous and requested documentation beyond the summaries, I could present the last 25 days instead of the previous three years. These highlights address most issues from the past three years more effectively and in an organized manner. This new method of collecting and organizing data can also be applied to future exhibits or motions.

From moments of biting my tongue to those where I felt ready to scream, this documentation and preparation phase has instilled a new calm in my responses. It has demonstrated that pausing, patience, persistence, and problem-solving can build a more stable foundation for what comes next.

The motto that emerged from this process was, "Let the facts scream so you can whisper."

My Invitation to Others in Similar Situations

Start organizing your materials now. Consider preparing the Excel file as a CSV for use with AI, or begin documenting incidents, events, texts, emails, and other items as they occur to facilitate cross-referencing. If it feels off, wrong, or unfair, or if a moment lingers in your mind, track it.

It's better to have it listed, dated, and saved than not. While the pages of my motion and spreadsheets may not be visible, the compiled and cross-referenced data will likely come to light. It's not about the small moments or incidents, nor the major blowout experiences. In isolation, they can be shifted, reshaped, and reinterpreted to support the other side or undermine yours. When you can illustrate patterns, themes, ongoing issues, elements, and recurring actions, those small pieces of evidence can create a stronger case.

Building and maintaining a tracking blueprint like this can benefit a lawyer, if you have one, or help you achieve better results with AI if you are self-representing. Ensure that what you add can be substantiated and withstand scrutiny from those attempting to discredit it.

There were emails I remembered that would have strongly supported my case, but that I could no longer locate. Rather than reference them without proof, I omitted them, as including unsubstantiated claims would have weakened the credibility of the material I could document and cross-reference.

By stating only what I can substantiate, I protect the integrity of my case and ensure that each statement can be supported, demonstrated, and cross-referenced with evidence.

Plan for your material to be attacked, distorted, scrutinized, and misrepresented, along with efforts to discredit both it and you. Despite clear evidence on your side, the other party may still try to make you or your material appear wrong.

Consider taking the time each day to track and document negative interactions and experiences as they occur. Review your emails and texts to identify prior materials that can be saved and incorporated into your new blueprint.

Small steps, research, and organization in five or ten minutes a day can help build a stronger defense and provide a solid foundation against those causing problems. Over time, these records can speak for themselves in ways a single conversation or hearing never will.

In many courts, and in many cases, outcomes rarely hinge on who appears most convincing in the moment. What can carry a case toward the best possible outcome is a clear, consistent record built over time. Documentation that is correct, substantiated, and compliant has less to argue and less to defend. It stands on its own, showing what happened, when it happened, and how often. That record is the proof. Being right is different from being able to demonstrate it.

APPENDIX D.
Preliminary Prompt Preparation as a First Step

Structured Protocols to Consider for Court-Ready AI Documentation

Preparation shapes whether AI becomes a strategic tool or an expensive gamble. While thorough and detailed prompt construction can require a sizable upfront time investment, a well-structured prompt can prevent cascading errors, reduce revision cycles, and turn hours of correction into minutes of verification.

Many complaints about AI inaccuracy often trace back to input quality, not system failure. Some users rush through prompts and accept outputs without verification. A plug-and-play approach asks a simple question and instantly accepts the first answer without considering what could be wrong, off, or incomplete.

Others request templates but fail to customize them for specific circumstances, treating prompts as one-size-fits-all solutions rather than frameworks requiring personalized adaptation. I have seen individuals request the right prompt and then use it as a template but choose not to update, modify, or personalize it to fit their specific request or situation. They also fail to account for changes, updates, and additions that occur over time.

A foundational issue stems from a limited understanding of AI architecture paired with unrealistic expectations about its performance and inference capabilities. Many AI systems operate on pattern matching and probability distributions, not mind reading. They require explicit context, defined constraints, and verification protocols to function reliably.

Taking a few steps back and focusing on preliminary prompt preparation may resolve many issues and lead to better results. While it can take some time initially, a well-prepared prompt can save a great deal of time down the line, as it delivers better results and stronger information.

This approach can prove valuable when building a master prompt for repeated use. Whether managing a court case with multiple motions, running a business operation, or tackling any situation where questions follow a sequence, a well-constructed master prompt can account for both expected and unexpected variables.

It can be updated as circumstances change, while remaining stable enough to deliver consistent, substantiated results with each use. This investment of time and effort upfront pays off by avoiding the obligation to rebuild the foundation with each query.

The preliminary work may seem tedious, but it can deliver stronger, more substantiated results than iterative, frustrating correction cycles. This upfront structure can also create accountability checkpoints that shift outputs from suggestions into stronger, proven, and vetted documentation.

Here are some of the elements I included in my master prompt for my motions and hearing information, for preparing and responding to emails, and for creating documentation and tracking for motions, exhibits, evidence, and incidents.

1. Mandatory Document and File Verification Protocol at the Start of Each Session

This is a significant issue, as some users may automatically presume that the conversations, uploads, and understandings from last week are still present or active today. Many AI models operate on session-based context windows with variable retention policies. Some systems maintain conversation history within active threads but require re-verification of files across sessions. Others offer variable memory features or context handling based on settings or subscription levels.

Persistence without verification invites gaps that compromise continuity and accuracy. Establishing a verification protocol and asking whether the AI has the prompt and all materials uploaded and accessible helps eliminate the **"I will work with what I have"** scenario that can lead to inaccurate output. This can prevent hallucinations or creative filling-in by the AI and ensures it operates as intended, using the information you want it to work from.

2. Batch Organization Systems

Grouping materials for reference into batches that you upload when you first send your prompt can help create a mental map of sorts for the AI to locate the information quickly. This can assist with cross-referencing and enable the AI to double-check that all those files are uploaded and accessible.

Batching reduces retrieval errors by creating logical file hierarchies within the AI's working memory. When files are uploaded without structure, the AI must scan all documents for each query, increasing token consumption and slowing response time. Organized batches allow the AI to target specific document sets, improving accuracy when cross-referencing dates, quotes, or evidence across multiple sources.

For legal work, consider batching by document type, correspondence files in one batch, court filings in another, and evidence exhibits in a third.

I had seven batches of files, PDFs, and documents to upload for my case. Since I would first enter the prompt at the start of a session, I asked the AI model not to proceed with my questions until it confirmed it had all the batches and each document was available for reference.

3. Version-Dating Confirmation for Logs and Documents That May Change

Some documents will not change, while others may have elements added each day, week, or month. Adding a version-dating confirmation ensures the AI uses the latest version and does not rely on outdated materials. This prevents citing outdated information.

Name files with version dates included in the file name. Using 'Email_Log_2026-04-07.pdf' instead of 'Email_Log.pdf' can prevent confusion when you upload different versions of the same document. In your prompt, specify that the AI should use only documents dated from a specified date or later. If citing information, verify that the document version date matches the most recent upload. This prompts the AI model to check document timestamps before referencing content.

For ongoing legal cases where evidence logs and communication records grow weekly, version-dating can help to prevent the AI from citing email exchanges or incidents documented in an earlier version. This is crucial when the most recent version contains additional context or corrections.

4. Zero-Assumption Protocols with Failure Consequences

This element serves as a foundation for reliable AI output and made a significant difference for me when I added it to my prompts. Incorporating this element can help explicitly prohibit AI from assuming, guessing, inferring, or filling in gaps. This part of the prompt can also state that if the AI makes an assumption, it fails the prompt.

This has helped me obtain clarification and more substantive responses, often leading into the next part of the prompt by asking clarifying questions. Adding this can compel the AI model to request clarification before generating output, preventing generic responses that are misaligned with specific circumstances.

Without this protocol, AI can often default to probability-based completion. Ask for 'a motion response,' and the AI may assume jurisdiction, filing deadlines, or procedural rules, filling gaps with guesses instead of facts. It can generate a motion citing Montana statutes when your case is in Vermont.

The zero-assumption protocol can prevent this.

Instead of guessing, the AI asks specific questions like, "Which jurisdiction?" "What filing deadline?" "What court rules apply?"

This can shift the focus from assumption to clarification and separate usable output from unverified guesses.

5. Clarifying Questions

This builds on the zero-assumption protocol above and involves adding an instruction to ask for clarifying questions if any element is not completely clear, substantiated, or proven.

This can help address the questions you have after using the master prompt. When you are preparing to submit a request and include the details of your question, it can be a way to get initial feedback questions before it offers an incomplete answer.

In your prompt, consider including, "Before generating output, ask clarifying questions about any ambiguous elements."

This encourages dialogue instead of assumption.

For example, if you request, "Draft a response to her email about the schedule change,"

the AI should ask questions like, "Which email?" "What date was it sent?" "What specific schedule change is referenced?" "What tone should the response be (cooperative, firm, or neutral)?"

These clarifying questions can prevent an AI model from inventing context or using incorrect source material.

Without this protocol, you may receive generic output based on probability.

With it, you have a better chance of getting stronger, targeted output built on verified specifics.

6. Mandatory Double-Check Protocol

It may seem redundant, but I advise it, and I use it myself. This requires double-checking and cross-referencing dates, citations, quotes, addresses, exhibits, facts, and grammatical elements. This adds systematic error detection through multiple validation passes.

Numerous AI models exhibit consistent failure patterns, including false citations, date transposition, quote modification, and context drift. You could have the latest and greatest AI model or the most popular prompt of the moment, but these errors still occur. Multi-pass verification can catch many of these errors before they reach the final output.

For example, I asked the AI model to cite an email from February 6, 2026. The first output cited November 18, 2025. The double-check protocol caught the error, corrected the date, and verified that the quote matched the original email verbatim. In court filings, dating errors can undermine credibility. The double-check can help prevent that.

7. Prohibited Language Scanner

This is about maintaining a professional tone and avoiding specific phrases that could be legally risky or used against you later. Having the AI model scan, remove, or replace risky language before the final output can help protect compliance, credibility, and uniformity.

In your prompt, consider specifying the following instructions: "Scan all output for emotionally charged language, absolute statements, claims or accusatory phrasing. Replace them with neutral, factual alternatives."

For example, the AI may draft, "She always ignores my requests,"

and the scanner catches it, replacing it with, "She has not responded to three consecutive requests dated July 15, 2025, February 15, 2026, and April 7, 2026."

The first version invites cross-examination and sounds reactive. The second version documents facts and can help to withstand scrutiny.

This becomes particularly valuable when emotions are running high. The scanner acts as a filter between your frustration and the permanent record. In my case, I included part of my 2,150-word restricted list as an attachment and instructed the AI to flag any violations before generating the final output.

8. Hearing-Ready Mindset

For court-based prompts focused on writing and responding to emails, add to that prompt that you require all work or emails be formatted for use in hearings as evidence. This marker can save time as you compile and prepare evidence for a hearing. It can help maintain admissibility, clarity, and strategic value upfront, preventing the creation of internal documents that are unsuitable for later use.

This is a preparation-focused and time-saving part of the prompt.

For example, without this protocol, you may draft the following message, "Hey, can we switch next Tuesday? Something came up."

With hearing-ready formatting, the same request becomes, "I am requesting a schedule modification for Tuesday, April 7, 2026. The current parenting plan designates this as your parenting time. I am available to discuss alternative arrangements that work for both of us. Please confirm receipt."

The second version contains dates, references the parenting plan, documents the request, and reads professionally when printed as part of a potential exhibit.

When every email may be read aloud in court, you may want to write differently from the start.

This protocol can prevent later rewriting of communications or having to explain casual phrasing under oath. This can save a great deal of time by preparing every email in the present moment to be useful at a future date, without requiring full rewrites later.

9. Strategic Objectives Linked to Every Action

Think of it as reinforcing the objectives and reasons for the results you seek. The primary goals are presented repeatedly, so the AI model can continue to understand both the big picture and the small details.

In your prompt, consider stating the overarching goal explicitly at the beginning and referencing it throughout your specific instructions.

For example, my master prompt opens with this strategic objective statement, "The primary objective is to generate court-admissible documentation that protects my parenting time, demonstrates consistent communication patterns, and provides verifiable evidence for custody proceedings."

Then, when requesting specific outputs like email responses or motion drafts, I reference back, "Draft this response in alignment with the primary objective stated above."

Without thoroughly stated strategic objectives, some AI models will treat each request as a singular and isolated item. It may draft a friendly, conciliatory email when your broader goal requires documented boundary-setting. By anchoring every output to stated objectives, the AI can maintain consistency and uniformity across dozens of communications over months.

In my case, this prevented tone shifts that could portray me as inconsistent or reactive across different documents.

10. Role Definition

Activating specific AI knowledge domains is already a common addition to shorter prompts.

Confirm you are not asking the AI to be what it cannot be.

For example, asking it to act as a lawyer is not the best choice, but a senior legal strategist can help you avoid many problems. Adding multiple roles can strengthen output too.

If you are dealing with a consistently difficult and negative communicator in an ongoing court case, you could add, "Act as a senior legal strategist and high-conflict communication expert."

Role definitions can direct an AI model toward specific areas of its existing training. Legal strategist roles can help some AI models access case law patterns, procedural knowledge, and compliance frameworks, while communication expert roles can activate conflict de-escalation techniques and linguistic analysis. Combining different roles can create intersectional expertise often unavailable from single-domain prompts.

Here is a practical example from my master prompt, "You are a senior legal strategist specializing in family law, a high-conflict communication expert, and a documentation specialist focused on evidence preservation."

This tri-role combination enabled the AI model to draft emails that were legally sound, framed to de-escalate potential conflict, and written in a tone suitable for admissibility as exhibits if required. Without defined roles, a generic AI model often defaults to conversational writing that may be unsuitable for court use or less effective without this structured guidance.

With proper roles assigned, every output in my case reflected both strategic legal thinking and communication psychology.

11. Verbatim Quote Preservation with No Paraphrasing

Many AI models are known to shortcut quotes. Including this additional element in a prompt can ensure that the exact quote from an email, text, or other document is preserved and verified.

In your prompt, consider specifying the following instruction, "When citing communications, reproduce quotes verbatim. Do not paraphrase, summarize, or modify any quoted text. Include full context with the sender, date, and timestamp."

Several AI models condense and paraphrase quotes to save space or improve flow, which can create legal liability.

For example, an email can state, "I cannot accommodate that request this week due to work conflicts, but I am open to discussing alternatives next week."

Some AI models may compress this to, "She said she cannot accommodate the request."

The compressed version loses critical context, sounds more absolute, and removes the offer to discuss alternatives.

I noticed this pattern in my first motion draft when the AI model shortened a quote that removed the other party's acknowledgment of fault.

The original email stated, "I understand I should have notified you sooner, but my schedule has been unpredictable."

The AI model's first response quoted only, "my schedule has been unpredictable," erasing the admission.

12. Requiring Professional Tone

It may seem redundant to request the tone and then reference the required tone and other elements for compliance; still, explicitly defining tone parameters creates wording that serves you and avoids language that could work against you.

That risk does not disappear simply because what you are sharing is accurate. Tone can shape how accurate information lands, and the wrong framing can undercut a truthful statement.

Professional tone in this context means calm, factual, and free of reactive language. It avoids sarcasm, accusation, and emotional escalation.

In your prompt, define this specifically, "Maintain a professional, neutral tone in all outputs. Use factual statements without emotional descriptors. Avoid rhetorical questions, sarcasm, accusations, or defensive phrasing."

If I am frustrated by a schedule change request and I have not set this protocol, I may instruct the AI model to draft a response like this, "I find it concerning that you continue to request last-minute changes without regard for my schedule."

With a professional tone enforced, the same response becomes, "I received your request for a schedule modification on January 10, 2026. The current parenting plan requires 48-hour notice for modifications. I am unable to accommodate this request due to the short timeframe."

The first version reads more reactively and can invite conflict escalation. The second version documents the request, cites the agreement, and declines without emotion. When read in court, tone can be a factor in determining whether you appear reasonable or combative.

Lastly, Read Through the Responses and Output

Review the AI model's output and verify it yourself before sending the email or uploading the document to the court. Despite the most carefully constructed prompt, elements may slip through the cracks, or the AI model may skip instructions.

Accepting output without verification invites risk and potential consequences.

Well-structured prompts reduce the frequency of errors but cannot eliminate the possibility entirely. Human review remains the final checkpoint. No prompt substitutes for your own verification.

This personal, not AI, double-check process can still save hours compared to drafting from scratch, and the output you receive will be substantially stronger than if you start without structure. I believe you must review what is produced and confirm its accuracy.

Why take the chance? Why trust it blindly? This work deserves diligence, not faith in a machine.

Do that due diligence yourself. This goes beyond crafting the most concise and detailed prompt. After your prompt is in its strongest form, you still have to verify what the AI model provides. As human beings, or at least those of us who seek the most accurate answers, we must insist on oversight and rigorously check every result before relying on it. No system delivers flawless results, and without human verification, you are not managing the risk; you are accepting it. Give diligence its due.

Building an evidence system with clear authority hierarchies, verification protocols, and hearing-ready standards that treat every output as a future court exhibit can change how AI functions in legal work. I have found that it distinguishes casual use from a more systematic legal documentation method.

Still, some casual users hope their output will withstand scrutiny with little double-checking and accountability. Systematic practitioners engineer prompts that can produce court-ready documentation with solid verification trails built in from the start.

A deeper dive into prompt creation, although it might take a little longer, can separate preparation from improvisation. Vetted structures built on detailed verification protocols have a better chance of withstanding judicial scrutiny. Documentation produced through these systematic methods becomes evidence that endures when memory fades and claims conflict.

APPENDIX E.
Holding Lawyers Accountable for Misconduct

Filing Bar Complaints to Expose Misconduct without Retaliation Risk

Lawyers are expected to advocate vigorously for their clients within the boundaries of the law. That is their job. The issue arises when a lawyer steps outside those boundaries.

Problems occur when lawyers disregard the rules, misrepresent their authority, or use intimidation tactics instead of advocating for their clients correctly. If you are representing yourself, you may not recognize these violations when they happen, or you may not know how to challenge them. That imbalance can create opportunities for misconduct that will go unchecked.

In exploring this firsthand, I observed that many who have experienced questionable attorney conduct believe they have to remain silent. Some of the reasons are practical and predictable. For example, when it comes to online reviews, some attorneys who receive negative reviews choose to respond with legal posturing to get those reviews taken down.

Without documented evidence of wrongdoing prepared correctly for possible litigation, a reviewer may face genuine legal consequences the moment a lawyer decides to act. That alone silences many people before they post. For those who do post, many of those reviews quietly disappear after legal pressure arrives. Consequently, individuals who share their experiences are silenced, and the lawyer remains unaccountable and avoids the bad reviews.

This pattern creates a system where questionable attorneys can operate without public or professional accountability. Clients and others who have experienced problematic conduct often lack safe avenues to warn others or document misconduct. The information and actions remain concealed, benefiting attorneys whose practices rely on clients being unaware of how they operate.

Absolute Privilege

Many people don't realize that bar complaints in the U.S. are protected by absolute privilege. Unlike public reviews or social media posts, statements made in bar complaints cannot lead to defamation claims, regardless of the outcome. Whether the complaint results in discipline or is dismissed, the attorney cannot legally retaliate against the complainant. This protection exists to encourage reporting without intimidation.

Learning about this protection changed my perspective. I had documented conduct that violated procedural rules and ethical boundaries. As a self-represented litigant, I initially lacked confidence in my analysis.

Using a detailed prompt I developed, I reviewed the documentation against the State's Rules of Civil Procedure and Bar ethical guidelines, as well as 17 other documents. The analysis confirmed that what had occurred warranted formal reporting.

Filing a bar complaint served multiple purposes beyond my individual case. It created a record that may warn future clients about how this attorney operates, at least in my case. It fulfilled an ethical responsibility to document questionable practices through appropriate channels. It sought accountability without seeking monetary compensation, as bar complaints do not award damages or settlements.

The complaint focused on conduct, not compensation. My goal was transparency and honesty.

Why I Filed

The specific conduct involved my former wife's attorney continuing to represent her for ten months after her appearance automatically terminated under state rule. She filed documents as "undersigned attorney," responded to communications as counsel, and presented herself as counsel of record throughout that period, all without filing a new notice of appearance.

The attorney's pattern also included adversarial language in communications and unprofessional conduct during a court-ordered meeting.

Regardless of whether she was reflecting my former wife's wishes or acting out of forgetfulness or unprofessionalism, my properly prepared and filed motions were denied because of it. The court ruled that service on an attorney whose representation had already terminated did not constitute proper service. Her continued unauthorized presence in the case directly caused that outcome and cost me both time and standing.

I filed the bar complaint not for revenge or case advantage (the motions were already denied) but because the conduct showed a course of behavior that could harm others. If this attorney operated this way with me, other self-represented litigants may face similar disadvantages.

Creating a documented record could serve others by establishing a pattern and providing the bar association with information to assess whether intervention or discipline is warranted.

How to File a Bar Complaint

Each state bar association has its own complaint process, although fundamental protections remain consistent across jurisdictions. Most state bars provide online complaint forms through their websites. The process generally requires identifying information about the attorney, a detailed description of the conduct at issue, and supporting documentation.

That documentation is crucial. Include copies of relevant court filings, email communications, letters, and any other materials that demonstrate the conduct you are reporting. Organize these chronologically when possible. Reference specific rules or ethical guidelines the attorney may have violated if you can identify them, though the bar will conduct its own analysis regardless.

Follow Directions with Attention to Detail

Read through the instructions and requirements. Including all you want to say without adhering to the required format can lead to the complaint being dismissed. Review exactly what is required and how to fill out each part, how to deliver it, and any other details listed.

Write Your Complaint Factually

Avoid emotional language or speculation about the attorney's motives. Focus on describing what happened, when it happened, and how it affected your case or violated procedural rules. Bar investigators will evaluate the conduct against professional standards. Your job is to present the facts and let the evidence speak.

A Protective Privilege

The absolute privilege protecting your complaint applies to statements made within the complaint and during the bar's investigative process. This protection does not extend to public statements you make outside the complaint process, so keep your reporting within the proper channels.

What to Expect After Filing

Bar complaints do not resolve quickly. Investigations can take months or longer, depending on the complexity of the issues and the bar's caseload. You will generally receive acknowledgment that your complaint arrived, followed by updates as the investigation progresses.

The bar association will review your complaint to determine whether the alleged conduct warrants investigation. If they proceed, they will contact the attorney for a response.

Again, the attorney cannot legally retaliate against you for filing, though they may dispute your characterization of events in their response to the bar. This protection does not apply if you choose to post on a review site, in a public forum, or on social media. Be aware of that distinction.

Outcomes Vary

The bar may find that no violation occurred and close the complaint. They may issue a private reprimand. In more serious cases, they may pursue public discipline ranging from formal reprimands to suspension or disbarment. You may or may not receive detailed information about the outcome depending on whether the discipline is public or private.

Understanding what filing accomplishes and what it doesn't is important. A bar complaint creates an official record of concerns about an attorney's conduct. It provides the bar association with information to identify similar conduct if other complaints arise. It fulfills your responsibility to report misconduct through proper channels.

What it does not do is change the outcome of your case, award you damages, or guarantee that the attorney will face discipline.

For me, filing served its purpose regardless of the outcome.

The conduct was documented.

The pattern was reported.

Other self-represented litigants who encounter this attorney in the future may benefit from that record if similar issues arise again. That possibility made the complaint worthwhile to me.

APPENDIX F.
Calming the Current Initiative: A Nonprofit Concept

Strengthening Co-Parenting Through Structured Support Systems

Support was unavailable at the beginning of my family court journey. Calming the Current Initiative is the nonprofit concept I'm developing to provide others with what I believe is lacking. While not operational at the moment, I share this vision to outline the principles and structure that may inspire others or offer a framework for future support systems.

This appendix differs from the others because it presents a vision rather than documentation or reference material.

Calming the Current Initiative

This nonprofit concept emerged from my own experience with a high-conflict legal situation. It is designed to support parents navigating overwhelming legal challenges when they may be unprepared or under-resourced.

The initiative will provide reliable resources and support systems to connect, correct, and calm parents committed to honorable conduct during difficult times.

Unlike standard pro bono legal resources, this initiative will pair participants with seasoned, vetted, ethical attorneys and counselors. The initial plan is for the nonprofit to cover legal retainers directly, ensuring professional representation and guidance. Applicants will be carefully vetted, with support contingent upon active and honorable participation.

A Multi-Level Support System

The initiative operates through a four-level support system, meeting parents where they are in their journey and providing appropriate guidance for their current stage.

Level 1. Full Legal Readiness

For parents who have diligently prepared, taken the high road, documented their experiences objectively, and are ready to engage legal support at the highest level.

Level 2. Guided Legal Preparation

For those requiring assistance with assembling evidence, organizing communication, and presenting their story constructively, this level helps them move closer to readiness for direct representation.

Level 3. Personal Reset and Redirection

This level provides support and counseling for parents prone to reactivity, struggling with conflict, or those whose conduct may undermine their own cases. Counseling encourages restraint, strategic planning, and non-retaliation during preparation.

Level 4. Early-Stage Orientation

Helping those at the beginning, whether blindsided by legal action or a divorce filing. This level provides guidance on how to slow down, take a breath, avoid impulsive mistakes, and build a solid foundation for the next steps with strength and perseverance, ensuring emotional reactions do not hinder progress.

Accountability and Responsibility

Clear accountability accompanies the support that will be offered. Parents must avoid verbal attacks, retaliation, and behavior that undermines their own position, demonstrating their commitment to honorable conduct throughout the process. Those who cannot follow the guidelines, escalate conflict, or undermine their case risk losing the nonprofit's backing and may jeopardize their attorney's involvement.

Intention, Purpose, and Guiding Principles

This initiative focuses on creating strong, healthy foundations for families to build upon rather than pursuing short-term wins or venting in ways that can negatively affect long-term outcomes. The initiative centers on preparedness for the journey rather than a linear approach fixated on the next email, filing, or legal battle. The focus is on restoration, responsibility, accountability, and truth to achieve a fair outcome for both parents and children.

The foundation is truth, love, and transparency brought to light, not hidden in the shadows.

The aim is to establish cooperation, compromise, and communication in a healthy way to honor the children involved.

This is about making it right, not being right, regardless of the opposition and what they have said or done.

The goal is to ensure that the new foundations created are solid enough to support a fair, balanced path forward for all involved.

This is about healing, forgiving, and letting go of the past to focus on the present and the future.

I hope this nonprofit will connect fathers, mothers, and families with support at different stages of their journey. I believe that by valuing preparation, humility, and endurance, its growth can mean fewer parents have to walk this difficult path alone. My intention is for it to provide steady guidance, clear structure, and real hope, so more families can find a healthier way forward.

APPENDIX G.
Restricted Language Categories and Definitions

Categorizing 2,150 Restricted Terms for Compliance and Authentic Voice

Language has determined how this story has been told, especially in areas where facts, safety, and credibility demanded precision. The boundaries in this section reflect patterns that emerged while drafting motions, incident records, and chapters, as well as while writing and responding to emails with my former wife, her attorney, and the courts. Experience showed that specific words and phrases can be taken out of context, used against me, or quietly reshape perceptions, create conflict, and erode trust.

These restricted terms do not appear in the Preface, Author's Note, Introduction, any of the numbered chapters, the Conclusion, the Epilogue, the Letter from Daddy, or the Coda. They surface only here and in a few related appendices, where more technical terminology or stronger wording is used to explain the framework and educate readers rather than to attack anyone. The pages that follow break this discipline into twelve clear groups so readers can see how specific terms were limited, why they were set aside, and how a similar structure could support their own writing, motions, or records.

These twelve categories define the structure behind the 2,150 words and phrases I chose to restrict while writing this book. They explain how certain terms can blur facts, invite legal or platform risk, or dilute the clarity and authenticity required in documentation that may later be reviewed in court. Appendix H contains the complete alphabetical list. The pages that follow focus on why each category exists and how this framework can be adapted to other motions, evidence systems, and personal histories.

Note on Language in This Appendix

Certain terms appear in this appendix to define categories and explain their purpose. These terms do not appear elsewhere in the book. Their use here provides clarity and instruction for readers who may adapt this framework.

I recognize that this list represents an unusual approach. Most writers would not restrict 2,150 terms from their vocabulary. This extensive framework served multiple purposes beyond simple word avoidance.

What began as a protective strategy evolved into a discipline I had not anticipated. It became a writing practice that pushed me toward clarity, precision, and authenticity. The list required me to slow down and kept me from using familiar shortcuts in wording that could have weakened the narrative from start to finish. When I could not rely on common expressions or overused phrases, I had to dig deeper for words that carried more accurate meaning.

This extra effort improved how I communicated both the hardships and the hope. I began thinking more carefully about what I intended to say rather than settling for language that felt close enough. The restriction became a tool for clearer thought, not only safer writing. It reminded me that my daughter's future access to the truth deserved intentional effort, not repetition of phrases designed for different contexts.

This framework helped me eliminate presumptions and protect elements of the narrative creatively, legally, and ethically. It differentiated this story from automated, algorithm-driven content in today's publishing environment.

Could I tell a complete, steady story while avoiding overused, reactive, or ambiguous language? Could strategic restraint strengthen authenticity rather than limit expression? Each chapter tested me and that premise. The restrictions pushed me to find alternatives, to describe experiences without resorting to emotional exaggeration, diagnostic labels, or legal accusations that could jeopardize this narrative's longevity.

Why This List Matters Beyond This Book

These categories originated in family law documentation, where word choice carries direct consequences for credibility, safety, and how records are interpreted over time. They evolved as I studied how specific words and phrases can feel satisfying in the moment, while creating legal vulnerabilities, platform issues, or gradual shifts in trust when taken out of context.

Over time, that work expanded beyond court-facing documents into a personal discipline that reduced fillers and avoided overused language. I organized what I learned into twelve categories and a list of 2,150 restricted words and phrases that shaped how this story was told.

This list addresses several layers at once and keeps the focus on steady, credible documentation across different settings.

Legal Protection Removing accusatory, diagnostic, and inflammatory terms can reduce risk while maintaining factual accuracy through subjective framing.

Platform Compliance Many restricted terms trigger content moderation on social media, which can limit book promotion and message reach.

Authenticity Benchmarks Eliminating AI marker language and corporate buzzwords supports distinctly human writing that is less likely to be dismissed as automated content.

Emotional Restraint Restricting exaggeration and amplification can maintain credibility, especially when documenting difficult experiences that could otherwise be perceived as overstated.

Pattern Documentation Focusing on observable behaviors rather than diagnostic labels allows for pattern recognition without unauthorized psychological claims.

The 12 Categories

1. AI Marker Language

Words, phrases, or syntactic patterns commonly generated by automated writing tools (AI, bots, or algorithmic text) can undermine organic narrative voice and authenticity. This category addresses the challenge of distinguishing human-written content from machine-generated text.

As AI tools become more common in writing and editing, certain phrases appear with predictable frequency, such as "delve into," "tapestry," "multifaceted," "in today's ever-evolving world," and "navigate the complexities of."

These terms can act as markers that indicate automated assistance rather than original human expression.

Removing AI marker language can enhance credibility. Readers, reviewers, and gatekeepers increasingly recognize these patterns. Their presence can raise questions about authorship and weaken the personal nature of a memoir. For a book centered on transparency and human vulnerability, eliminating these automated patterns was non-negotiable.

In legal or advocacy contexts, AI marker language can suggest the writer relied on tools to generate positions rather than expressing genuine experience. This can create openings for opposing parties to challenge authenticity. Strategic removal of these terms protects against that vulnerability while maintaining a natural human voice.

2. Buzzwords, Crutch Terms, and Trendy Adjectives

Corporate, marketing, or industry jargon, along with overused descriptors or filler language, can dilute meaning and signal unoriginality. This category targets language that sounds impressive but communicates little. Terms like "synergy," "leverage," "robust," "cutting-edge," and "game-changing" populate corporate communications, marketing materials, and business literature.

They can create an impression of sophistication while often obscuring real meaning.

In memoir and narrative nonfiction, buzzwords can distance readers from authentic experiences. They can insert a commercial-style filter between the writer and the audience. When documenting personal challenges, family struggles, or legal battles, buzzwords can feel performative rather than genuine. They can signal that the writer is trying to impress rather than communicate truth.

Removing these terms requires more specific, grounded language.

Instead of describing situations as "robust," I worked to identify what made them substantial. Rather than leaning on "transformative" as a shortcut, I documented what changed and how. This restriction became a steady challenge that strengthened precision and eliminated empty modifiers that add syllables without meaning.

3. Clichés and Overused Expressions

These include recycled idioms, figures of speech, or sayings that reduce originality and weaken clarity or meaning. Clichés are shortcuts. They allow writers to gesture toward meaning without doing the work of precise description, like "at the end of the day," "when all is said and done," and "the bottom line."

Readers often gloss over these phrases because they have encountered them so many times that they function more as filler than communication.

This book addresses experiences that resist easy summarization. Parenting challenges, communication breakdowns, legal proceedings, and faith journeys deserve specific language, not recycled phrases that flatten depth into repeated patterns. Clichés can minimize the distinct nature of an individual experience by suggesting that all difficult situations fit the same templates.

Eliminating clichés required finding original ways to express common experiences. That effort honored the precision of what happened and respected readers by offering fresh language rather than predictable patterns. It acknowledged that the story my daughter and I have shared could not be adequately captured through borrowed expressions designed for entirely different contexts.

4. Diagnostic and Mental Health Labels

Clinical, mental, or psychiatric terminology used to label, diagnose, or pathologize behaviors or individuals without professional credentials or authorization. Using diagnostic language without appropriate credentials creates legal and ethical vulnerabilities. Terms like "narcissist," "borderline," "bipolar," "sociopath," or "disorder" carry clinical meanings that typically require professional evaluation.

When non-professionals apply these labels in written narratives, they risk defamation claims and credibility challenges.

Removing diagnostic language from the narrative chapters offered additional legal protection to this book while still allowing me to document observable patterns. Instead of labeling someone with a disorder, I described specific behaviors I witnessed. Rather than stating clinical diagnoses, I shared my subjective experiences and observations. This approach helps maintain factual accuracy while avoiding unauthorized psychological assessments.

The restriction also served authenticity. Readers can recognize when writers borrow clinical language to add weight to personal grievances. Describing what I saw and experienced without diagnostic shortcuts respected both the complexity of human behavior and the limits of my expertise. It acknowledged that patterns can be documented without claiming professional diagnostic authority.

5. Reactive or Sensationalized Language

Highly charged, reactive, or sensationalized terms can escalate tone, undermine objectivity, and trigger content moderation.

This category addresses language that aims to provoke emotional responses more than to communicate facts. Words like "brutal," "destroy," "catastrophic," "devastate," or "obliterate" can intensify the emotional temperature of writing. While they may feel satisfying to use, they can create problems for credibility, platform compliance, and legal protection.

Escalated wording can give opposing parties tools to characterize the writer as reactive, biased, or unreliable. In family law contexts, especially, emotionally loaded terminology can be used against the writer to suggest instability or exaggeration. Removing these terms helped maintain a steady tone that better served the narrative over time.

Platform moderation systems increasingly flag some of these charged terms for review or restriction. Books that include certain words may face challenges with social media promotion, advertising, or distribution on certain sites. Strategic removal of some of these words can preserve options for sharing the book's message across multiple channels without triggering automated content warnings and penalties.

6. *Hedging, Minimizing, or Evasive Language*

Qualifying phrases, uncertainty markers, or deflecting terminology can weaken directness, obscure responsibility, or undermine clarity. This category targets language that excessively softens positions or avoids clear communication. Phrases like "sort of," "kind of," "to some extent," "it seems like," or "arguably" can introduce unnecessary uncertainty.

While hedging language sometimes serves appropriate caution, overuse can make writing feel tentative or unclear.

This book is written to communicate directly without excessive hedging. Where I observed specific behaviors, I described them. Where I felt certain emotions, I named them. Removing unnecessary qualifiers helped the narrative maintain appropriate confidence without crossing into absolute claims or accusations.

The distinction matters. Subjective framing uses "I witnessed" or "I experienced" to establish perspective. Hedging language relies on softer phrases that avoid committing to a clear position. Strategic use of direct subjective statements can serve both legal protection and narrative strength better than excessive hedging.

7. Insulting or Defamatory Terms

Language that attacks character, makes allegations, diminishes others, or carries high risk for legal or reputational consequences. This category addresses words and phrases that cross from observation into attack. Terms like "liar," "fraud," "criminal," "unfit," or various insults can create legal exposure through defamation claims.

When frustration feels warranted, written accusations can still follow a book permanently and create vulnerabilities for the story.

Removing accusatory language required finding ways to document concerning behaviors without labeling the person. Instead of calling someone a liar, I documented instances where statements contradicted evidence. Rather than claiming that she was not acting in a safe or responsible way, I described specific actions that concerned me. This shift from labels to observations can protect both the writer and the narrative.

The restriction can also enhance credibility with readers. Insults and accusations can make writers appear vindictive rather than truthful. When difficult experiences are documented through specific behaviors, rather than character attacks, readers can draw their own conclusions. That approach respects reader intelligence and can strengthen the narrative's persuasive power through restraint rather than inflammatory language.

8. Family and Relationship Labels

Stigmatizing or judgmental terms used to characterize family members, parenting roles, or relationship patterns in ways that can oversimplify, demean, or misrepresent complex situations.

This category addresses language that reduces people to labels within family contexts. Terms like "controlling," "manipulative," "unstable," "toxic," or similar characterizations can flatten the complexity of family relationships into simplistic narratives. While these labels may feel accurate in moments of frustration, they can create legal vulnerabilities and undermine nuanced storytelling.

Removing relationship labels from this book required describing specific behaviors and patterns rather than applying judgmental shorthand. Instead of labeling a co-parent with a dismissive term, I focused on documented actions and their effects. Rather than characterizing entire family interactions with a single word, I shared in a different way, intending for readers to form their own assessments.

This approach honored the reality that family situations can involve multiple perspectives and that my role was to share my experiences, not to define other people or their experiences through reductive terminology.

9. Legal Accusations and Allegations

Language that implies unlawful activity, makes formal accusations, or suggests legal violations without evidence, documentation, or professional legal support. Using legal accusation language without proper foundation creates significant risk. Terms that suggest criminal behavior, violations of law, or formal legal wrongdoing can invite defamation claims and damage credibility. Words like "fraud," "perjury," "contempt," "violation," or similar legal terminology carry specific meanings that require evidence and often professional legal determination.

I avoided legal accusation language throughout the narrative chapters to protect both the book and myself. Instead of claiming someone committed perjury, I noted when statements contradicted documented facts. Rather than alleging violations, I described situations and behaviors. This approach documents troubling patterns without making unsupported legal claims.

The distinction between observation and accusation matters tremendously in family law contexts. Describing what I witnessed and documented serves the narrative without creating possible attack points.

10. Exaggeration and Amplification Terms

Intensifiers, superlatives, or hyperbolic language can inflate descriptions beyond accurate representation or undermine credibility through overstatement.

This category targets words that amplify unnecessarily. Terms like "always," "never," "constantly," "extreme," "devastating," "horrific," or "unbelievable" can push descriptions into exaggeration territory. While difficult experiences may feel deserving of strong language, overstatement can backfire by giving readers or opposing parties reasons to question accuracy.

Removing amplification language helped me maintain credibility through restraint. When challenging situations were described without hyperbole, the facts carried their own weight. Specific details about what happened proved more persuasive than emotional intensifiers, allowing readers to trust that the goal was to communicate what occurred rather than perform distress for effect.

The restriction also served as an additional form of legal protection. Absolute claims like "always" or "never" can create openings for counterexamples that undermine entire arguments. More precise wording that accurately describes patterns and frequency is harder to challenge than sweeping statements. My goal in removing amplification terms was to strengthen both the narrative's credibility and its legal defensibility.

11. Filler

Vague, repetitive, or non-specific language that lacks real substance or detail.

This category addresses words and phrases that take up space without adding meaning. Common fillers include "very," "really," "quite," "actually," "basically," "literally," or phrases like "the fact that" and "in order to." These terms can make writing feel padded and imprecise, distancing readers from direct communication.

Removing filler language required finding more specific alternatives or restructuring sentences entirely. Instead of saying something was "very important," I identified why it mattered and worked to be more precise with my wording and phrasing choices, or I removed the filler altogether. Rather than using "really" to emphasize, I let the description itself carry emphasis, which tightened the writing and improved clarity throughout the book.

The restriction enhanced the writing experience for me. I believe fillers can slow comprehension and sometimes make writing feel uncertain or unfocused. Eliminating these terms created space for more precise language and stronger descriptions, resulting in cleaner prose that I hope respects both the subject matter and the reader's time.

12. Personal Preferences, Opinions, and Miscellaneous Negative Judgments

Some of the words and phrases I set aside did not fall neatly into the earlier categories. They were excluded for reasons of tone, style, personal value, or because they did not fit the positive, authentic intent of this narrative. In this group, I placed colloquialisms, taste-based exclusions, and terms that I flagged for my own personal compliance when they felt inappropriate for this book.

This final category became a repository for language that did not fit the other eleven groups but still seemed worth removing. Some terms felt tonally wrong for what I was trying to achieve here, although they may work in other writing contexts or for other authors. Others carried connotations that pushed the story toward judgment in ways that did not match the book's intent. Still, others appeared on moderation lists or showed up so frequently in drafts that they started to sound like performance rather than genuine expression.

Personal preference plays a legitimate role in shaping my writing discipline and authenticity. I don't think every restriction has to function like a universal rule or serve multiple strategic purposes at once. Some language does not fit the voice, tone, or values a writer wants to communicate.

For me, this category helped protect the parts of my voice that are authentic, while clearing out words and phrases that stemmed more from habit, culture, or automated patterns than from how I speak and write when I am thinking strategically and creatively. It allowed me to maintain the framework's protective and practical functions without dulling down or sanding off the elements that sounded like me.

For other writers, the specifics of this category may look different. An important question is not whether someone else would ban the same terms, but whether certain words and phrases detract from the core intent, important relationships, or the future audience that matters most. Treating personal preference as a deliberate filter rather than a rigid rulebook may help keep the writing honest, while still allowing room for individual voice, conviction, and style.

The miscellaneous nature of this final category does not diminish its value. Taken together, I believe these choices supported a more distinct voice and a more careful positioning for my story. They functioned as small refinements that helped separate this narrative from content that could come across as careless, reactive, or out of step with the protective intentions that guided each chapter.

What They Represent

These twelve categories represent different challenges that language can create for narrative writing, especially when words carry legal, emotional, or platform-related consequences. The categories overlap in places, and some terms can fit into more than one group. The structure is meant for practical reference, not academic precision.

Applying this framework required a sustained attention that I did not devote to any of my other books. I reviewed every chapter multiple times to identify and remove restricted terms. The process slowed the writing, but also improved the final result by demanding clearer thinking and more specific descriptions throughout.

Appendix H contains all 2,150 restricted words and phrases arranged alphabetically for reference. When reviewing drafts or revising content, this list allows writers to scan for specific terms without sorting through categories. The explanations in this appendix provide context for why these terms appear on the list, while the alphabetical compilation in Appendix H makes the framework easier to see and can help writers choose which words and phrases to include in their own restricted list.

This approach will not fit every writing situation or every writer. The extent of these restrictions reflects the particular mix of legal context, emotional history, and platform realities surrounding this book. Other writers in similar circumstances may choose to adapt specific categories or only certain parts of the framework, rather than adopt all of it.

The categories and list are offered as options, not requirements.

In some cases, I chose not to omit certain words and phrases that could have been placed into the twelve categories. In those instances, these words and phrases remained because they carried my natural cadence or a recognizable pattern that has appeared in my other books or in the way I speak.

The goal was not to erase personality. It was to remove language that created risk, distortion, or distraction while keeping the wording and phrasing that still felt honest, grounded, and consistent with how I write.

Together, these restrictions shaped how the story could be told in a more authentic light. I hope this disciplined approach helps to distinguish my writing from the abundance of today's automated and false content, much of which is produced instantly and churned out daily. It also made this the most challenging project I have ever undertaken.

APPENDIX H.
Alphabetical List of Restricted Words and Phrases

Complete Reference of 2,150 Terms Avoided for Voice and Strength

All 2,150 restricted words and phrases are listed below in alphabetical order for reference when reviewing drafts or adapting portions of this framework. Appendix G explains the twelve categories and the rationale behind each term's removal.

They appear in AI-generated content, corporate jargon, reactive writing, filler language, and vague expressions that hinder clear communication and can undermine authenticity and credibility.

A note on explicit language: This appendix contains a small number of profane and explicit terms listed solely for reference and platform compliance awareness. Those terms appear with letters separated by dashes in both the written and audio versions of this appendix. In the written text, the dash format breaks letter strings that automated content scanners may flag. In the audiobook recording, these terms are read as individual letters rather than spoken as complete words. Both choices were made to protect distribution across print, digital, and audio platforms while preserving the completeness of this reference.

This extensive restriction served my specific circumstances and goals. It also offers a working example for other authors and writers who may want to strengthen their voice and consider removing some of these words and phrases from their own work. Those who choose to adapt this approach can select from individual categories or remove specific terms that fit their own situations rather than adopting the entire list.

A.

A bit

A bit of

A bitter divorce

A clean slate

A closer look at

A deeper understanding

A little

A little bit

A lot

A lot of people believe

A means to an end

A no-brainer

A number of

A perfect storm

At certain times

A testament to

A word to the wise

About last night

A-b-d-u-c-t

Abject

Abortion

Above and beyond

Absolute

Absolute truth

Absolutely

Absolutely always

Absurdity

A-b-u-s-e

A-b-u-s-e-d

A-b-u-s-e-r

A-b-u-s-i-v-e

A-b-u-s-i-v-e parent

Abysmal

Accordingly

According to AI

Accusatory

Accuse

Accused

Accuser

Actionable

Actually

Added fuel to the fire

Addict

Addicted

Addicting

Addiction

Addicts

Additionally

Adept

Admit

Adulterer

Adultery

Adulting

Aesthetic

Afraid

Against all odds

Aggressor

Aiding a crime

Aiding and abetting

Aims to explore

Alcoholic

Alcoholism

Alienate

Alienated

Alienating

Alienating parent

Alienation

Alienator

Align

Aligned

Aligning

Aligns

All about control

All hell broke loose

All of the

All of a sudden

All over the map

All the feels

All the time

All walks of life

All-consuming

All-or-nothing

All-or-nothing thinking

Alleged

Allegedly

Alleges

Almost

Alter ego

Always

Always happens

Amaze

Amazed

Amazes

Amazing

Amazingly

Amoral

An axe to grind

And it came to pass

Another nail in the coffin

Antisocial personality disorder

Anxiety

Anxious

Anxiously

Anxiousness

Anything

Anyway

Anyways

Apocalypse

Apocalyptic

Arguably

As a matter of fact

As a result

As a whole

As far as I'm concerned

As per usual

As previously mentioned

ASD

Ask myself

Asked myself

Asking myself

ASMR

ASPD

Asperger's syndrome

Aspersion

A-s-s

A-s-s-a-u-l-t

Assume

Assumed

Assumes

Assuming

Assumption

Assumptions

Assumptive

Astonish

Astonished

Astonishing

Astonishingly

As we have seen

At a crossroads

At its core

At its finest

At my wit's end

At risk

At that point

At that time

At the end of the day

At the point

At the same time

At the time

At this moment in time

At this point

At this stage

At this time

Augment

Augmented

Augmenting

Autistic spectrum disorders

Award-winning

Awesome

B.

Backstabber

Bad dad

Bad faith

Bad father

Bad feeling

Bad influence

Bad influence on the child

Bad mom

Bad mother

Bad parent

Bad vibe

Bad vibes

Bae

B-a-l-l-s

Bandwidth

Bang for your buck

Bash

Bashed

Bashing

Basic

Basically

Basics

Basket case

B-a-s-t-a-r-d

Beacon

Beat

Beating

Beginning to

Begs the question

Behind the eight ball

Believe it or not

Belligerence

Belligerent

Benchmark

Bend over backwards

Best-in-class

Best practices

Bet

Betrayal

Better safe than sorry

Between a rock and a hard place

Beyond belief

Beyond horrific

Beyond measure

Beyond redemption

Beyond repair

Beyond saving

Beyond the pale

Beyond words

Bias

Biased

Best ever

Billion

Bias or corruption in this court

Billions of times over

Bipolar

Bipolar 1

Bipolar 2

B-i-t-c-h

Bite the bullet

Blackmail

Blackmailed

Blackmailer

Blackmailing

Blame-shifting

Blasted

Blatantly illegal

Bleeding-edge

Blessing in disguise

Bolster

Bolstered

Bolstering

Bombshell

Boots on the ground

Borderline

Borderline personality disorder

Bottom-feeder

Bought the judge

BPD

Brain rot

Brainwashed

Brainwashing

Breaking generational cycles

Breaking news

Breaking the stigma

Breakthrough

Breathtaking

Bring to the table

Broken home

Broken record

Broke the law

Bruh

Brutal

Brutally honest

Burning question

Bussin

Buy

By the end of the day

By the same token

By the way

C.

Cake walk

Calling out the system

Calling them out

Can of worms

Cap

Captivate

Captivated

Captivating

Cataclysmic

Catastrophe

Catastrophic

Catharsis

Cathartic

CBT

Certainly

Certifiable

Changing the game

Character assassination

Character flaw

Charlatan

Cheat

Cheated

Cheater

Cheating

Checkered past

Check this out

Chef's kiss

Child a-b-u-s-e

Child a-b-u-s-e-r

Child neglect

Chronic blaming

Circle back

Circle of trust

Clap back

Clearly

Clearly illegal

Climate change

Clinically insane

Closing this chapter

Coach

Coached

Coaching

C-o-c-k-s-u-c-k-e-r

Coercion

Coercive

Cognitive behavioral therapy

Cognitive deficits

Cold shoulder

Collage

Collude

Colluded

Colluding

Collusion

Come on

Commandeer

Commandeered

Commandeering

Commendable

Committed fraud

Committed perjury

Compelling

Compelling narrative

Competing narrative

Complete failure as a parent

Completely

Completely impossible

Completely shattered

Completely useless

Complex truth

Complicit

Comprehensive

Compulsive

Con artist

Con man

Condemn

Conditional love

Conjecture

Consequentially

Consequently

Conspiracy

Conspiracy against me

Conspiratorial

Constantly

Contemplate

Contemplated

Contemplating

Contempt

Content is king

Controlling

Controlling or coercive a-b-u-s-e

Cooked

Core competency

Corrupt

Corrupted

Corrupting

Corruption

Countless times

Coward

Cowardice

Cowardly

Craft

Crafted

Crafting

Crafts

Crash course

Crazed

Craziness

Crazy

Crime

Disabilities

Disability

Disabled

Disaster

Discover

Discovered

Discovering Discovery

Discriminated

Discrimination

Discriminatory

Disgrace

Disgraced

Disheartened

Disheartening Dishonest

Dishonesty

Disloyal

Disney dad

Disney father

Disney mom

Disney mother

Disney parent

Disney World dad

Disney World father

Disney World mom

Disney World mother

Disneyland dad Disney-land father

Disneyland mom

Disneyland mother

Disorder

Disparage

Disparaged

Disparagement

Disparaging

Disregard for right and wrong

Disrupt

Disrupted

Disrupting

Disruption

Disruptive

Disruptive innovation

Disruptor

Disrupts

Distraught

Distress

Distressed

Distressing

Distrust

Disturb

Disturbed

Disturbed thinking patterns

Disturbing

Disturbingly

Does that make sense

Do the work

Domestic a-b-u-s-e

Domestic v-i-o-l-e-n-c-e

Don't rock the boat

Done it a thousand times

Done this hundreds of times

Drama king

Drama queen

Dramatize

Drill down

Drinking problem

Drip

Drive

Driven

Driver

Drives

Drives me up the wall

Driving

Dropped

Drops mic

Drove

D-r-u-g-s

D-r-u-n-k

D-r-u-n-k-e-n-n-e-s-s

DSM-5

Dude

Due to the fact

D-y-i-n-g

Dynamic

Dynamics

Dysfunction

Dysfunctional

Dysfunctional family

Dysfunctioning

E.

Each and every

Each and every time

Easier said than done

Eat your words

Economic a-b-u-s-e

Ecosystem

E-j-a-c-u-l-a-t-e

E-j-a-c-u-l-a-t-e-d

E-j-a-c-u-l-a-t-i-n-g

E-j-a-c-u-l-a-t-i-o-n

Elephant in the room

Elevate

Elevated

Elevating

Embark

Embezzle

Embezzler

Embezzling

Emotional a-b-u-s-e

Emotional a-b-u-s-e-r

Emotional blackmail

Emotional bypassing

Emotional carnage

Emotionally damaged

Emotionally demolished

Emotional distress

Emotionally disturbed

Emotional instability

Emotional labor

Emotional volatility

Emotionally charged

Emotionally eviscerated

Emotionally unavailable

Emotionally unavailable parent

Emotionally unstable

Emphasizes

Empower

Empowered

Empowering

Enable

Enabled

Enabler

Enables

Enabling

Endeavor

Endless times

Endlessly repeated

Enemy

Enlightening

Enthusiastically

Entitle

Entitled

Entitlement

Entitling

Epic fail

Era

E-r-e-c-t-i-o-n

ERP

Essential

Essentially

Esteemed

Evade

Evaded

Evades

Evading

Evasion

Even

Even so

Ever-evolving

Every fiber of my being

Every single time

Every time

Everybody

Everybody knows

Everyone

Everyone knows

Everyone wants to know

Everything

Everything happened for a reason

Everything is energy

Everywhere

Evidence-based

Evil

Ex

Ex-husband

Ex-wife

Exceptional

Exceptionally

Excessive

Excessive preoccupation with oneself

Excessive preoccupation with others

Excessively

Excited

Excitedly

Excitement

Exciting

Exciting opportunities

Exclusion

Excrutiating

Excrutiatingly

Exemplary

Experienced it thousands of times

Explained it a thousand times

Explained this hundreds of times

Exploit

Exploitation

Exploitative tendencies

Exploited

Exploiter

Exploiting

Exposure and response prevention

Extorting me Extortion

Extortion attempt

Extortionist

Extreme

Extreme behavior

Extreme emotional reactions

Extremely

Extremes

Eye for an eye

F.

Fabricate

Fabricated

Fabricating

Fabrication

Fabrications

Facts of life

Fair enough

FAFO

Fake

Faked

Fake news

Faker

Faking

False accusations

Familiar

Familiarity

Familiarize

Familiarized

Familiarizing

Fear

Feared

Fearing

Fears

Feeling strange

Feels strange

Fell through the cracks

Felt strange

Felt this a million times

Fiasco

Fight

Fighter

Fighting

Fights

Financial a-b-u-s-e

Find myself wondering

Findings

First and foremost

Firstly

F-l-a-c-c-i-d

Flesh it out

Flex

Flying monkeys

Follow your heart

FOMO

For all eternity

For all intents and purposes

For all practical purposes

For her own sake

For his own sake

For instance

For one thing

For some reason

For the most part

For the purpose of

For the sake of

For whatever reason

For what it's worth

Force

Forced

Forceful

Forcing

Forever ruined Forward-thinking

Foster

Fostered

Fostering

Fosters

Fought

Found myself wondering

Framed

Frantic

Fraud

Fraudster

Fraudulent

Fraudulent behavior

Fraudulent scheme

Frequently

Fright

Frightened

Frightening

Frighteningly

Frightens

From here on out

From my perspective

From now on

F-u-c-k

F-u-c-k-e-d

F-u-c-k-e-d up

F-u-c-k-e-r

F-u-c-k-i-n-g

F-u-c-k-i-n-g up

F-u-c-k up

Full stop

Fully aligned

Fully seen and heard

Furthermore

Future faking

G.

Gambling

Game changer

Game-changing

Garbage human

Gaslighter

Gaslighting

Gaslighting behavior

Gaslit

Gatekeeping

Generational trauma

G-e-n-i-t-a-l-i-a

G-e-n-i-t-a-l-s

Get a leg up

Get the ball rolling

Get your ducks in a row

Ghosting

Gifted

Give hope

Give or take

Giving 110%

Go against the grain

GOAT

Goes without saying

Going forward

Gold digger

Goofy

Grandfather clause

Grandfathering

Grandiosity

G-r-a-p-e-d

G-r-a-p-i-n-g

Greedy

Gross sense of entitlement

Groundbreaking

Guaranteed results

Guessed

Guessing

Guilty

G-u-n

G-u-n-s

Gutless

Gyat

G-y-p-s-y

H.

Habitual liar

Hack

Had me wondering

Handicap

Handicapped

Happens a million times

Haranguing

Harass

Harassed

Harassing

Harassing me

Harassment

Harassment by her

Harassment by him

Hard no

Harmful

Harness

Harness the power of

Harnessed

Harnessed the power of

Harnessing

Harnessing the power of

H-a-t-e

H-a-t-e-d

H-a-t-e-f-u-l

H-a-t-e-r

H-a-t-e-s

H-a-t-i-n-g

H-a-t-r-e-d

Have the last laugh

HCPs

He deliberately

He's evil

Healing journey

Healing my inner child

Healing my trauma

Healing process

Heard it a million times

Heard that hundreds of times

Heartbreaking reality

Heartbreaking truth

Heartless

Heartlessly

Heavy drinker

Heavy drinking

Helicopter dad

Helicopter mom

Helicopter parent

Helmed

Hence

Her Truth

High-conflict people

High-conflict person

High-conflict personalities

High-conflict behaviors

High-conflict personality disorder

High-conflict ex

High-functioning

High-level overview

High-vibration

Highly

Highly curated

Hijack

Hijacked

Hijacking

Hijacks

His Truth

Histrionic personality disorder

Hit

Hit the ground running

Hitting

Holding space for

Hold down the fort

Hold myself accountable

Hold space for my emotions

Holistic

Home wrecker

Honestly

Hoovering

Hopeless

Hopelessly

Horrible

Horrific

Horrifying

Hostile

Hostility

How do you sleep at night

However

Hundreds of times, if not thousands

Hypocrite

Hypocritical

Hysterical

I.

I am wondering

I assume

I beg to differ

I can only imagine

I can't help but

I can't tell you how many times

I couldn't help but

I couldn't help but wonder

I did a thing

I do not trust her

I do not trust him

I don't know who needs to hear this

I don't trust her

I don't trust him

I feel you

I felt like

I find it interesting

I find myself

I find that interesting

I found myself

I get this question a lot

I guess

I guess you could say

I had this strange feeling

I have to admit

I kind of realized

I mean I meant

I need

I need to

I needed to

I realize

I realized

I sort of felt

I suppose

I think that

I want

I want to

I wanted

I wanted to

I wonder

I wondered

I would like to

I would love to

I'd like to

I'd love to

I'm always being asked

I'm frequently asked

I've been asked time and again

I've lost count of how many times

I've lost count of the times

Iconic

If I am being honest

If I had a dollar

If I may speak frankly

If I'm honest

If the shoe fits

If the shoe were on the other foot

Illegal

Illegal behavior

Illegal conduct

Illegal scheme

Illegally

Illuminate

Illuminated

Illuminating

Illumination

Immoral

Impact

Impacted

Impactful

Impactful journey

Impacting

Impacts

Impairment

Implicit bias

Important to note

Impose

Impossibility

Impossible

Imposter

In a lot of ways

In a nutshell

In a sense

In a sort of way

In a world that

In a world where

In any way

In conclusion

In contrast

In essence

In fact

In many cases

In many ways

In my experience

In my head

In my mind

In my opinion

In order to

In our modern world

In point of fact

In some cases

In some respects

In some ways

In spite of

In spite of this

In summary

In terms of

In the digital age

In the end

In the event that

In the ever-evolving landscape of

In the following sections

In the midst of

In the nick of time

In this chapter, we will

In this story, we explore

In today's day and age

In today's ever-evolving world

In today's fast-paced world

In today's society

In today's world

Incapable

Incentivize

Incompetence

Incompetent

Incredible

Incredibly

Indifference

Indifferent

Industry leader

Inflection point

Inexcusable

Infinite times

Inflammatory

Inflated self-importance

Inhumane

Inner child work

Innovative

Innovative solutions

Innumerable times

Insane

Insanity

Insight

Insights

Instability

Instead of asking

Institution

Instrumental

Intellectual disability

Intense conflict I-n-t-e-r-c-o-u-r-s-e

Interesting

Interestingly

Intimate partner a-b-u-s-e

Intimidate

Intimidated

Intimidates

Intimidating

Intimidation

Intricacy

Intricate

Intricately

Intrusion

Invalidation

Invaluable

Ironic

Ironically

Irony

Irreconcilable differences

Irredeemable

Irregardless

Irreparable

Irresponsibility with obligations

It appeared to me

It felt like

It happens every single time

It is important to note It is my belief

It is not fair

It is strange

It is what it is

It leaves me asking

It leaves me wondering

It left me asking

It left me wondering

It seemed like

It seems like

It was strange

It's a no-brainer

It's a question I get often

It's an uphill battle

It's giving

It's not my fault

It's strange

It's worth noting

It's my belief

It's not fair

IYKYK

J.

Jail

Jaw-dropping

Jipped

Junkie

Just

Justice

Justifiable

Justifiably

Justification

Justified

Justifies

Justify

Justifying

Just saying

K.

Keep up with the Joneses

Keep your eye on the ball

K-i-d-n-a-p

K-i-d-n-a-p-p-e-d

K-i-d-n-a-p-p-e-r

K-i-d-n-a-p-p-i-n-g

K-i-l-l

K-i-l-l-e-d

K-i-l-l-i-n-g

K-i-l-l-s

K-i-l-l two birds with one stone

Kind of

Kind of like

Know like trust

L.

Lack of empathy

Lack of remorse and guilt

Landscape

Lay down the law

Leading-edge

Leaning into vulnerability

Leaning into the discomfort

Left to wonder

Legally unsound

Legend

Legendary

Left me on read

Let me be clear

Let me tell you the truth

Let's delve into

Let's go

Let that sink in

Leveling up my healing

Leverage

Leveraged

Leveraging

Liar

Libel

Libeled me

Libelous

Libelous accusation

Lie

Lied

Lied under oath

Lies

Life-changing experience

Light at the end of the tunnel

Likable

Like a ton of bricks

Literally

Literally always Literally never

Literally pointless

Little did I know

Live and learn

Live and let live

Live my best life

Lived reality

Living hell

Living my best life

Long and short of it

Long time no see

LOL

Looking back

Loose cannon

Loser

Love bombing

Low energy and fatigue

Lowkey

Low-hanging fruit

Low-life

Low-vibration

Lunacy

Lunatic

L-y-n-c-h m-o-b

Lying

Lying to the court

M.

Madness

Main character energy

Maladjusted

Malcontent

Malevolent

Malfeasance

Malicious

Malicious intent

Maliciously

Malign

Maligned

Malpractice

Manhandle

Manhandled

Manhandling

Manifest the life I deserve

Manifestation journey

Manifesting my reality

Manipulate

Manipulated

Manipulating

Manipulation

Manipulative

Manipulator

Many people have asked

Mark my words

Masochist

Massive

Maybe it was just me

Master the art of

Mastermind

M-a-s-t-u-r-b-a-t-e

M-a-s-t-u-r-b-a-t-e-d

M-a-s-t-u-r-b-a-t-i-n-g

M-a-s-t-u-r-b-a-t-i-o-n

Measure

Measured

Measures

Measuring

Meddler

Meltdown

Menace

Menacing

Mental breakdown

Mental case

Mentally broken

Mental disability

Mental disorder

Mental health condition

Mental health journey

Mental health professionals

Mental illness

Mental instability

Mentally disabled

Mentally ill

Mentally unfit

Mentally unwell

Mentally incompetent

Mentally unstable

Merely

Metaphorical

Metaphorically

Meticulous

Mic drop

Microaggression

Million

Millions of times before

Mind-blowing

Mind-boggling

Misinformation

Mission-driven

Mogging

Moist

Monster

Monstrous

Morally bankrupt

More or less

More times than I can count

Moreover

Mosaic

Most likely

M-o-t-h-e-r-f-u-c-k-e-r

Move the needle

Moving forward

Moving into a new season

MVP

Multifaceted

M-u-r-d-e-r M-u-r-d-e-r-e-d

M-u-r-d-e-r-e-r

M-u-r-d-e-r-i-n-g

M-u-r-d-e-r-s

Must have

My authentic truth

My bad

My healing journey

My lived truth

My truth

N.

N-a-k-e-d

Narc Parent

Narcissism

Narcissist

Narcissists

Narcissistic

Narcissistic ex

Narcissistic fantastical shell

Narcissistic personality disorder

Narcissistic supply

Narrative control

Naturally

Navigate the complexities of

Nearly

Need

Needed

Needing

Needless to say

Needs

Needy

Neglectful parent

Negligence

Negligent

Neither here nor there

Nervous

Nervously

Nervousness

Neuropsychological evaluation

Never

Never works

Nevertheless

New level of healing

Next-gen

Next-level

Ninja

No can do

No one in their right mind

No redeeming quality

No-win

Paranoid

Parental alienation

Parental alienator

Parroting

Partial truth

Part-time parent

Partner a-b-u-s-e

Passionate

Passionate about

Passionately

Passive-aggressive

Patchwork

Pathetic

Pathological

Pathological liar

Pathological narcissism

Pathos

Peculiar

Peculiarly

P-e-n-i-s

People ask me all the time

People often ask me

People say

Perfect

Perfect truth

Perfected

Perfection

Perfectionist

Perfectly

Performative ally

Perjurer

Perjury

Persecute

Persecuted

Persecuting

Persecution

Persistent lying and deceit

Personal truth

Personality disorder

Perspectival truth

P-e-r-v-e-r-s-e

P-e-r-v-e-r-s-i-o-n of justice

P-e-r-v-e-r-t

P-e-r-v-e-r-t the truth

P-e-r-v-e-r-t-e-d

P-e-r-v-e-r-t-e-d the truth

P-e-r-v-e-r-t-i-n-g

P-e-r-v-e-r-t-i-n-g the course of justice

P-e-r-v-e-r-t-i-n-g the truth

Phony

P-i-s-s

Pivot

Pivotal

Pivotal moment

Pivoted

Pivoting

Plain as day

Play a significant role in shaping

Play the victim

Played a significant role in shaping

Playing the victim

Playing with fire

Plays a crucial role

P-o-i-s-o-n

P-o-i-s-o-n-e-d

P-o-i-s-o-n-o-u-s

P-o-r-n

P-o-r-n-o-g-r-a-p-h-y

Post-traumatic stress disorder

Powerful reminder

Powwow

P-r-e-d-a-t-o-r

Prejudice

Prejudicial

Preoccupation with blaming others

Pretender

P-r-i-c-k

Privilege

Problematic behavior

Prize

Probably

Project

Projected

Projecting

Projects

Propaganda

Proven track record

Providing valuable insights into

Provocation

Provoke

Provoked

Provokes

Provoking

Psycho

Psychological

Psychological a-b-u-s-e

Psychological evaluation

Psychological fitness

Psychologically damaged

Psychology

Psychopath

Psychopathic

Psychopathy

Psychosis

Psychotic

Psychotic break

PTSD

Pulled the rug out from under me

Punitive

Punitive damages

Purpose-driven

Pushing the envelope

P-u-s-s-y

Put a pin in it

Put the cart before the horse

Q.

Quack

Quick question

Quiet quitting

Quite

Quite honestly

Quite literally

R.

Racism

Racist

Radically honest

Radically vulnerable

R-a-p-e R-a-p-e-d

Rather than asking

Raving

Raving mad

Raw and unfiltered

Raw and unfiltered truth

Reach out

Reactive a-b-u-s-e

Read between the lines

Read that again

Really

Realm

Reap what you sow

Reclaim my power

Reclaiming my voice

Reckless disregard for the truth

Recklessly

Refuses to follow the law

Remains to be seen

Remarkably

Remarked

Reparenting myself

Repeated this thousands of times

Reprobate

Restless

Restlessly

Restlessness

Results-driven

Results-oriented

R-e-t-a-r-d

R-e-t-a-r-d-e-d

Revolution

Revolutionary

Revolutionize

Revolutionized

Revolutionizing

Rewriting my narrative

Rewriting reality

Rich tapestry

Ridicule

Ridiculing

Rigged court

Rigged process

Rigged system

Ripped me off

Ripped my life apart

Rizz

Robust

Rock bottom

Rockstar

Rude awakening

Ruined my life

Ruining my life

Running in circles

S.

Sabotage

Sabotaged

Sabotaging

Saboteur

Safe to be seen

Safe space

Said it a million times

Said no one ever

Sale

Scalable

Scalable solution

Scam

Scam artist

Scammer

Scare

Scare tactics

Scared

Scared stiff

Scared to d-e-a-t-h

Scaring

Scariest

Scary

Schizophrenia

Schizophrenic

Scorched-earth tactics

Scum

Scumbag

Seamless

Seamlessly

Seamlessly integrate

Second to none

Secret

Secretive

Secrets

Seemingly strange

Seen it a billion times

Seen it a million times

Seen that thousands of times

Selective memory

Self-oriented perfectionism

Sells you down the river

Self-perfection

Self-perfectionism

Serious

Seriously

Seriousness

Serves as a testament

Set the record straight

S-e-x

S-e-x-u-a-l-i-t-y

S-e-x-y

Sham

Shame

Shamed

Shameful

Shamefully

Shaming

Sharing my story

Shattering loss

She deliberately

Shed light

Shenanigans

She's evil

S-h-i-t

Shock

Shocked

Shocking

Shockingly

Shot in the dark

Showcasing

Show up as my authentic self

Show up authentically

Show up fully

Shrug

Shrugged

Shun

Shunned

Side hustle

Sigma

Significant milestone

Similarly

Simply

Sink or swim

Sit with the discomfort

Skibidi

Slammed

Slander

Slandered

Slandered me

Slandering

Slanderous

S-l-a-v-e

S-l-a-v-e-r-y

Slay

Slightly

Slur

Slurred

Slurring

S-l-u-t

Smear

Smear campaign

Snowplow parent

So excited

So many people want to know

So to speak

Sociopath

Sociopathic

Sociopathy

Sold down the river

Solutioning

Solutions-oriented

Some things

Somehow

Something

Somewhat of a

Sorry not sorry

Sort of

So there's that

Soul-crushing

Speak of the devil

Speak my authentic truth

Speaking my truth

Special needs

Spectacular

Spectrum

Speculate

Speculated

Speculating

Speculation

Speculative

Spied

Spinning your wheels

Spite

Spirit animal

Spiritual bypassing

Spited

Spiteful

Spitefully

Spitefulness

Split personality

Spousal a-b-u-s-e

Spy

Spying

Staggering

S-t-a-l-k

S-t-a-l-k-e-d

S-t-a-l-k-e-r

S-t-a-l-k-i-n-g

Stand in my truth

Start from scratch

State-of-the-art

Stealing

Step into a new chapter

Step into my power

Step into my truth

Stole

Strangely

Strategic advantage

Streamline

Stress

Stressed

Stressed out

Stressing

Strike

Strikes

Striking

Strikingly

Struck

Struck me

Stuck in a vicious cycle

Stuff

Stun

Stunned

Stunning

Stunningly

Subjective truth

Subsequently

Substance a-b-u-s-e

Substance use risk

Sue

Sued

Suffer

Suffered

Suffering

Sugar daddy

Sugar momma

Sugar mommy

S-u-i-c-i-d-a-l

S-u-i-c-i-d-e

Suing

Super excited

Superhero

Surprise

Surprised

Surprising

Surprisingly

Surveil

Surveillance

Surveilled

Surveilling

Surveils

Sus

Swept under the rug

Swindler

Symphony

Synergies

Synergize

Synergy

Systemic

T.

Table this

Take the bait

Tapestry

Target audience

Tasked

TBI

Tell my authentic story

Tell the truth

Tell you the truth

Telltale signs

Terrible parent

Terrified

Terrify

Terrifying

T-e-r-r-o-r

T-e-r-r-o-r-i-s-m

T-e-r-r-o-r-i-s-t

T-e-r-r-o-r-i-z-e

T-e-r-r-o-r-i-z-i-n-g

Testament

Testaments

That being said

That's ghetto

That's a good question

That's a great question

That's an excellent question

The bottom line

The calm before the storm

The fact is

The fact of the matter is

The fact that

The fact was

The grass is always greener

The ick

The itis

The judge is biased

The judge is corrupt

The judge is unfair

The n-a-k-e-d truth

The reality is

The reality is that

The same old story

The simple truth is

The truth is

The truth that

The truth was

The universe had other plans

The whole truth

Their truth

Then again

There is no

There is no excuse

There is no reason

There was no

Therefore

Thief

Thing

Things

Think outside the box

Thinking outside of the box

This day and age

This or that

This point in time

Thought leader

Thought leadership

Thought-provoking

Thought-provoking insights

Thousands

T-h-r-e-a-t

T-h-r-e-a-t-e-n-e-d

T-h-r-e-a-t-e-n-i-n-g

T-h-r-e-a-t-s

Three sheets to the wind

Thrill

Thrilled

Thrilling

Through the lens of

Throw in the towel

Time and again

Time and time again

Time is of the essence

Time will tell

Times a million

Times ad infinitum

T-i-t-s

To a certain extent

To a degree

To be clear

To be fair

To be frank

To be honest

To be honest with you

To be perfectly honest

To explain this more directly

To say the least

To some extent

To summarize

To tell you the truth

To the best of my knowledge

Told you a million times

Told you a thousand times

Told you hundreds of times

Told you time and time again

Tons of

Too good to be true

Took on a life of its own

Too little too late

Too numerous to mention

Tore our family apart

T-o-r-m-e-n-t

T-o-r-m-e-n-t-e-d

T-o-r-m-e-n-t-i-n-g

T-o-r-t-u-r-e

T-o-r-t-u-r-e-d

T-o-r-t-u-r-i-n-g

Total disaster

Total nightmare

Totally

Totally unbearable

Touch base

Toxic

Toxic co-parent

Toxicity

Toxic positivity

Traducement

Trailblazed

Trailblazer

Trailblazing

Train wreck

Train wreck of a parent

Traitor

Transformation

Transformative

Transformative power

Transformed

Transforming

Trash

Trauma

Trauma bonding

Trauma-bonded

Trauma-informed

Traumatic

Traumatic brain injury

Treasure trove

Trials and tribulations

Triangulation

Tribe

Tried and true

Trigger

Triggered

Triggering

Trolled

Trolling

Truly

Trusted by

Trust the universe

Truth be told

Truthfully

Truthfulness

Trying to ruin my life

Turned the page

Turning the page on this chapter

Turnkey

Two birds one stone

Two cents worth

Two-faced

Typical

Typically

U.

Ultimately

Unachievable

U-n-a-l-i-v-e-d

U-n-a-l-i-v-i-n-g

Unapologetically me

Unbalanced

Unbelievable

Unbelievably

Unconscious bias

Underrated

Under the g-u-n

Underscored

Underscores

Underscoring

Undertake

Undoubtedly

Unethical

Unethical attorney

Unethical lawyer

Unethically

Unfit

Unfit dad

Unfit father

Unfit mom

Unfit mother

Unfit parent

Unforgivable

Unforgivable act

Unhinged

Unimaginable

Unique

Universal truth

Unleash

Unleashed

Unleashing

Unlock

Unlocked

Unlocking

Unpack

Unpacked

Unpacking

Unpaid emotional labor

Unparalleled

Unprecedented

Unprofessional

Unprofessionalism

Unsafe parent

Unstable

Unstable personality

Unspeakable harm

Unsupported accusation

Untruthfully

Untruthfulness

Unvarnished truth

Unworkable

Using the child as a pawn

Usual

Usually

Utilization

Utilize

Utilized

Utilizing

Utmost

Utterly destroyed

Utterly hopeless

Utterly intolerable

V.

V-a-g-i-n-a

Vain attempt

Value-added

Value proposition

Validating my experience

Validation I never got

Vengeful

Very

Very important

Very interesting

Vibe

Vibe check

Vibrant

Vicious

Viciously

Victim

Victimize

Victimized

Victimizing

Victims

Vilification

Vilified

Vilify

Vilifying

Villain

Villainess

Vindictive

Vindictiveness

Violate

Violated

Violating

Violation

Violation of ethical rules

Violations

V-i-o-l-e-n-c-e

V-i-o-l-e-n-t

V-i-o-l-e-n-t-l-y

Viral

Virtually

Virtue signaling

Vital

Volatile

W.

Wacko

Wait for it

Waiting for the other shoe to drop

Wakeup call

Walked back

Was left wondering

Waste of space

Watch now

W-e-a-p-o-n

Weaponize

Weaponized

Weaponized incompetence

Weaponizing

Weaponizing incompetence

Weaponizing the system

W-e-a-p-o-n-s

Wearing the pants

Weather the storm

Weekend parent

What experts are saying

What many are saying

What matters most

What people are saying

What's more

Whatever

Whatsoever

Wheelhouse

When all is said and done

Whenever

Whether or not

Whoever

Whole nine yards

W-h-o-r-e

Wicked

Wickedly

Wild goose chase

Will explore

Win-win

Wished

Wishing

Witch

Witch hunt

With all due respect

Without exception

Woke

Wonder

Wondered

Wonderful

Wonderfully

Wondering

Wonders

Worked up

World-class

World-class leader

World-ending

Worried

Worries

Worrisome

Worry

Worrying

Worst

Worst dad

Worst father

Worst mom

Worst mother

Worst nightmare

Writing on the wall

Wrongdoer

Wrongdoing

X.

Xenophobic

Y.

Yellow-bellied

Yet

You can't judge a book by its cover

Your truth

#'s

(Em dash)

100%

30,000-foot view

67

Whether you adopt this complete framework or select portions that suit your specific situation, what worked for me was rooted in intention and restraint.

Choose words intentionally.

Pause for reflection and patience.

Consider the meanings and how those words might be used outside your intention.

Protect your narrative through thoughtful restraint.

Let clarity, transparency, authenticity, and truth guide your story. Amplify what you hope to say, while remembering how easily words can be lifted, twisted, or taken out of context.

APPENDIX I.
Titles and Topics from the Digital Gift Basket

Over One Thousand Titles Demonstrating Consistent Connection and Care

Connection required consistency when distance separated me from my daughter. Over 27 months, I created audio messages, videos, and graphics to stay present in her life and build a record she could revisit at any time. The following pages list the titles and topics of more than 1,000 of those pieces, described in Chapter 54, "Daily Digital Messages Archived to Outlast Distance and Time."

A Note on the Titles

The titles were created for the Digital Gift Basket Archive filing system. Each one consists of short phrases or keywords that reflect the specific theme of the graphic, video, or audio, allowing my daughter to search for particular pieces or themes later. Dates and file extensions (.mp3, .wav, .mp4, .mov, .jpg, .png) have been removed for readability in this appendix.

To My Daughter

Through these titles, you can find messages, images, audios, or videos you may want to see again or watch for the first time. You should have the file-sharing archive, links to the audio and video files, and the web address for all the graphics.

You can enjoy them anytime you choose. These daily graphics, weekly videos, and audios became our rhythm, a thread of consistency through separation and reunion. I will continue making them for as long as you like or until you tell me to stop.

The titles reflect the range of what these were designed to share with you, bringing laughter, smiles, calm, or reflection. They include memories of our time together, lessons from conversations that were challenging, reminders of fun talks, encouragement on hard days, celebrations on good days, and more.

I also love looking through them for myself. They connect me to you at different moments.

To Other Readers

This list outlines how I maintained connection while building a collection for my daughter to revisit over time. Each piece of content represents a message I created and shared daily and weekly. They came from my heart and what I felt would be useful for my daughter in those moments. They are not AI-generated themes or content created by anyone else; they came from me to her, in authenticity, humility, and love.

Section 1

Weekly Audio Messages

Over 100 Audio Messages

001. Ask me what you want to know, and call anytime.

002. Handling concerns and being thankful.

003. Doing your best with no pressure.

004. The morning you were born.

005. A Daddy-daughter audio about praying.

006. The difference between being right and making it right.

007. You are so independent and strong.

008.   An alphabet description of you on my birthday.

009.   Your strength strengthens me.

010.   It is okay to be angry with me.

011.   Enjoy your train ride today.

012.   I am praying for your understanding.

013.   Have a great first day in third grade.

014.   Please be patient with me.

015.   Stand your ground with your good behavior.

016.   I love our connection, and I feel it when we're apart.

017.   Listen and watch when you want. No pressure.

018.   Hearing your voice changes my world for the better.

019.   No guilt approaches from me to you. That is not how I work.

020.   A favorite memory from our visit last week.

021.   What do you want to do when you grow up?

022.   Making mistakes is part of any game.

023.   Bella Luna and my beautiful lady baby.

024.   I am so proud of your efforts in school.

025.   Being a good sport when it comes to sports.

026.   My love for you is unconditional.

027.   Don't keep it held in where it can hurt more.

028.   How about a new list for our next visit?

029.   A new Christmas ornament.

030.   Stand your ground and be strong.

031.   Integrity and kindness.

032.   Make your word your bond.

033.   Christmas day memories with you.

034.   What should we make our 2025 word or words?

035.   This week has meant so much to me.

036.   Two sides to every story.

037.   The road not taken.

038.   I wouldn't change a single moment.

039.   Please and thank you.

040.   My life is yours. I live for you.

041. Keep filling me in on your world. I love it.

042. The donkey fable.

043. Our Christmas 2024 visit memories.

044. Your letters this week.

045. "Don't do me like that" song recollections.

046. You have such an outstanding memory.

047. Doing puzzles together.

048. My unconditional love for you.

049. You have a brilliant and resilient mind.

050. He is risen. Happy Easter.

051. That school breakfast together and a dental surgery Daddy-daughter visit.

052. Wisdom and intelligence.

053. Be you, and try not to be concerned about what others think.

054. A musical memory about performing in Minneapolis.

055. Not giving up, and my first pro recording session.

056. My first time facing concerns on a stage.

057. Consider some summer fun learning.

058. I am so thankful for your health.

059. A couple of thoughts about crushes and boyfriends.

060. You can talk about girl topics with me if you want to.

061. What do you want to do together for our next Daddy-daughter visit?

062. The shortest times with you still mean the world to me.

063. Ask me if you have questions.

064. I knew your cries so well.

065. Handling the hormones and moods as they come.

066. There is great power in being comfortable alone.

067. A couple of ideas for falling asleep and relaxing.

068. Your beauty, inside and out, has moved me every day since you were born.

069. Standing strong and planting the good seeds.

070. Some cover songs were recorded for you.

071. I love how you take care of me and how you care for me.

072. The best time we have had recently, and talking about believing.

073. I love our stretching together on FaceTime.

074.   Life after the womb story.

075.   Some ideas for your birthday party.

076.   Stand strong as you plant seeds and build your foundation.

077.   I am so proud to be your father.

078.   You did so well with problem-solving the other night.

079.   I have so much faith in you and all you will do.

080.   Be courageous enough to be you, not to copy others.

081.   Your accountability is becoming so strong.

082.   Problem-solving plans can reduce or eliminate concerns.

083.   You are the right weight, width, height, and shape for you.

084.   I love you, and all that makes you who you are.

085.   Happy Thanksgiving 2025. I am so thankful for you.

086.   Being the science officer and detective of your patterns.

087.   I am here to support every dream you have.

088.   Keep up with accountability in the hard times.

089.   So much reminds me of you.

090.   A visiting story recap in the style of Dr. Seuss.

091.   Keep recognizing those patterns, as you have been.

092.   Adding those commas with the so's and the buts.

093.   Committing to the rules at school and at home.

094.   The title I love and am most proud of being called is your dad.

095.   Memories of scents and sounds that bring us together at times.

096.   Your cries and wanting to make you feel comforted and safe.

097.   Stay true to yourself around others. Do not be afraid to be you.

098.   I love learning from you and learning about you.

099.   Following through even when no one is leading you.

100.   Keep asking questions and stay curious always.

101.   The impact of a moment on many moments.

102.   Do not say it, if you do not mean it.

(I continue to make these audios for her each week.)

Section 2

Weekly Video Messages

Over 90 Video Messages

001.   A video for you from your daddy.

002.   What are you up to, lady baby?

003.   I miss our walks so much.

004.   I hope you enjoy your first flight and have fun.

005.   You are the most beautiful girl, inside and out.

006.   I am excited for you to go to New York City.

007.   Tell me all about New York City, I'd love to know.

008.   Have fun in Washington, D.C.

009.   Was it fun flying at night?

010.   I look forward to taking you to this park and many other places.

011.   Who can you forgive today?

012.   There is a big difference between "not happening" and "not right now".

013.   Look at all these dolls.

014.   I am here for you, Zoey.

015.   Thank you, video from a thankful Daddy.

016.   What is on your list for our next visit?

017.   Mad, sad, glad, and concerned feelings.

018.   Taking a break from the phone for Yom Kippur.

019.   I loved our conversation and problem-solving last night.

020.   I love you more than all the stars in the sky.

021.   This is a quick look at Las Vegas.

022.   Can you help me decorate the new place here?

023.   Ask me directly if it is about me, and you want the true answer.

024.   You can share anything with me, anytime you like.

025.   I love praying for you and how it makes me feel.

026.   You help to heal me when I am sick, my doctor.

027.   I would love to know about your dreams.

028.   It's okay if you are angry with me. Share what you feel.

029.   You create such outstanding connections.

030.   Walk with one foot on the ground trick.

031.   A plan for our Valentine's Day.

032.   You can share what you want to share with me.

033.   I love reading with you.

034.   You come first for me. You are first.

035.   A reading marathon pace copy.

036.   Happy Valentine's Day, my love.

037.   Keep challenging yourself.

038.   No more feeling boxed in anymore for you.

039.   You give me courage.

040.   Love your neighbor as yourself.

041.   That might be God.

042.   You are software, not hardware.

043.   The brave can be concerned and have doubts, too. It's ok.

044.   I am better when I am with you.

045.   That was such a special daddy-daughter visit. Thank you.

046.   The way you share with me means so much to me.

047.   Focus on the fix to move on from the problem.

048.   Thank you for the care package, Doctor Zoey.

049.   Sharing this or sharing that. I love connecting however you want.

050.   Congrats on finishing third grade.

051.   Take care of yourself and recognize these facts.

052.   So many memories of you stay with me throughout the day.

053.   I love how I could calm you and how you responded to me.

054.   Prerecording some videos for June because of the surgeries.

055.   What new foods can you try in the month of July?

056.   Happy Fourth of July and some July 4th memories.

057.   Our blueberry muffins and other food.

058.   I like picking our outfits out together.

059.   We do not have to talk about the doctors or my health.

060.   Not now does not mean it will not be. I promise.

061.   I love you too much to expect too little from you.

062.   Your favorites are for you to choose. No one else.

063.   Be you, and only you.

064.   I love our connection; distance does not separate our hearts.

065.   You are part of every moment for me, and the best moments of my life.

066.   I love you for every moment, now and forever.

067.   My new affirmation list for you.

068.   Thank you for such a wonderful visit.

069.   More information about publishing our children's book.

070.   It was great listening to you read.

071.   Thank you for calling and for your creativity.

072.   The powers of approval and disapproval.

073.   Let's create some goals together for the short and long term.

074.   Growing out my beard and hair for you is fun.

075.   The first add it to the book, or kick it to the curb recipe for you.

076.   You have already had such an influence on the world and me.

077.   Where else should we go? What else should we see?

078.   Remove the negative and solve with the positive.

079.   I am sorry.

080.   Counting down the days till I see you.

081.   Your mind is so powerful and creative.

082.   Our talks inspire me, make me so happy, and make me so hopeful.

083.   You do not have to share if you choose not to.

084.   Give yourself grace. Do your best, but also...

085.   Watching you sleep was so calming and beautiful.

086.   Back up from a problem or concern to see a bigger picture.

087.   Which wolf wins? A story to think about.

088.   Forgiveness can be a gift for yourself as much as for others.

089.   Doing your best is not about perfection; it will look different every day.

090.   The smallest steps every day can create the biggest results over time.

091.   Look at the difference positive change can make over a year.

092.   Stretching after those bumps and bruises.

093.   A look at my temporary recording studio you asked for.

(I continue to make these videos for her each week.)

Section 3

Daily Graphic and Visual Messages

Over 800 Messages

1 to 100

001.　Our Daddy-daughter airport goodbye.

002.　Only a day and I miss you so much.

003.　Hello from Daddy Turkey.

004.　A Thanksgiving array of pictures for my sweet girl.

005.　You will be my queen always. My lady baby.

006.　Happy Thanksgiving, Zoey 2023.

007.　Daddy bear loves you beary, beary much.

008.　I will always be your biggest fan, Zoey. For as long as I live.

009.　A Christmas tree with ornaments of us.

010.　I love every moment with you.

011.　You are my most magnificent unicorn.

012.　My brightest light, my brilliant daughter. My best friend

013.　Daddy loves you so much. Please know that.

014.　No matter where I am, you'll always have my whole heart.

015.　Your smile always makes me smile.

016.　An alphabet of words that describe you to me.

017.　Spelling words for the week with a weird sentence.

018.　I know school isn't always fun, but you're getting smarter.

019.　There is nothing you can do that will ever change my love.

020.　Moving walkway in the DC airport and remembering you.

021.　I love you in every way and every day.

022.　The thought of you fills me with joy.

023.　More spelling words and a funny sentence with them.

024.　Have fun at the Nutcracker.

025.　Did you know this about German chocolate cake?

026.　Happy birthday to Taylor Swift.

027.　An alphabet of love poem from Daddy.

028.　Remember to love yourself, you are worth it.

029. Hello Zoey, from blueberry chicken cake.

030. I pray for you every morning, every night, and day.

031. A long letter from Daddy for my Zoey.

032. You are the best daughter in the world.

033. I miss you and how you make me feel.

034. Hi Zoey, from a funny monkey.

035. I am sorry you are sick. Get well soon.

036. You have the most beautiful blue eyes, Zoey.

037. I will always be here to catch you, Zoey.

038. Merry Christmas 2023 note from Daddy.

039. I love, love, love you... The size of Texas.

040. You make my world, my work, and my life amazing.

041. Looking at pictures of you lights up my world.

042. Thank you, Zoey, for being so helpful, kind, loving, and being you.

043. I love you, I love you, I love you, I love you, I love you.

044. You can ask me, tell me, or share anything, anytime with me.

045. Happy new year, 2024, Zoey. May it be the best one to date.

046. You will always be my beautiful and amazing lady baby.

047. Hot chocolate, muffin, and conversations at a cafe we loved.

048. I thank God for you every morning and every night.

049. I loved reading the cone, cone, cone book with you.

050. Another spelling list and a weird poem for you.

051. Playing Monopoly with you always made me smile.

052. You are the most beautiful girl inside and out.

053. A welcome-back-to-school poem for you.

054. Praying you have a happy and colorful day.

055. Did you know Taylor Swift loves cheesecake?

056. Your doll is on a waterfall as you requested.

057. Dream, believe, and do not worry. You are ok.

058. You are stronger than you think you are.

059. You are a unique girl.

060. The seeds we have planted together will grow.

061. You are an elegant and stunning girl.

062.   Thinking of how you made me coffee and how good it was.

063.   We found out you were coming anniversary.

064.   Your presence is a present. You are a gift.

065.   I love all the first times we had together and will have.

066.   Your hugs are everything to me, Zoey.

067.   I whale always love you, and that is no fish tale.

068.   Your 100th day of school in 2nd grade.

069.   I am so proud of you and how you communicate.

070.   A picture and memory from four years ago today.

071.   We can work to control our feelings when we have to.

072.   You are so beautiful to me, words from a Joe Cocker song.

073.   Thinking of your laugh and smile today.

074.   Macaroni everywhere the bed. That was six years ago today.

075.   I love you, cactus, and googly eyes.

076.   Big chairs in Cocoa Beach 2019 with Daddy and daughter.

077.   Look, it's cactus Taylor Swift.

078.   You make me so happy, Zoey, in the hardest and saddest times.

079.   You are my laundry lady baby. Remember this picture?

080.   Remember always that you mean everything to me.

081.   Nana's birthday in 2015 is when we told her you were coming.

082.   I miss my water girl and how you used to bring me water.

083.   Should I keep growing the beard? You are in charge of it.

084.   I love sharing ice cream shakes with you.

085.   What dog keeps the best time?

086.   Happy Super Bowl Sunday, Zoey.

087.   Congrats on the Chiefs winning the Super Bowl.

088.   This is my Hebrew name. It means comforter.

089.   Happy Valentine's Day 2024, I love you so much.

090.   I'm sending you manatee hugs today.

091.   Zoey, I will be here for you always.

092.   I miss our blanket-folding mornings.

093.   Swimming with you was always incredible for me.

094.   You have always been a knock-out.

095.   That time you flew an airplane, sort of, as a baby.

096.   You were a keynote speaker for a moment in Miami.

097.   We are sunglasses buddies, making them look cool.

098.   Always here for you and always proud of you.

099.   The Lord your God will always be beside you.

100.   100th graphic. Everything is going to be ok, I promise.

101 to 200

101.   To see you and to hear you is everything to me.

102.   May the Lord bless you and protect you.

103.   Weird cat says, "Hi, Zoey. What a strange-looking cat."

104.   A Daddy-daughter riddle for you with three letters.

105.   Daddy-daughter riddle. Can you spot the mistake?

106.   Thank you for being the most wonderful daughter.

107.   Daddy-daughter riddle. A question you cannot say yes to.

108.   Driving with you at your school was so cool.

109.   You make me want to do my best to get better.

110.   2 Timothy 1.7. A bible verse for you today.

111.   How many seconds are in a year, Zoey?

112.   I love you forever. You make life worth living.

113.   I miss sharing my iced coffee with you.

114.   I love going on walks with you.

115.   Popcorn the unicorn says hi, Zoey.

116.   Thinking of you and your beautiful artwork today.

117.   Our Daddy-daughter time gets me through the hard times.

118.   Your Hebrew name and the meaning behind it.

119.   I enjoyed watching the Monty Python knights who say "Ni" skit with you.

120.   Wild nines and how they add up in funny ways.

121.   Happy St. Patrick's Day 2024, Zoey.

122.   Some information about your Tishrei birthday month.

123.   Have you seen a Donk lately? I like the names we gave some birds.

124.   It's okay to be mad with me. I still love you.

125.   I love playing games like Uno with you.

126.   Everything I do is for you.

127.   Remember, no assumptions. Always make sure to ask before you conclude.

128.   Please share your thoughts with me if you want to.

129.   Those Denny's birthday pancakes together were so fun and delicious.

130.   I loved making those fun lunches together before school.

131.   What is your favorite TV show right now?

132.   It's okay to be confused, sad, or angry. Feel the feelings instead of hiding them.

133.   I love you berry much, my fruity, funny girl.

134.   This seal thinks farts are funny.

135.   Happy Easter, Zoey 2024. He is risen.

136.   Happy April Fool's Day, my silly daughter.

137.   Happy National Peanut Butter and Jelly Day, Zoey.

138.   I love thinking of a few of the times when we watched the sunrise together.

139.   Could I have 33 seconds with you to see you for a few moments?

140.   Congrats on all the A's on your report card. Outstanding job.

141.   Which side of a horse has the most hair?

142.   I am so proud to be your dad, Zoey.

143.   I look forward to reading with you again.

144.   Today I'm here to remind you how special you are to me.

145.   It was so fun watching you laugh at the word "vodka."

146.   What kind of bagel can travel?

147.   I hope your field trip to the science center is fun.

148.   I will never make you call me, ever. Call when you want.

149.   What's your mood today, Zoey?

150.   Happy Monday, my beautiful, brilliant girl.

151.   I think you are purrrrrfect, Zoey.

152.   Spelling words and a funny sentence with all of them.

153.   You are so kind, caring, and loving, my wonderful lady baby.

154.   I love the airport time with you and all the memories of you.

155.   Happy weekend. I hope it is lots of fun with your friends.

156.   Doing Mad Libs has been so much fun with you.

157.   This is a cool trail near where I am staying that I hope to visit.

158.   This is the street and the view from where I am staying for a while.

159.   Bowling with you has always been so much fun.

160.   I watched Phineas and Ferb last night and thought of you.

161.   Washing the car with you was always the best. I miss that.

162.   Nine years ago today, I learned you were going to be a girl.

163.   Friendly's is opening a restaurant near you. Let's go there one day.

164.   I had a great dream about us snuggling last night.

165.   This is one of the views from my walk the other day.

166.   I will always give you all the space you want, but know I am still here.

167.   A view from a pretty library today that made me think of you.

168.   A picture of a cool hotel fireplace from this morning.

169.   John says "hello" and I hope your day is going well.

170.   Emily and Jackson are two of John's kids, and they say "hi."

171.   This is snaky, the snake. She seems friendly and colorful.

172.   This might not all make sense right now, but know that...

173.   Some affirmations I would love for you to say out loud and see how they feel.

174.   Hello taco. Do you know that you are my happiness?

175.   Zoey, your love is like a rainbow to me.

176.   This snuggling duck and dog reminded me of us snuggling together.

177.   It was always wonderful going to the train and the museum with you.

178.   This is the view from the library I am working at today.

179.   This is April, and she says, "Hi, Zoey."

180.   Think for yourself and try not to assume without all the understanding possible.

181.   What is your favorite TV show now? Has it changed from last time?

182.   I still think of this fun dessert we made up one night for our movie night.

183.   Only five days of school to go in second grade. You will be done soon.

184.   I look forward to going to Culver's again with you soon.

185.   The last week of second grade. Wow.

186.   Those Biscuit books and the way you said "woof, woof, woof" made me smile.

187.   You can still tell me anything or everything. I am here for you.

188.   Some Passover pictures from a Seder I went to last night.

189.   Congrats on finishing second grade.

190.   Do you have a favorite book you are reading right now?

191.   I've been missing you so much, my little bean.

192.   Happy Memorial Day 2024, and have a blessed and fun day.

193.   Donuts with you at that old donut shop were always wonderful.

194.   I made sure to leave the Walmart stars, like you used to.

195.   Do you know what this puzzle is saying, Zoey?

196.   Popcorn the unicorn says "hi" and still farts rainbows.

197.   There is another Zoey besides you in our family tree.

198.   FaceTiming with you from the Grand Canyon six years ago today.

199.   Why do bees have sticky hair?

200.   How is your summer so far, Zoey?

201 to 300

201.   Where did the one-legged waitress work?

202.   Thinking about cake pops and memories of sharing them with you.

203.   Why did the golfer bring two pairs of pants?

204.   I walk around this fountain and think of you.

205.   I imagine holding you and snuggling with you so often.

206.   What do you call a toad parked where it shouldn't be?

207.   I am sorry for what has happened.

208.   You deserve the best and all the love in the world.

209.   Love yourself the way I love you. You deserve that love.

210.   How about this pink unicorn super truck?

211.   Almost eight years ago, your first time in the ocean.

212.   A list of some of your great-grandmothers from your family tree.

213.   Why did the math book look sad?

214.   A challenge for you to stand strong and tall at all times.

215.   When does a joke become a dad joke?

216.   So thrilled you are my volleyball girl, and playing volleyball.

217.   Who can you forgive today, and what can you let go of?

218.   "Look at me," and bubbles in the park from many years ago.

219.   Have a great time at Busch Gardens today.

220.   What did the big flower say to the little flower?

221.   I would love to have a Daddy-daughter picnic and dance with you.

222.   This morning was so great because you called.

223.   A fountain and thinking of walking around fountains with you.

224.   A funny hair picture of you from eight years ago.

225.　　What did the horse say after it tripped?

226.　　Everything beautiful makes me think of you.

227.　　Happy July. I miss you so much and can't wait to see you.

228.　　I think you have the cutest bed head, and your hair always looks good.

229.　　You are my best birthday present ever.

230.　　Happy Fourth of July 2024. I hope you have a blast.

231.　　Zoey, still be kind when others are not.

232.　　I think someone is peeing on a plane right now.

233.　　We should do a Daddy-daughter talent show sometime.

234.　　I look forward to seeing your fashion show of new clothes.

235.　　Memories of snuggling in bed with you fill me up.

236.　　You have the biggest, most beautiful blue eyes I have ever seen.

237.　　This sunrise has me thinking of you, and happy crying.

238.　　Third grade starts in one month. Are you looking forward to it?

239.　　What does a cow use to do math?

240.　　You can still tell me anything you want or nothing. It's up to you.

241.　　What is your favorite song right now?

242.　　"Hello Muddah, Hello Faddah" song memories.

243.　　What brand of shoes do chickens wear?

244.　　It's so hard being away from you, Zoey. I am missing you so much.

245.　　The hardest eight months of my life have been being away from you.

246.　　Always loved watching Alf with you. That was a funny show.

247.　　I am so happy that you are going to New York City.

248.　　New York City has some of the best bagels and pizza.

249.　　An image of you in Atlanta in a big kitchen and in big boots.

250.　　A fact about the Statue of Liberty that you might like.

251.　　Good Morning America is near where you will be on your trip.

252.　　I hope you enjoy the Empire State Building.

253.　　A picture from seven years ago, and I still love reading with you.

254.　　Marshmallow the monkey says hello, Zoey.

255.　　I love thinking of the rainbows that we saw together.

256.　　Our hot chocolate googly eyes always made you laugh.

257.　　I miss playing Battleship with you and other games.

258.   I remember your first birthday brain freeze.

259.   Drying and combing your hair as we talked is a great memory for me.

260.   Enjoy your cool hotel in Washington, D.C. It's a nice place.

261.   It's so wonderful that you're going to Washington, D.C.

262.   You and I at your first haircut before starting school.

263.   Do you remember the 'Where is Zoey?' game?

264.   You are my happiness, my healing, my strength, my everything.

265.   You are so awesome, amazing, smart, incredible, and beautiful.

266.   A water fountain that made me think of you the other day.

267.   I was thinking about that talk I gave your class last November.

268.   I miss snuggling and nuzzling with you.

269.   Happy first day of school, 3rd grade. I know this year will be great.

270.   You are always on my mind, with so much love and hope.

271.   Every road for me leads to you.

272.   The way you look at me heals me and helps me get better.

273.   Try to never assume. Share your view, ask, and understand.

274.   Thinking about your first day of preschool. It is such a great memory.

275.   Keep doing things the right way even when it's hard.

276.   Please be patient with me, amazing times will come. I promise.

277.   Ask me anything anytime, and I will always share with you.

278.   Ducks don't enjoy being stressed. A dad joke.

279.   Always be honest and speak the truth. It will serve you well.

280.   I've never loved anyone the way I love you, and I never will.

281.   When you make a promise, be sure to follow through.

282.   In my dreams, I hold you close. A poem for you about you.

283.   Your belly button is kind of like your old mouth.

284.   We had so much fun washing the car together over the years.

285.   Watching you on the horse was amazing for your birthday.

286.   Where do math teachers go on vacation?

287.   Everything beautiful makes me think of you.

288.   I'm the luckiest Father in the world to have you for a daughter.

289.   I pray for you and know that God is with you.

290.   My dearest Zoey, this is a poem called "This is my wish."

291. A Zoey poem from Daddy. I love how much I love you.

292. Please remember who I am and what I stand for.

293. Keep trying new things when you can experience them.

294. There is a big difference between 'never' and 'not now'.

295. Your volume speaks volumes, so pay attention to how loud you are.

296. Every day I look at your pictures and think of you.

297. Never settle for second best because you deserve the best.

298. It was fun creating our nickname design poster together.

299. It's okay to forget at times, but know that my love is always here for you.

300. Every morning, I pray and give thanks for you.

301 to 400

301. You can do anything, be anything, learn anything.

302. My daughter is my hero, and you have been since you were born.

303. Change can be a good thing. Be patient and trust in God.

304. Thank you for being my daughter and greatest blessing.

305. Happy birthday, Zoey, my outstanding nine-year-old.

306. You have always been that missing piece in my life.

307. Thank you for spending your ninth birthday with me.

308. So much fun visiting that hotel again and taking pictures.

309. Zoey, you rock. You are the biggest rock star to me.

310. It was so much fun on the water slide with you.

311. That was so cool playing Mario Kart with you.

312. How many lips does a flower have? A dad joke for you.

313. That was one hungry duck at the Hyatt at lunch.

314. Looking into your eyes is everything to me.

315. My heart is always connected to yours.

316. The M&M store on your birthday was a blast.

317. You are so artistic and creative, Zoey.

318. When you are in my arms, I feel so alive.

319. Never forget that you are loved more than you know.

320. What a giant pumpkin that was that we saw.

321. Happy Rosh Hashanah, and Happy Jewish New Year.

322. You won bowling on your birthday, and I tried to win.

323.   Sending you a virtual high five that is powerful.

324.   I never got tired of watching the train with you.

325.   I love how athletic and strong you are.

326.   School is out for the hurricane, and I miss hurricanes with you.

327.   Always know how much I love you and cherish you.

328.   Beautiful girl, you were made to do great things.

329.   Happy International Day of the Girl Child, Zoey.

330.   Can I see your Taylor Swift Halloween costume fashion show?

331.   Why was Cinderella such a bad football player?

332.   You've been snuggled in for many years with me.

333.   Congrats on your win over the Panthers. Can you show me pictures?

334.   What do you call a funny mountain, Zoey?

335.   Why is bacon called bacon when you cook it?

336.   If you pour ice water on a hot dog, it's a chili dog, right?

337.   Do you have a football game tomorrow?

338.   Your nighttime FaceTime calls are like hugs for me.

339.   What did the T. Rex use to cut wood?

340.   I miss your strong neck rubs and strong hands.

341.   I like that we have the same favorite candy bar.

342.   Stand on the truth and by the truth always and forever.

343.   Let's finish up our book soon, when you have time.

344.   I heard you had a great dentist visit. That's wonderful.

345.   Be strong and ask for what you need.

346.   It's National Chocolate Day, Zoey.

347.   You can tell me if there is anything or anyone you are afraid of.

348.   Here is your Halloween trick-or-treat bag coming in the mail.

349.   Happy Halloween, and have a great time trick-or-treating.

350.   What is the leading cause of dry skin? Towels.

351.   The pumpkin was so big in Las Vegas. Have a look.

352.   How was your Halloween weekend, Zoey?

353.   Albert says hi and have a great Monday.

354.   Let your light shine, Zoey, and know that you are amazing.

355.   Here is a reminder that you are Fanta-stick.

356. So much of what you are, lady baby, is in this graphic.

357. My love will always grow, no matter what.

358. What do clouds wear under their shorts?

359. What do you get when dinosaurs crash their cars?

360. Why doesn't the sun have to go to college?

361. I live to love you, my beautiful girl. And it is a great life.

362. This new sign is on the front door for you.

363. Why aren't iPhone chargers called Apple juice?

364. This is our place if you ever come to visit me here.

365. My real home and my true home are where you are.

366. Can I see your school pictures? I love pictures of you.

367. Picture from the airport a year ago, and us playing there that day.

368. What should we do on our next Daddy-daughter FaceTime date?

369. I'm so proud of how you communicate and how big a heart you have.

370. This is what my school lunch used to look like when I was younger.

371. Let's talk about the hotel for the visit. Let's choose together.

372. Thank you for such an amazing Daddy daughter FaceTime date.

373. I am looking for a hotel with an indoor pool for us, as you asked.

374. Thank you for helping me place all the pictures on my walls.

375. How about this Daddy-daughter holiday schedule and plan?

376. Why do pilgrims' pants fall down? Another Dad joke for my daughter.

377. Happy Thanksgiving 2024, and I look forward to our Thanksgiving.

378. Zoey, I wish you would hug me and never "Lego."

379. Would you like to go to another buffet place again?

380. Call me anytime that you want to, need to, or have to. I am here.

381. Hand Santa-tizer is how Santa stays healthy.

382. A Daddy-daughter Snickers date together. Sound good?

383. Why was the letter 'E' the only one to get presents?

384. What did sushi A say to sushi B? Wasabi.

385. How I feel before and after. What do you think?

386. Did you get this year's ornament that I sent?

387. I love all the blanket folds we did together in the mornings.

388. Why can't you give Elsa a balloon? Because she will let it go.

389. Where does Santa stay during vacations?

390. I have a super special fireworks surprise for you on our visit.

391. Only two weeks till I get to see you again.

392. That looks like a serious leek. What do you think?

393. What is your favorite Taylor Swift song or album at the moment?

394. Do you have a favorite food right now? I am curious.

395. What is one thing you wish you could have for Christmas this year?

396. I adore you. I love you. I miss you.

397. Do you still like Jello cake? How about this one?

398. I still think it's a small bowl. How about you?

399. Did you get the shirt I sent you with the heart on it?

400. They delivered the fireworks surprise for you. This will be fun.

401 to 500

401. Anything special you want to add to our to-do list together?

402. Should we play mini golf again on this visit?

403. Merry Christmas Eve 2024, Zoey.

404. Merry Christmas 2024, Zoey.

405. I will see you at ten am, and I am excited to see you and hold you.

406. I have loved all our Daddy-daughter dates.

407. It was nice to see Nana before picking you up.

408. What do you think of this gingerbread house?

409. Be careful when you follow the masses.

410. Happy New Year's Eve with our bubbles.

411. Happy New Year, 2025, Zoey. May this year be full of blessings for you.

412. Here is the stone layout that you asked for.

413. I kept my Gatchaland socks too.

414. You are right about the Arby's tagline.

415. "I before e" rule except in these funny words.

416. Say hi to penguin banana. What do you think of this guy?

417. I am looking forward to our book together.

418. I am a girl dad first before anything else.

419. Here is a graphic of Enzo and Zeebee playing golf together.

420. I love your gifts and have that blanket you sent on my bed.

421.   Stay true and stand with integrity and truth.

422.   You add life to my days every day and in every way.

423.   What can kids make? A riddle and a joke for you.

424.   You are so talented, and I love your art. Thank you for sending it to me.

425.   A pickle and cheese snack to try.

426.   What does a painter do when he is cold?

427.   Try to stay in a growth mindset rather than a fixed mindset.

428.   Did you know o'clock is short for of the clock?

429.   Stick, stick, stick, stick, stick, stick.

430.   More brownies to make teeth fall out.

431.   No one knows me better than you, and I love that fact.

432.   Try dividing fifty by half and add twenty trick.

433.   If I am in second place, here's a riddle for you.

434.   I cannot wait to take you to Meow Wolf and experience it with you.

435.   We can work on some ideas for remembering together.

436.   Would you like me to send this hotel key card, too, for your collection?

437.   This was the view and what was across from my hotel in Las Vegas.

438.   Are these the right books for the last of your reading challenge?

439.   I trust you more than anyone else in the world.

440.   I think you would like this water show in Las Vegas.

441.   A factory that only makes okay products is called what?

442.   How do you organize a party in space?

443.   You are my favorite person to do everything and nothing with.

444.   This is a funny pickles chart for burgers.

445.   I look forward to golfing with you again.

446.   The most scared I ever was in my life...

447.   At every age and every moment, you have always been so beautiful.

448.   How about some dill pickle lemonade?

449.   Even far apart, we are always connected.

450.   What do a racecar and a kayak have in common?

451.   Did you know butterflies taste with their feet?

452.   You always slept so well as a baby.

453.   It was amazing how you would share food even when you were little.

454.   I am so proud of my A+ girl.

455.   I can't wait for the next hurricane with you.

456.   A new café and memories of you at our old café.

457.   I loved how you would say bazgeddi instead of spaghetti.

458.   Happy Presidents' Day 2025, Zoey.

459.   You were so strong climbing on those bars back then.

460.   I never knew real love and trust till I knew you.

461.   Our McDonald's FaceTime with Uber Eats was fun.

462.   Why can't a nose be twelve inches long?

463.   Tell me when you get things I send you. Let me know that you got them.

464.   I'll always do my best for you.

465.   This is a dog joke about love.

466.   A tropickle fish joke.

467.   What is your favorite class right now?

468.   Mail me anything you like.

469.   I will be your boxcutters if you need me to be.

470.   A tiny pickle and a jumbo pickle.

471.   Here is where I am on the map.

472.   A funny-looking penguin and a reading challenge.

473.   I look forward to playing volleyball with you.

474.   Making a waterbed a bouncier bed and other silly thoughts.

475.   A funny joke about maps backwards.

476.   Did you know Yoda from Star Wars had a last name?

477.   Do you know what days are the strongest?

478.   What are your top five favorite shows right now?

479.   You are my most precious star.

480.   You are so strong, brave, and smart. I hope you can see that in yourself, too.

481.   Did you know a jellyfish's mouth and butt are the same opening?

482.   I love music more when I'm with you and listening with you.

483.   Did you know mice can't fart or burp?

484.   Nothing in this world can measure the size of my love for you.

485.   A reminder that you are allowed to have privacy.

486.   Happy St. Patrick's Day 2025, my little pickle.

487.   Our favorite donut shop is still there. I hope we can visit it again.

488.   Rubber duck from that superhero show you watched.

489.   Bangkok's full name is the longest-titled city.

490.   The way you look at me makes me feel like the luckiest Dad.

491.   Having some pickle juice and thinking of my favorite little pickle.

492.   What feels like a world away sometimes.

493.   A backwards flying hummingbird.

494.   You are so much smarter and stronger than you realize.

495.   Cricket from Big City Greens was funny.

496.   Hanging upside down on the inversion table.

497.   Have fun on your fieldtrip today.

498.   I remember how Bluey used to say this.

499.   A funny joke about butts, you might get a kick out of.

500.   Watching Sid the Science Kid with you is a great memory.

501 to 600

501.   There is a part of me that only you will ever see.

502.   Reading all those stories this year has been amazing.

503.   We now have a plan C for the April 2025 visit.

504.   Happy first sleepover day, and have a great time.

505.   Can you guess who this is when he was seventeen?

506.   I will see you tomorrow night, Zoey.

507.   Please drink more water. It will help.

508.   Thank you for sending the tests and art.

509.   I had so much fun at that Daddy-daughter school breakfast with you.

510.   You are brave, strong, amazing, and you will do great with the surgery.

511.   Your bravery is so incredible.

512.   It was great talking and doing work together the other day.

513.   Our talks are the best, and I love how you share.

514.   That picture of you and Darth Vader is in a frame and up on my shelf.

515.   I found pickle juicers in the airport.

516.   In those moments of mean, work on planting a seed of nice.

517.   Your strength and love will impact more people than you could imagine.

518.   Your love is my medicine and helps me heal. Thank you.

519. Happy Easter, Happy Passover, and Happy Feast of Unleavened Bread.

520. A couple of Daddy jokes about tires.

521. Still have your New York City bear on my laptop bag.

522. A Bible quote about being less stressed and less pressured.

523. Why did the math book look sad? Another Dad joke.

524. So proud and honored by how much you share with me.

525. Do you think pickle pizza might be good?

526. Watching Netflix in the car with you as you rested was so special.

527. You are going to have a great fast test day this week.

528. A picture and memory of your first time in the hot tub.

529. I look forward to going on a boat with you again, like in this photo.

530. Have a great test day. I know you will do amazing.

531. I hope the testing went well, lady baby.

532. A cow is not called a cow till it gives birth.

533. We can work on focusing together.

534. New month, so let's try something new.

535. Have a great math testing day.

536. Fourth grade is going to be fantastic for you.

537. Do you know why you can never tell a burrito a secret?

538. When we only speak for a few seconds, it is still so great for me.

539. The simple moments with you mean the world to me and Babybel cheese.

540. I had you with me for the first surgery procedure.

541. What is the seventh letter in the alphabet? A trick question.

542. A picture of one of the first real bands I was in.

543. The Lord will help you. You only have to be still and trust.

544. What do you want to do for Father's Day?

545. Sometimes ignoring their behavior can make them stop.

546. How many dots do you see?

547. My view today for you to see. Do you like it?

548. Look for the patterns to recognize and realize what you need to do.

549. How was your awards show?

550. Did you know people eat more bananas than monkeys?

551. Have a great end-of-year celebration at school today.

552.   Every day for the next seven days.

553.   "There's a hole in the bucket." Dear Liza, dear Liza.

554.   Some self-care day ideas for you.

555.   Why do seagulls fly over the sea? Shouldn't they be called baygulls?

556.   So proud that you are trying new things.

557.   Last day of school for third grade.

558.   Monkeys jumping on the bed. Do you remember that book and song?

559.   Truth does not mind being questioned.

560.   Hug o' War poem by Shel Silverstein.

561.   Toothbrush studies to laugh about.

562.   The house I lived in when I lived in Las Vegas.

563.   Some wisdom to think about, lady baby.

564.   Every day is a lesson if you are willing to learn.

565.   A teaching from Jesus called the beatitudes.

566.   Difference between stumbling blocks and stepping stones.

567.   How change is created to make things better.

568.   Some more words of wisdom from your Daddy.

569.   Did you know astronauts don't burp in space?

570.   Have you had any new ideas or dreams of what you want to be?

571.   What is the only letter of the alphabet not used in US state names?

572.   This is the house I grew up in with Nana and your uncle.

573.   This is a funny picture of me when I was 14.

574.   You can still tell me anything you want.

575.   Father's Day 2025. You are my heart, my light, my Zoey.

576.   Did you know kangaroos can't walk backwards?

577.   I love playing board games with you.

578.   Making pickle waffles with you someday, perhaps.

579.   Remove any letter from the word seat, and it will make these words.

580.   You are the person I trust the most.

581.   No hurricane has ever crossed the equator.

582.   What word starts with e and ends with e and has one letter in it?

583.   We have been touching heads since you were little.

584.   Work to maintain good eye contact and use respectful words.

585.   A picture of Daddy with a band from 2000, as you asked for.

586.   This is the gospel in twenty bullet points.

587.   Love is patient, love is kind.

588.   A picture of a band I played with in 1994.

589.   I love all the memories of this day at the Hyatt.

590.   An old picture from a TV interview in Pennsylvania.

591.   How about a fruit salad frog? Kinda weird, huh?

592.   Now and then, read your Bible as you did before.

593.   You are not in my life; you are my life.

594.   Happy Fourth of July 2025.

595.   A picture in a recording studio from 2000.

596.   The blocks are the same color.

597.   Be careful who you trust.

598.   Don't worry about anything.

599.   Fear and faith, and how faith can take away fear.

600.   Hope means sometimes we have to hold on and believe.

601 to 700

601.   Your first pancake in March 2016.

602.   It's super kitty.

603.   You are my warrior, and such a strong young woman.

604.   Cute kitty with a flower.

605.   Let's always be honest with each other.

606.   Look for these kinds of green flags.

607.   A prayer for you from head to toe.

608.   Switching your mentality.

609.   Do you know what M&M's stand for?

610.   Did you know this about Monopoly?

611.   Your next move matters more than your last mistake.

612.   Stop using your energy to worry.

613.   Make sure you know the difference in how people talk to you.

614.   How about this look and hairstyle?

615.   It is better to walk alone than with a crowd.

616.   Spell rabbit without using the letter r.

617. I "hop" you have a great day, my little bunny.

618. Zoey, I can promise these things.

619. Privacy is power, and you have a right to that power.

620. An important lesson for life and communication to consider.

621. May you be filled with the Holy Spirit every day of your life.

622. Do not be afraid. Do not fear, and do not worry.

623. Believe in yourself, Zoey. Believe in you as I do.

624. Feel it in your soul and find that centering.

625. Experience and feel all the feelings you can.

626. A beautiful Bible verse for you.

627. Doing your best will look different every day.

628. Everything comes to you at the right time.

629. Be patient and consider this when feeling restless.

630. Always pray to have eyes that see the best.

631. My favorite memory from that hospital visit.

632. Are you experiencing a lack of vitamin me?

633. You are not fully grown until you know these things.

634. Discipline is choosing between these two things.

635. A few emergency numbers in the bible to check out.

636. Some sentences to read and consider for your life.

637. No mountains in your neck of the woods.

638. Every day God thinks of you.

639. Your first visit to Steak and Shake.

640. Always say a prayer when you are having doubts.

641. Law of attraction and connecting with positive people.

642. Doctor Enzo and nurse chicken duck.

643. Why do crabs never volunteer? Dad joke.

644. Try to avoid making big choices when you are angry.

645. Remember these three things in hard times.

646. Switching your mentality from the bad to the good.

647. Close your eyes and then barely open them. What do you see?

648. Some people who leave your life can be for the best, sometimes.

649. The things you can control and the things you cannot.

650. Strong people break too. It is okay to feel broken for a moment.

651. Try to do everything with a good heart.

652. Sometimes, home can be another person.

653. What types of cats teach college classes?

654. When you are honest, even when others aren't, it is the right choice.

655. Ice cream made in Ziplock bags. We should try this.

656. God will put his angels in charge of you to protect you.

657. Don't give up. Even water can break rock over time.

658. Faith does not always take you out of the problem.

659. We both know what to do with this bird.

660. The Zoey Decathlon and ten fun events to try.

661. Have you heard of the new movie Constipation? A Dad joke.

662. A ten-dollar bill for an almost ten-year-old girl.

663. How is this for a cool hairstyle for your dad?

664. Seconds, days, and years, so much more together than apart.

665. You may not understand right now, but it will become clear.

666. Mr. Snugglebonk Woofenstuff and our creative, funny ideas.

667. I will see you tonight, lady baby.

668. I took out the teeth as you asked.

669. Happy 10th birthday to the most amazing girl.

670. There is so much power in your beliefs and faith.

671. Have an amazing volleyball game tonight.

672. Have a great birthday party this weekend with your friend.

673. A new affirmation list I made for you to try out.

674. More things that are in and out of our control.

675. Speaking the truth is key. Stand on the truth and not a truth.

676. A picture of us together six years apart.

677. I loved playing trash with you. That was a fun game.

678. My double-digit girl is still my number one.

679. A prayer for both of us to pray, perhaps.

680. That was so much fun at Abbott's with you on your birthday.

681. All the birthday balloons and balloons and balloons.

682. Two beautiful girls; you and your Mommy.

683.   Can I see some of the pictures from your party?

684.   You are so beautiful, lady baby, inside and out.

685.   That was such a fun game we played together during the rainstorm.

686.   A stem idea. Cut up foam and rubber bands for the egg drop.

687.   A messy peanut butter and jelly sandwich beard.

688.   This is Roo, who came and kept me company today.

689.   Did you know this fact about Abraham Lincoln?

690.   My new screensaver of us on my computer. What do you think?

691.   Did you know that farting is healthy and good for you?

692.   Above all, I wish to be remembered as your dad.

693.   Look, they have a life-size one too. How funny.

694.   How do you make four balanced squares from these sticks?

695.   Did you know that honey never spoils?

696.   This cutie says, "Have a great day."

697.   Did you know M&M's were the first candy eaten in space?

698.   Can you guess what this is? A riddle for you.

699.   What should we call the cup holders we created?

700.   A pretty cool math trick to test out.

701 to 800

701.   Some affirmations I would like you to remember.

702.   Always work to be a first-rate version of yourself.

703.   This is what you looked like at ten weeks old.

704.   What country is this, Zoey? Can you figure it out?

705.   Another "what country is this?" riddle.

706.   A silly riddle for you this morning.

707.   A word count and word find for you.

708.   I love you, and I am doing all I can to get better for you.

709.   What is this picture saying with Tom?

710.   What do you think this picture is saying today?

711.   Can you find the mistake in these words?

712.   What is this picture puzzle saying to you?

713.   Can you spell another animal in three moves?

714.   Another picture for your mind.

715.   Lotta "Gots" and heroes for these pictures.

716.   Can you figure out what this one is trying to say?

717.   Can you name three consecutive days without...?

718.   What do you think is being shown here?

719.   Can you find what's wrong with this picture?

720.   How many holes can you find in this shirt?

721.   Do you know which celebrity this is?

722.   Can you find the 12 ducks in this image?

723.   Giving you two riddles and all my love.

724.   How about two more riddles today, as requested?

725.   A numbers riddle to dig into, Zoey.

726.   Four different puzzles, for Friday the Fourteenth.

727.   Another riddle, to search out the meaning.

728.   A couple more for you to figure out.

729.   Can you figure out this four-word phrase?

730.   Thank you for every moment we share online.

731.   What could wear cotton? Another funny riddle.

732.   Thank you for the amazing hairbrush. I love it.

733.   More riddles you requested, to think about and solve.

734.   Three more riddles for you to answer.

735.   A city and a country to figure out, riddle.

736.   A few more turkey riddles for your turkey break.

737.   How about five riddles at once?

738.   A set of three picture puzzles and a quote.

739.   Happy Thanksgiving, Zoey. Gobble, gobble.

740.   Some more riddles to figure out and play with.

741.   How about a Daddy-daughter word find today?

742.   What are your best guesses for these images?

743.   How would you measure four gallons? A test.

744.   How tall is the cat? Another hard riddle for you.

745.   Two more riddles, and something to know always.

746.   Zoey, what are these pictures saying to you?

747.   It's not an alligator. Do you know what it is?

748.   Another one to figure out, and a fun graphic for you.

749.   How about this dad joke and riddle?

750.   Have a great fast test day tomorrow. You will do great.

751.   Fast test day riddles and a joke.

752.   I love, love, love you, my amazing lady baby.

753.   All my love is yours, and a few more riddles for you.

754.   Ten days till I see you. I wish it was today.

755.   I hope you have a wonderful weekend.

756.   A riddle to think about for a moment.

757.   A picture riddle and some Christmas jokes.

758.   What are these puzzles saying?

759.   Only five more days, Zoey, till I see you.

760.   The second one is how I feel about you.

761.   You are both of these riddles.

762.   Only two days left till I see you.

763.   Good morning, my beautiful girl.

764.   What are these puzzles saying?

765.   Time with you is perfection to me.

766.   Happy Christmas Eve to the most amazing daughter.

767.   Merry Christmas, Zoey 2025.

768.   You make life worth living for me. I love loving you.

769.   I loved showing you where you were born, the other day.

770.   Seven and a half years ago and yesterday, a picture of us.

771.   I loved watching the sunrise with you on the beach.

772.   You are the greatest gift I have ever received.

773.   Our time together is everything to me.

774.   Happy New Year, Zoey. May it be a great one.

775.   This will be our best year ever together.

776.   Can you figure out these two riddles?

777.   Last vacation day, I hope it is a great one for you.

778.   Have a great first day of school back from break.

779.   Our ten-year-apart sunrise pictures on the beach.

780.   What goes up but never comes back down? Riddle.

781.   What five-letter word becomes shorter? And other riddles.

782.   A trio of riddles for you today, and park pictures.

783.   I loved making ice cream with you; what a workout, too.

784.   Some weird "Did you know?" facts you might enjoy.

785.   Another picture of the same place, but ten years later.

786.   This will be a great day for you, my beautiful lady.

787.   I am so proud to be your Daddy. You are unstoppable.

788.   I love how your mind works and the way you think.

789.   Some more word riddles to think about and figure out.

790.   You are not a princess, but our family had a castle.

791.   What two things can you never eat for breakfast?

792.   You may not be an official princess, but you are one to me.

793.   A few more riddles to figure out, lady baby.

794.   If I lost every other memory and could only remember you...

795.   Your bravery, tenacity, intelligence, and love inspire me every day.

796.   Keep being the girl who makes things happen.

797.   You give me hope that keeps me going.

798.   When we are close, I feel so much calmer, at peace, and centered.

799.   Fun is amplified when I am with you and watching you have fun.

800.   Patriots and Seahawks in the Super Bowl 11 years later.

801 to 831

801.   How many squares are in a Rubik's Cube, and lifting up from an issue.

802.   You are a true original, and no one is like you.

803.   Try adding this statement to your affirmations and prayers.

804.   Look at the way the color changes over time. Pretty cool.

805.   You are in my thoughts and in my heart every day.

806.   This was such a wonderful night with you. Thank you.

807.   Sometimes falling forward is still a positive step and helps with forward motion.

808.   Ten ideas for my ten-year-old to try for better days and better ways.

809.   Nothing will ever change my love for you. I will always love you without end.

810.   Test it, double-check it, research it, and dig deeper to find out if something is true.

811.   It is okay to have favorites.

812.   Happy Super Bowl Sunday! Go Patriots.

813.   I love loving you.

814.   Can you make twenty words out of "waterfall"?

815.   Poutine and fries yesterday.

816.   I know that I got something in my life perfectly right. You.

817.   I got six just like you said, and switched up the flavor.

818.   Happy Valentine's Day 2026, Zoey.

819.   The snowstorm was wild last night.

820.   They make cookies the size of pies up here.

821.   Final information and numbers of the book.

822.   Finding greater calm, peace, and truth.

823.   Can you spot the five mistakes in this image?

824.   There is no better doctor than Doctor Zoey.

825.   The power of consistency every day can make all the difference.

826.   When we use positive words to lift each other up.

827.   I will never stop fighting for you.

828.   Home is not where I live; it is where I belong, and I belong with you.

829.   Four time zones in one day.

830.   Nothing compares to being close to you.

831.   You are brilliant, intelligent, aware, and astute.

(I continue making these graphics for her each day.)

APPENDIX J.
Mapping 349 First-Word Launches Across the Book

Architecting How Original Structural Openings Shape Each Section of the Book

Spanning 349 structural openings across 75 sections of this book, every first word is distinct. Each chapter's title, opening thought, closing thought, pull quote, and body begins with a distinct word. The front matter, back matter, and appendices follow the same rule across their available positions.

Some sections feature five tracked positions, while others have fewer. The Preface, Author's Note, Introduction, numbered chapters, Conclusion, and Epilogue use these original first words for the title, opening thought, closing thought, pull quote, and chapter start. The Coda and Letter from Daddy include only title and chapter body first words. The appendices combine the title, subtitle, and chapter start first words.

Below is the complete structural map for the book and the first words that anchor each position.

Section Title	Chapter or Sub Title	Opening Thought	Closing Thought	Pull Quote	Chapter Start
Preface.	Authoring	My	Steadfast	Details	Vulnerability
Author's Note.	Practicing	Growth	Humility	Legacy	Restraint
Introduction.	Grounded	Truth	Renewal	Moments	Perspective
Chapter 1.	Clarity	Difficult	Embracing	Despite	Wisdom
Chapter 2.	Red	Whispered	Authenticity	Deflection	Uncertainty
Chapter 3.	Conflicts	First	Overlooking	Swinging	Friction
Chapter 4.	Recognizing	Naming	Rejection	Balance	Cycles
Chapter 5.	Shadows	Pursuing	Forgiveness	Learning	Fathers
Chapter 6.	How	Wellness	Healing	Acknowledgment	Frequent
Chapter 7.	Façades	Refusal	Helping	Hiding	Avoiding
Chapter 8.	Choosing	Prioritizing	Revelation	Regardless	Writing
Chapter 9.	Surrounded	Problematic	Voices	Unchallenged	Observed
Chapter 10.	Living	Reduced	Realizing	Playing	Absence
Chapter 11.	Marrying	Vows	Mistakes	Committing	Distinguishing
Chapter 12.	Rewriting	Belief	Yesterday's	Eliminating	Letting
Chapter 13.	Navigating	Denial	Proper	Safety	Subtle
Chapter 14.	Unexplained	Precautions	Intriguing	Covert	Strange
Chapter 15.	Resisting	Sharing	Reasoning	Becoming	Recording
Chapter 16.	Strategic	Receiving	Continued	Packing	Elements
Chapter 17.	Rejecting	Questions	Carefully	Failing	Information
Chapter 18.	Objective	Overt	Limited	Proof	Accountability
Chapter 19.	Preserving	Records	Satisfaction	Permanent	Curious
Chapter 20.	Recognition	Mirrors	Sound	Reading	Confrontational
Chapter 21.	Abandoned	Honesty	Consequences	Deeds	Quitting
Chapter 22.	Using	Legal	Painful	Conversations	Tension
Chapter 23.	Patterns	Dialogue	Resolve	Replies	Exposure
Chapter 24.	Reflecting	Substance	True	Quiet	Mirroring

Section Title	Chapter or Sub Title	Opening Thought	Closing Thought	Pull Quote	Chapter Start
Chapter 25.	Rushing	Urgency	Outcomes	Apparent	Pressure
Chapter 26.	Performing	Genuine	Decency	Working	Early
Chapter 27.	Searching	Positive	Memories	Food	Reflections
Chapter 28.	Breaking	Flexibility	Openness	Once	From
Chapter 29.	Frustrating	Silent	Careful	Stirring	Signs
Chapter 30.	Refusing	Trying	Commitment	Distortions	Surviving
Chapter 31.	Conviction	Faith	Prayer	Devotion	Resistance
Chapter 32.	Three	Before	Guided	Later	Caution
Chapter 33.	Enduring	Human	Comprehending	Kindness	Harshness
Chapter 34.	Offering	Emotional	Distance	Steady	Unease
Chapter 35.	Structure	Rules	Healthy	Punishments	Spanking
Chapter 36.	Monitored	Love	Control	Revealing	Ongoing
Chapter 37.	Instructions	Clear	Lessons	Defensiveness	Core
Chapter 38.	Married	Persistent	Certain	Relentless	Throughout
Chapter 39.	Warmer	Acting	Caretaker	Making	Socially
Chapter 40.	Boundaries	Discipline	Strong	Hearing	Differing
Chapter 41.	Too	Detecting	Hope	Resilience	Planted
Chapter 42.	Interrogation	Private	Present	Pressing	Raising
Chapter 43.	Combative	Coexisting	Unwelcome	Exhaustion	Specific
Chapter 44.	Fortifying	Evidence	Futility	Validating	Strangers
Chapter 45.	Clarifying	Vague	Modifications	Enforcing	Requests
Chapter 46.	Biting	Direct	Speaking	Calculated	Keeping
Chapter 47.	Jabs	Zero	X-rays	Linear	Unhealthy
Chapter 48.	Legitimate	Cooperation	Primary	Custody	Knowing
Chapter 49.	Creating	Unscrupulous	Avoidance	Laying	Centering
Chapter 50.	Visits	Planning	Coordinating	Negotiating	Managing
Chapter 51.	Laziness	Watching	Hesitation	Ensuring	Shortcuts

Section Title	Chapter or Sub Title	Opening Thought	Closing Thought	Pull Quote	Chapter Start
Chapter 52.	Words	Phone	Responding	Attempting	Evasive
Chapter 53.	Persisting	Notice	Cancellation	Facing	Traveling
Chapter 54.	Daily	Developing	Across	Consistency	Bridging
Chapter 55.	Sustained	Peace	Actions	Patience	Growing
Chapter 56.	Trust	Grace	Compassion	Conduct	Compositions
Chapter 57.	Strategy	Rulings	Setbacks	Spotlighting	Positioned
Chapter 58.	Praying	Weighing	Accepting	Repeated	Recalling
Conclusion.	Standing	New	Resolution	Remember	Gratitude
Epilogue.	Recasting	Awareness	Strength	With	Initially
Letter From...	Through				To
Coda.	Anchored				Being
Appendix A.	24	Identifying			Communication
Appendix B.	Traits	Documenting			Transparency
Appendix C.	Building	Organizing			Order
Appendix D.	Preliminary	Structured			Preparation
Appendix E.	Holding	Filing			Lawyers
Appendix F.	Calming	Strengthening			Support
Appendix G.	Restricted	Categorizing			Language
Appendix H.	Alphabetical	Complete			All
Appendix I.	Titles	Over			Connection
Appendix J.	Mapping	Architecting			Spanning

Chapter Title or Section First Words: 75

Opening Thought or Subtitle First Words: 73

Chapter First Words: 75

Closing Thought First Words: 63

Pull Quote First Words: 63

Total First-Word Positions: 349